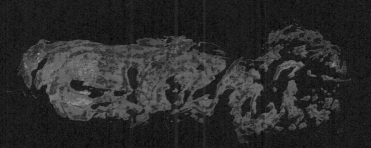

The Illustrated
BRONTËS
of Haworth

The Illustrated

BRONTËS
of Haworth

Scenes and characters from the
lives and writings of the Brontë sisters

Brian Wilks

Introduction by Victoria Glendinning

WILLOW BOOKS
COLLINS, 8 Grafton Street, London W1
1986

Dedication
For Sue
who made it possible

**British Library Cataloguing in Publication
Data**

The illustrated Brontës of Haworth.
   1. English fiction—19th century
   I. Brontë, Charlotte   II. Brontë, Emily
   III. Brontë, Anne   IV. Wilks, Brian
   823'.8'03   PR1304

   ISBN 0–00–218192–4

**Designed, conceived and produced by
Robert Adkinson Limited, London**
Editorial Director   Clare Howell
Editor   John Gilbert
Art Director   Christine Simmonds
Picture Researcher Sheila Corr

Phototypeset by Tradespools Limited, Frome
Illustrations originated by East Anglian Engraving
Limited, Norwich
Printed and bound by Brepols, Turnhout, Belgium

CONTENTS

Introduction

by Victoria Glendinning

'If men could see us as we really are, they would be a little amazed', wrote Charlotte Brontë. She meant that men misunderstood women, reinventing them according to their own masculine theories of what women are or should be like. But if we, men or women of the 1980s, could see the Brontës themselves as they really were, we might indeed be a little amazed.

It's hard even to get a true picture of their parsonage home in the poverty-stricken little town of Haworth, as it was in the first half of the nineteenth century. Nowadays Haworth is a tourist-trap and a literary shrine; the parsonage itself, now the Brontë Parsonage Museum, has been embellished and enriched by the generosity of American benefactors. On each side of the steeply sloping main street, Brontë books and Brontë pictures and Brontë biscuits and Brontë souvenirs are displayed to tempt the visitor. Major roads and a motorway roar within a few miles, and not far away are the great conurbations of West Yorkshire and, over the hills to the west, those of the Lancashire manufacturing towns – the results of the industrial revolution which was changing the face of Britain during the Brontës' own lifetime. The illustrations in this book go a long way towards enabling us to reconstruct the past, just as Brian Wilks's text illuminates the lives, the writings, and the perverse imaginations of three extraordinary sisters and their brother.

The main street in Haworth, one of the steepest streets in England.

The Brontës' world was a small, isolated one, and they themselves were small as well. Emily was considered to be tall; but since the average height of women was several inches less then than now, and since a dress of Charlotte's preserved in the Museum would only fit a slim eleven-year-old of today, even Emily's height must have been modest by our standards. The parsonage too is small, with just two rooms, the dining-room and the parlour, neither of them spacious, on either side of the stone-flagged passage on to which the front door opens; and a kitchen behind. Upstairs, just two bedrooms – and that third room, scarcely bigger than a closet, into which the little girls crowded to play their secret games. There was of course no running water, no inside lavatory. Before the two elder girls Maria and Elizabeth died, and then their Aunt Branwell, there were eight people – and a variety of pets – living in this snug but constricted little house, and that's not counting two servants, with whom the family lived on affectionate terms.

The front door opens almost directly on to the churchyard. Even though, when the Brontës lived there, it was not so stacked and packed with slanting tombstones as it has since become, this was nevertheless a monumentally grim outlook. There were no other families of their own level of education in Haworth, which compounded the motherless children's isolation and self-containment.

It all sounds like a recipe for a tough childhood, perched there above the unhealthy squalor of the main street. The nearest buildings of any stature, symbolically enough, were the church where their father or his assistant curates held services, and the Black Bull where Branwell Brontë was to drink himself to death.

But Branwell, the only boy in the family, was also the only emotional casualty. Charlotte, Emily and Anne loved their family and their home intensely and suffered when they were away from it. The tiny house was alive with physical and mental activity. Beyond the town, the young Brontës had the wild windswept moors, not only as the outward setting of their daily lives, but as their inner landscape, which filled the imagination of Emily in particular. There was a Mr Greenwood, a little deformed man, who kept the stationer's shop just below the Black Bull; the Brontës bought all their paper, pens and ink from him, and he had a special admiration for Emily. He would watch her walking out alone to the moors and coming back hours later, elated, her face 'holy, heavenly'.

The high moorland above Haworth, once a year a sea of purple heather.

Within the house, they had books, newspapers, magazines, and an unusual father who wrote himself, talked to his children, and took their aspirations seriously. Mr Brontë wrote to Mrs Gaskell, Charlotte's first biographer: 'I do not deny that I am somewhat eccentrick.' If he were not, he thought, 'I should in all probability never had such children as mine have been.' Hypochondriacal and nearly blind, this strange man, who came from humble northern Irish beginnings, outlived all his children.

Part of the magic that the Brontës have for us is that they never grew old. Like Keats and Shelley, who died even younger, they seem romantically preserved in perpetual youth. This is exaggerated, in fact. Branwell was 31, Emily 30 and Anne 29 when they died, all within a few months. It was tuberculosis that carried off the girls, and Charlotte only survived them for five years, succumbing a few months after her marriage. It is difficult to think of any Brontë as a married woman — maybe even for Charlotte herself, who took a long time to make up her mind, and wrote to her best friend three months after her wedding: 'Indeed, indeed, Nell, it is a solemn and strange and perilous thing for a woman to become a wife.'

Their limited experience of the world and their way of life makes us think of them as younger than they really were. Anne's diary entries, at the age of 26, seem childishly innocent: 'Emily is upstairs ironing. I am sitting in the dining-room in the rocking-chair with my feet on the fender. Papa is in the parlour.' Even Charlotte, when she went to London, seemed immature and unworldly to the few sophisticated literary people she met, and even she remains mysterious. If she had lived, as Virginia Woolf remarked, she might have become 'a figure familiarly met with in London and elsewhere, the subject of pictures and anecdotes innumerable, the writer of many novels. . . .'

As it was, the girls produced just seven novels between them, and a quantity of poems — not counting the fantastical sagas of imaginary kingdoms which they and Branwell worked on obsessively as a strictly private activity, their secret game. The published novels became classics — by which one means that they are sufficiently powerful and sufficiently universal in appeal to be read and enjoyed by people whose experience would seem to be quite different from the experience of the characters in the books, or of their authors. Countless novels were published in the past century, including thousands by women, but only a small

Introduction

proportion have survived, and few so triumphantly as those by the Brontë sisters.

For a long time now their novels – especially Charlotte's *Jane Eyre* and Emily's *Wuthering Heights* – have been given to young people to read as part of their studies in English literature: they have become 'set books', read in schools and universities as well as for private pleasure at home. This would have astonished the Brontës' contemporaries. Critics at the time, who did not know at first that the novels were written by women, generally fell under their spell and acknowledged their power, but frequently denigrated them for 'coarseness' and 'grossness'. Anne Brontë's *The Tenant of Wildfell Hall* was judged by Charles Kingsley, author of *The Water Babies*, as 'utterly unfit to be put into the hands of girls'.

What shocked these solemn critics in part was the Brontës' innocently unashamed acceptance of women's passions, women's unhappiness, and women's frustration and anger. When Mrs Gaskell asked Charlotte for her views on 'the condition of women', Charlotte replied that there were 'evils' in the social system 'which no efforts of ours can touch: of which we cannot complain: of which it is advisable not too often to think.' For a start, they saw their brother being given money, and every opportunity, to make his way in the world, and wasting both the money and the opportunities.

Yet Branwell was central to their emotional and artistic lives. For nineteenth-century girls of the middle class, brothers were the only young males with whom they had physical contact. The fierce rough-and-tumble of the nursery and the schoolroom set the pattern for a pre-adolescent eroticism which might never be displaced by any mature sexual experience. It was so for the Brontës. Emily, for example, could not have created Heathcliff were it not for the fact that she had a brother, and that brother the dearly loved, doomed and difficult Branwell.

But too much nowadays is written about the real-life sources of fiction, the real people on whom characters and situations in books are modelled. The Brontës may have based their characters on people they knew, and on themselves, and exploited too their experiences as pupils and governesses, as members of a family – everything that added up to what Charlotte called the Real, 'something as unromantic as Monday morning'. But what their writing really shows us, like a blaze of light, is the power and the primacy of the romantic imagination. They wrote, these inexperienced virgins, about desire, sadistic love, adultery, madness, illegitimacy, incest, all the passions of the mind and the heart. Again Branwell is a key. Anne Brontë's *The Tenant of Wildfell Hall* would never had been written had the sisters not had to cope with his troublesome decline into alcoholism. Protected as they were from much of life, the little life they knew was intense and often raw. Intuition and imaginative genius showed them the rest.

Anne Brontë has always been described as 'gentle'; she is stereotyped as the mild, pious, less-talented youngest sister. This typecasting is largely Charlotte's fault. Outliving her sisters, she was able to present her lovingly edited version of their characters to posterity. She may also have been enviously surprised by 'gentle' Anne's achievement. Anne was not really so timid. Her novels prove it. She writes as sharply and ironically as Charlotte about the unfairly different ways that girls and boys were educated, and about the secondary position women stoically took in a male-centred world. She was not so home-loving as Emily; she insisted, when she was dying, on travelling to Scarborough where she had once been happy, and spending her last days within sight and sound of the sea. What Anne had, to perfection, was the approved demeanour of submission. Underneath lay the 'snappish fierceness' that a contemporary critic diagnosed in her fiction, and which Charlotte chose to forget.

Emily submitted to nothing, not even to her mortal illness. (Having read the unbearably painful account of her dying, it is a shock, at Haworth, to look at the sofa where she denied death to the last second.) Emily was, most likely, more strange and amoral, more freakish even, than Charlotte described her.

Charlotte's own passionate nature was also glossed over by a loving survivor. Mrs Gaskell saw four letters which proved that Charlotte had been unhappily in love with a married man, M. Heger, the owner of the girls' school in Brussels where she worked for a time. Not only had Charlotte been in love, but she had confessed her love. Mrs Gaskell, with the noblest of motives, suppressed this evidence of strong feeling, and it was not until 1913, when the four letters were published in *The Times*, that the world knew of this central drama in Charlotte's life, which it is still hard to see in proportion: as Brian Wilks writes in this book, 'too much and too little has been made of Charlotte's time in Brussels.'

Yet the stereotypes of the three sisters as they have come down to us have their own mythological value. I think all women, reading about the Brontës, find themselves identifying with one or another: with quiet, disregarded Anne, with wild, proud Emily, or with Charlotte, the one who negotiated with the outside world of publishers and fellow-writers. As Brian Wilks says, the Brontës 'have hypnotized the world'.

I always have to remind myself that the three Brontë sisters are not buried in Haworth churchyard, or out on the moors. Anne's grave is in Scarborough, the others lie in the family vault in the church. If for me their spirits at least are out in the open, it is because of the last paragraph of *Wuthering Heights*. Of this gothic tale of obsessional love, the poet Rossetti wrote that 'the action is laid in Hell — only it seems places and people have English names there.' But there are glimpses of a pagan heaven, as well; and that last lyrical paragraph about the graves of three people at peace after torment is among the most beautiful in our language.

'I lingered round them, under that benign sky; watched the moths fluttering among the heath and hare-bells; listened to the soft wind breathing through the grass; and wondered how anyone could ever imagine unquiet slumbers for the sleepers in that quiet earth.'

9

I

THE BRONTËS OF HAWORTH

It is not in my power to give any assurance of the substantial existence of Miss Helstone. You must be satisfied if that young person has furnished your mind with a pleasant idea: she is a native of Dreamland, and such can have neither voice nor presence except for the fancy, neither being nor dwelling except in thought.
Charlotte Brontë to George Smith, 15 January 1850

The most surprising thing about the Brontë sisters is that all of them became writers. To cherish such an early dream is common, to realize the dream is rare. What was it that first stimulated, then encouraged and supported the dream? Something in their circumstances fostered a love of words and provided the means whereby ideas could burgeon and flourish. Somewhere an apprenticeship with words was served that gave access to the technical skills necessary for writing lyric poetry and the sustained prose of a novel. That apprenticeship was undertaken in Haworth Parsonage where four children played with literature as others play with toys.

Central features of the circumstances that influenced the Brontës as they matured are the family, the parsonage in its graveyard, the little township of Haworth, the county of Yorkshire, and in a broader sense, England and Europe between 1820 and 1860. From Haworth and the isolated companionship of the parsonage nursery, a path leads to the literary salons of London and the reviews in Parisian literary journals. Yet it is a two-way traffic, for the culture of Europe was flowing into the small house long before the women there had published any books.

To be a member of the Brontë family meant being totally immersed in literature and the interplay of ideas. It meant taking art seriously and seeing the whole of life through the eyes of poets and painters. The mixture was heady and not always beneficial. It proved too rich for the only boy of the house. Whereas it fed the imagination of the girls, in Branwell's case it seems to have resulted in satiation. The close companionship enjoyed by the young women was not enough to sustain him. While the sisters gained increasing mastery over words, the brother gradually lost control altogether; false starts, unfinished pro-

Opposite Haworth Moor.

[handwritten marginalia: girls blossomed in the environment of literature and painting & poetry but Branwell didn't]

The Brontës of Haworth

jects, hasty jottings, tormented babbling were the sad outcome of his 'Scribblemania.' Branwell Brontë's failure is a counterpoint to his sisters' success, his apparent self-destruction a response to the same passions and circumstances.

The Rev. Patrick Brontë dominated his family but he was not the tyrannical figure portrayed by popular biography. Above all, it was his love of literature, music and painting, his interest in politics and his zeal for education, that established the workshop for writers in Haworth Parsonage. The children saw his printed works on their shelves and read his articles in the newspapers that they fetched from stationers in nearby towns. Whatever his shortcomings, he imparted a love of learning to each of his children and, more importantly, allowed them space in which to develop and explore their own ideas.

The parsonage home, however, was inevitably isolated from the rest of Haworth. The children's links with the real activities of the parish were restricted to their father's study, his office as chairman of the parish committee and his role of spiritual guide. It was not possible for them to mingle normally with the other children of the township. Haworth was unusually bereft of what we would now call any middle-class people. Almost the entire population was made up of workers, either in wool-processing, in quarries, or in low-level farming. Gentry had no interest in the township; even the mill-owners cared little for the welfare of the parishioners. Conditions in the town while the Brontë sisters lived there were appalling: the sanitation system was primitive and there was no piped water. The now-picturesque Main Street then ran as an open sewer, and local infant mortality was twice the national average. Haworth was a microcosm of the effects of industrial overpopulation and overcrowded housing. The comparatively sheltered and cultured upbringing of the Brontë children set them firmly apart from the people and children of the parish, although they were not oblivious to the conditions of the undernourished, ill-clothed, poorly housed workers who were their near neighbours.

Haworth lies at the edge of a large tract of moorland in Yorkshire, on the borders of Lancashire. It is perched upon the roof of England, high above sea-level, exposed to extremes of weather. In all, a dangerous place. The open moorland, which the Brontë children roamed, and which they made a private paradise, was one of the most powerful shaping forces of their childhood and an enduring delight of their maturity. It can be said without exaggeration that the wild wind off the moor permeated their writing as the rains soak the peatbogs on the moors themselves. In this landscape where nothing obscures a view of the rising and setting sun, the rolling moors became an informing image for their literary works. The seclusion of the parsonage fireside, a haven against the wind, is always set against the threat of an exposed wilderness reminiscent of *King Lear*.

Yorkshire was passing through all the rapid and far-reaching changes of the Industrial Revolution; populations of nearby woollen and clothworking towns would quadruple during the girls' lifetime. And as Yorkshire changed, so too England and Europe were caught up in

A page from one of Charlotte Brontë's early books.

economic boom and depression as the waves both of social and industrial revolution made themselves felt. All was grist to the Brontës' imaginative mill. The place where they lived, the people they saw around them, the immediate family, the attempts to overcome their social isolation in the small, economically depressed parish – these were the separate elements that made their circumstances unique. Always just outside things, at the edge of ordinary life, the family engendered individual minds, fostered a singularity of vision that was eventually to astonish the world.

In their writing, T'Parson's Charlotte, T'Parson's Emily and T'Parson's Anne – for that is how they were known in Haworth – celebrate the remote Yorkshire parish where they lived. But they do not write of the parish and the moors as travel writers guiding tourists, they write of the tension between loneliness and belonging, between solitude and society; above all, they follow the impulse of their imaginations, not the narrow strictures of any actual world.

In exploring the world of their fiction in the light of their biographies we must heed the warning that Charlotte gave George Smith, her publisher: that her characters, like the houses and plots of her stories, are '. . . a Native of Dreamland, and such can have neither voice nor presence except for the fancy, neither being nor dwelling except in thought'. We can, however, explore with confidence the remarkable and at times eccentric world of Haworth Parsonage, the crucible in which such rare works were refined and the mould in which they were cast.

The following pages tell the story of what was happening to the Brontë sisters as their books were published. Establishing their common experience as children of Haworth Parsonage, the tale of their extraordinary lives is set against passages from their works which illustrate their preoccupations, feelings and hopes. The illustrations accompanying the text draw together features of family life and experiences that were of importance in the sisters' creative development and maturing.

Nothing will fully explain the creative process that began in a remote moorland parish in the middle of the 19th century. This marriage of fact with fiction may illuminate and celebrate the lives of three of the most puzzling yet most loved women writers of English literature.

Portraits of Branwell, Charlotte, Anne and Emily Brontë.

II

THE EARLY YEARS

The Brontë sisters have hypnotized the world. Their novels, their fame, the story of their extraordinary lives, all conspire to bring visitors in their hundreds to the front door of their parsonage home in Haworth, Yorkshire.

Haworth does not appear in any of their fiction and yet it lies at the heart of all. The small depressed wool-processing township to which their father and mother brought them in 1820 affected them as surely as they now capture the imaginations of readers around the world. The home in a corner of a graveyard was like a magnet to them, its moorland setting high upon the backbone of England, the Pennine Chain, never far from their thoughts wherever they might be:

'That wind pouring in impetuous current through the air, sounding wildly, unremittingly from hour to hour, deepening its tone as the night advances, coming not in gusts, but with a rapid gathering stormy swell, that wind I know is heard at this moment far away on the moors at Haworth. Branwell and Emily hear it and as it sweeps over our house down the churchyard and round the old church, they think perhaps of me and Anne . . .'
Charlotte Brontë. Roe Head Journal

Remarkable as the house was, and remains to this day, the family of the parsonage from 1820 until 1860 was even more remarkable. To be a member of the Brontë family was to belong to a group of people unique in the history of literature. Life in the parsonage was lived in the crossfire of vivid imaginations and singular personalities held in close proximity. No ordinary house, it bred no ordinary talent, being a context of circumstances that served minds of extraordinary vision.

Mrs Gaskell best describes the township the family knew:

Opposite The bridge on the moors above Haworth parsonage, a spot well known to the Brontë children, now known as the 'Brontë Bridge'.

'It can hardly be called *country* any part of the way. For two miles the road passes over tolerably level ground, distant hills on the left, a *beck* flowing through meadows on the right, and furnishing water power, at certain points, to the factories built upon its banks. The air is dim and

The Early Years

lightless with the smoke from all these habitations and places of business. The soil in the valley (or *bottom* to use a local term) is rich, but, as the road begins to ascend, the vegetation becomes poorer; it does not flourish, it merely exists; and, instead of trees, there are only bushes and shrubs about the dwellings. Stone dykes are everywhere used in place of hedges; and what crops there are, on the patches of arable land, consist of pale, hungry-looking, grey-green oats. Right before the traveller on this road rises Haworth village; he can see it for two miles before he arrives, for it is situated on the side of a pretty steep hill, with a background of dun and purple moors, rising and sweeping away yet higher than the church, which is built at the very summit of the long narrow street. All around the horizon there is this same line of sinuous wave-like hills; the scoops into which they fall only revealing other hills beyond, of similar colour and shape, crowned with wild, bleak moors — grand, from the ideas of solitude and loneliness which they suggest, or oppressive from the feeling which they give of being pent-up by some monotonous and illimitable barrier, according to the mood of mind in which the spectator may be.'
Life of Charlotte Brontë. *Chapter 1*

Mrs Gaskell was right to emphasize the harshness of the semi-industrial landscape. Charlotte Brontë used to remind strangers that Haworth was 'ringed with mills as well as moors'. The moorland is still there, thirteen miles of almost totally uninhabited wilderness, treeless and but sparsely clothed with heather, fit grazing only for hardy upland

Haworth Parsonage as it was during the Brontë family's lifetime, before the building of the north wing and the planting of trees in the graveyard.

sheep. But around the little town itself were mills and quarries, even some open-cast coal workings.

More than the little town, it was the old parsonage built in a corner of the churchyard, the juxtaposition of its rooms and the life established in them by the family that most shaped and directed the Brontë sisters' development as writers. Again it is Mrs Gaskell, with her own sure novelist's eye, who sets the scene:

'The parsonage stands at right angles to the road, facing down upon the church; so that, in fact, parsonage, church and belfried schoolhouse, form three sides of an irregular oblong, of which the fourth is open to the field and moors that lie beyond. The area of this oblong is filled up by a crowded churchyard, and a small piece of garden or court in front of the clergyman's house ... The house is of grey stone, two stories high, heavily roofed with flags, in order to resist the winds that might strip off a lighter covering ... Everything about the place tells of the most dainty order, the most exquisite cleanliness.'
Chapter 1

Portrait by George Richmond of Elizabeth Gaskell, author of *The Life of Charlotte Brontë*, the celebrated biography commissioned by Patrick Brontë in 1855.

In winter, because of the hilly terrain and poor roads of the region, the Rev. Brontë's parish, with its huddle of houses up the side of the steep main street, was frequently cut off from the outside world. Yet that vulnerability did not turn the Brontë family into lonely recluses. Comparative isolation in an austere, challenging environment merely spurred them to greater effort, notably to keep well-informed, not only about affairs of the immediate locality but of Yorkshire and the greater world beyond. In this respect the parsonage became a cultural haven, a home with books, newspapers, engravings and music. This had wider implications for the village, since the parson, himself alert and informed, could shape attitudes and offer a lead to his parish. Patrick Brontë was chairman of the parish committee for forty-two years – still a record in those parts – and thus had daily dealings in the everyday realities of village life. The administration of poor law charities; the setting up of vigilantes in the absence of regular policing; campaigning for piped water to combat outbreaks of cholera and typhoid; these were among the many matters referred to Papa's study and brought to the front door of the children's home.

The remoteness of the community and the unaccustomed lack of aristocratic interest in the area enhanced the importance of the clergyman who, together with the doctors, alone represented an educated group. Such a group would often find itself arraigned against the only other people with an interest in the place: the mill-owners.

Today there is visible evidence of the Brontë family's work. Beside the house is the school, one of three in the area that the Rev. Brontë brought into being; the bells in the belfry are those he had hung. The parish registers and minute books record his baptizing, marrying and burying of parishioners, and also give details of many parish meetings concerning secular and social matters.

The Early Years

The Irish prelude

The most unlikely and remarkable single event in the whole story of the Brontë family was the entry in the registers of St John's College, Cambridge of Patrick Brontë as a sizar (subsidized undergraduate) in 1802. The arrival of the first-born child of illiterate parents, now 25 years old, at the ancient seat of learning culminated a programme of heroic self-education, and was to lead, half a century later, to a change in the direction and course of English literature. Wordsworth's college would unknowingly nurture a poor scholar with an unbounded application and enthusiasm for learning. Patrick Brontë's love of poetry, his competence in Greek and Latin, and his lifelong curiosity about science and medicine can all be traced to his days at Cambridge.

The path to Cambridge began in a small thatched cabin at Emdale, near Loughbrickland in County Down, Ireland. On St Patrick's Day 1777, a first child was born to Eleanor McClory, a Roman Catholic who had renounced her faith to become a Protestant, and Hugh Brunty. The boy Patrick somehow learned to read, devoured major works such as Milton's *Paradise Lost*, and came to the attention of local clergy who encouraged his studies and eventually made it possible for him to become an untrained teacher in the local church schools. This apprenticeship, together with his own zest for learning, set the seal on his life. From his early teaching days in the one-room schoolhouse at Drumballyrony, the parish where he lived, to the time, years later, when he lectured as a guest at the Mechanics Institute in Keighley, Patrick Brontë's theme was the same: the value of education for the poor and the mysterious influence of circumstances.

It was a letter from the Rev. Thomas Tighe, parson of Drumballyrony parish, that introduced Patrick Brontë to Cambridge; and it was in Tighe's church that the same Patrick, a newly ordained clergyman, preached one of his first sermons after graduation.

Patrick Brontë's ministry took him away from Ireland, never to return. First he served at Weatherfield, in Essex, where again he taught in Sunday school and preached in the church. From here he went north,

The Cottage at Emdale, County Down, where Patrick Brontë was born in 1777 of peasant stock.

Sunday School Class. Painting by Max (or Mayer) Issac, 1823–91.

to Wellington in Shropshire, and then in December 1809 arrived in Yorkshire to serve as additional curate in Dewsbury. Yorkshire was to be his home, the centre of his life's work and the nursery of his remarkable children.

From Dewsbury he went to St Peter's Hartshead-cum-Clifton, his first church, where he had complete charge of a parish that saw considerable unrest during the Chartist riots – events that provided daughter Charlotte with source material for her novel, *Shirley*.

While at Hartshead he undertook to examine the Religious Knowledge of pupils at a newly formed Methodist school near Leeds, entailing a walk of some ten miles at various times of the year. On one such visit he met and fell in love with the headmaster's niece, Maria Branwell of Penzance, who was in Yorkshire on holiday. The courtship was brisk and letters passed from Woodhouse Grove School to the curate at Hartshead. Maria wrote with great affection to her 'Dear Saucy Pat', sure that 'no one ever loved . . . with an affection more pure, constant tender and ardent than that which I feel'.

Meeting for the first time in August 1812, Maria and Patrick married in Guisley Church on Tuesday 29 December of the same year.

The birthplace and Haworth

None of the Brontë sisters were born in Haworth itself. After their marriage Patrick and Maria lived first in Hightown near Dewsbury and then in Thornton near Bradford where Patrick Brontë was in charge of the Old Bell Chapel. It was in Thornton that Charlotte (1816), Patrick Branwell (1817), Emily Jane (1818) and Anne (1820) were born. The

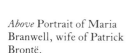

Above Portrait of Maria Branwell, wife of Patrick Brontë.

Centre Charlotte Brontë's flattering reworking of the portrait of her mother.

Right William Morgan, lifelong friend of Patrick Brontë, and critic and publisher of his early poetry.

The Early Years

family moved to Haworth in 1820, by which date the Rev. Brontë had published several books of prose and verse and had begun to contribute regularly to local newspapers.

Shortly after their arrival at Haworth, Mrs Brontë was taken seriously ill, and the family of six children (two older girls, Maria and Elizabeth, completing the group) were left motherless in September 1821. Sadly, the officiating minister at her funeral was William Morgan, who had married Maria's cousin at the same ceremony as that of the Brontës only nine years previously.

Maria's elder sister, Elizabeth Branwell, eventually moved to Haworth to help her brother-in-law bring up the family. Aunt Branwell, as the children always called her, stayed for the rest of her life. To all the children she was a support and stimulating presence. Branwell, the only boy, considered her 'for twenty years as my mother', and at her death wrote that he had now 'lost the guide and director of all the happy days connected with my childhood'. Although little of fact is known of Aunt Branwell, her contribution to the children's development should not be underestimated. After the death of the two elder sisters in 1825, Aunt Branwell and the four children were drawn even closer together and her influence was notable.

There is considerable misunderstanding about the health of the Brontë children. It is commonly held that they were always sickly, consumptive and touched with the mark of an early death. Nothing could be further from the truth. If death stalked them daily in the parsonage, as some biographers would have us believe, death must have been very bored. For after the loss of Mrs Brontë in 1821, and the

Above The Old Bell Chapel at Thornton, near Bradford – Rev. Brontë's second living. It was in this chapel that Charlotte, Patrick Branwell and Emily Jane were christened.

Below St Michael and All Angels, the parish church at Haworth, as it was circa 1850. The buildings to the left of the tower are the schoolroom and the schoolmaster's house that Patrick Brontë had built.

HAWORTH CHURCH.

Right The National Church Sunday School, Haworth, opened in 1832 with the Schoolmaster's house built on at the end.

Below Profile shade portrait of Aunt Elizabeth Branwell, the Brontë children's aunt, who came to care for them after their mother's death in 1821.

deaths of the elder girls in 1825, no one died in the parsonage for seventeen years. All the Brontë children were strong at birth. For a woman to bear six live children in the first quarter of the 19th century is in itself quite remarkable; that all those children survived not only their first years but into their tenth year (Maria was $10\frac{1}{2}$ when she died, Elizabeth 9) is evidence that they were extremely resilient. Charlotte, at the time of Branwell, Emily and Anne's deaths in 1848–9, believed that their health had been steadily undermined in maturity, perhaps from living so close to a poorly drained, over-filled graveyard.

'We had very early cherished the dream of one day becoming authors' *Charlotte Brontë. Biographical Notice to 1850 edition of* Wuthering Heights

The dream of one day becoming authors, shared by all four of the surviving children, and realized by three of them, wove its spell in and out of their daily lives. The strange ingredients of this achievement included a childhood and adolescence at the corner of a graveyard (frequented by body-snatchers), the roaming of spectacular, wind-swept moorland, with precious days of golden sunshine by secret waterfalls, and, most important of all, the sharp interplay of like minds in close proximity. In such an environment the Brontë children educated themselves and prepared with unwavering diligence to compose prose and verse.

By setting the characters and scenes of their fiction against the context of their lives and surroundings we may come to understand more of the springs that fed the steady progress of their development from childhood fantasies to best-selling novels. From their encounters with great literature, their explorations of painting and drawing, their love of music and the shared enrichment of their lives as a consequence of their father's total involvement in the affairs of a poor parish, but above all from the mere fact of being a Brontë living in Haworth Parsonage, there sprang the seven novels that since the first days of publication have fascinated the world.

By E. J. B. to _____ Oct 27th 1.841.

III

THE BELLS' POETRY ANTHOLOGY

'The bringing out of our little book was hard work. As was to be expected, neither we nor our poems were at all wanted.'
Charlotte Brontë. Introduction to the 1850 edition of *Wuthering Heights* and *Agnes Grey*.

In 1846 Charlotte Brontë collected together poems written by herself, Emily and Anne and endeavoured to find a publisher. The anthology appeared in May of that year at the author's own expense. This first publishing venture was not a success. In spite of favourable reviews in the *Athenaeum* and the *Critic*, the book failed to find an audience. Only two copies were sold of this edition.

The anthology, however, is not without significance. It marks the culmination of a long process of preparation, writing and experiment. It was also the occasion for the adoption of the pen-names Currer, Ellis and Acton Bell.

Charlotte recorded the manner in which the idea of a poetry anthology came to her:

'One day, in the autumn of 1845, I accidentally lighted on a MS volume of verse in my sister Emily's handwriting. Of course, I was not surprised, knowing that she could and did write verse: I looked it over, and something more than surprise seized me, – a deep conviction that these were not common affusions, nor at all like the poetry women generally write. I thought them condensed and terse, vigorous and genuine. To my ear, they had also a peculiar music – wild, melancholy, and elevating.'
Biographical Notice to the 1850 edition of Wuthering Heights *and* Agnes Grey

Charlotte's discovery was regarded by Emily as impertinent prying; her writings were private: '. . . it took hours to reconcile her to the discovery I had made, and days to persuade her that such poems merited publication. I knew, however, that a mind like hers could not be without some spark of honourable ambition, and refused to be discouraged in my attempts to fan that spark to flame.'

Opposite Watercolour by Emily Brontë, thought to be of her tame merlin hawk, Hero.

The Bells' Poetry Anthology

Typically, Charlotte took it upon herself to organize Emily and it is unfortunate that only her account of events survives. She explained that once Anne learned of the plan to attempt publication she too offered poems for inclusion. The older sister is once more condescending: 'I could not but be a partial judge, yet I thought that these verses too had a sweet sincere pathos of their own.'

The poems were therefore collected and a letter sent out:

28th January 1846

to Aylott and Jones – Publishers
London

Gentlemen,

May I request to be informed whether you would
undertake the publication of a Collection of short
poems in one vol.oct.

If you object to publishing the work at your own
risk – would you undertake it on the Author's account?
I am gentlemen, Your obdt. hmble.Servt.

C. Brontë

Aylott and Jones replied that they would only publish the work at the author's risk, and thus it was undertaken for the cost of £37.

The poems were selected and it was at this point that the poets decided to disguise their identity. The sisters kept a common surname but thinly veiled their identity and sex by adopting Currer for Charlotte, Ellis for Emily and Acton for Anne. The surname seems to have been borrowed from Arthur *Bell* Nicholls, then their father's curate in Haworth. Thus the Messrs Bell enter English Literature.

There is much conjecture as to why the sisters adopted the Bell pen-names. Charlotte and Anne both felt the need at different times to explain:

'Averse to personal publicity, we veiled our names under those of Currer, Ellis and Acton Bell; the ambiguous choice being dictated by a sort of conscientious scruple at assuming Christian names positively masculine, while we did not like to declare ourselves women, because – without at the time suspecting that our mode of writing and thinking was not what is called "feminine" – we had a vague impression that authoresses are liable to be looked on with prejudice . . .'
Charlotte Brontë. Biographical Notice to the 1850 edition of Wuthering Heights *and* Agnes Grey.

Anne, whom Charlotte frequently suggested was too feeble to express herself with conviction, was the first to explain in print the distinction between the three Bell writers: this she did in the preface to the second

POEMS

BY

CURRER, ELLIS, AND ACTON

BELL.

LONDON:
AYLOTT AND JONES, 8, PATERNOSTER-ROW.

1846.

Title page of the First Edition of the Poems of Currer, Ellis and Acton Bell.

edition of *The Tenant of Wildfell Hall*, her second published novel:

'I would have it to be distinctly understood that Acton Bell is neither Currer nor Ellis Bell, and therefore, let not his faults be attributed to them. As to whether the name be real or fictitious, it cannot greatly signify to those who know him only by his works. As little, I should think can it matter whether the writer so designated is a man, or a woman as one or two of my critics profess to have discovered . . . in my own mind I am satisfied that if a book is a good one, it is so whatever the sex of the author may be. All novels are or should be written for both men and women to read, and I am at a loss to conceive how a man should permit himself to write anything that would be really disgraceful to a woman, or why a woman should be censured for writing anything that would be proper and becoming for a man.'
Anne Brontë. Preface to second edition, 1848, of The Tenant of Wildfell Hall

The adoption of the pen names Currer, Ellis and Acton Bell in 1846 was inadvertently mischievous in effect and unfortunate for the literary reputation of its individual authors. The Messrs Bell industry, which never existed, was by this single event given an apparent reality which today colours our response to the separate writings of singular minds. Nowhere is this more evident, or unhelpful, than in the evaluation of the poetry written and published by the Brontë family.

We know that Charlotte was moved to resolve some of the more irritating difficulties that the pen-names had created when she sped to London with Anne to astonish George Smith, her publisher, with 'ocular proof' that the Messrs Bell were in fact 'three sisters'. There is nothing collaborative about the published work of the Brontë family. Charlotte's zealous 'tidying up' of Emily's work and her stern censure of Anne's *Tenant of Wildfell Hall* (both, significantly, after the death of each writer) could arguably be regarded as interference but not held out as evidence of collaboration.

The little anthology, whatever its intention (perhaps merely the satisfaction of seeing manuscript poems in book form) led to confusion and an unhelpful emphasis on the corporate nature of the Bells', and thereby the Brontë sisters', writing.

The sisters could not have known that within two years of the anthology first appearing the hounds of the reading public would be in full cry seeking the identity of the mysterious brothers Bell. With hindsight, it is easy to foresee the muddle that the unsubtle and half-hearted disguise (the correspondence with Mr Currer Bell was, after all, directed to Miss Charlotte Brontë) was likely to create. Newby's attempt to pass off Ellis and Acton as the same writer as Currer, understandably with a view to making his authors sell as fast as their 'brother' Currer, did not, of course, help matters.

Among the reasons given for the publication of the poems (at considerable cost, for £37 could represent a year's wages) one is notably absent from biography and criticism: the desire to emulate their father and their brother Branwell. Papa's published books, including several collections of verse, were on his study shelves. Branwell had succeeded four years earlier in having a group of poems printed in *The Halifax Guardian* and *Huddersfield and Bradford Advertiser* with a further poem in *The Leeds Intelligencer* at the same time. The poems published in Halifax had also been published a few days previously in another Bradford newspaper. These poems, printed over the pen-name *Northangerland*, represent the first appearance in print of the children of Haworth Parsonage. The sisters were perhaps keen to see their works out in the world alongside those of their father and brother. Knowledge of these poems may also partly explain the exclusion of Branwell from the new anthology.

Typical of Branwell's poems is *Caroline's Prayer*, published in the Bradford newspaper in 1842 and not since reprinted in any form until now:

Some of Patrick Brontë's publications. A pioneer in the field of popular education, his works were readily accessible to all his children, whose literary and artistic activities he encouraged.

CAROLINE'S PRAYER

On the Change from Childhood to Womanhood

My Father, and my childhood's guide,
    If oft I wandered far from thee;
Even though thine only son has died
    To save from death a child like me.

O! still – to thee when turns my heart,
    In hours of sadness – frequent now –
Be thou the God that once thou wert;
    And calm my breast, and clear my brow.

I'm now no more a little child
    O'er shadowed by thine angel wing,
My very dreams seem far more wild
    Than those my slumbers used to bring.

I farther see – I deeper feel –
    With hope more warm, but heart less mild,
And former things new shapes reveal.
    All strangely brightened or despoiled.

I am entering on Life's open tide;
    So – farewell, childhood's shores divine!
And, Oh my Father, deign to guide
    Through these wide waters, Caroline.

Northangerland

Drawing by Patrick Branwell Brontë of his fictional hero, Northangerland, which bears a striking resemblance to the existing drawings of himself. Northangerland was the pen-name he assumed in publishing his poetry in local newspapers.

Branwell's poem, with its theme of transition from childhood to maturity, echoes the familial aspect of his sisters' poetry. The 'Bell' anthology, which would scarcely have commanded much interest in the light of its authors' subsequent publications, is nevertheless a rare work.

In drawings and diary papers, Emily and Anne described the scene in their drawing room when writing was in progress; the subjects, style and manner of the poems suggest a close companionship in ideas as well as physical proximity.

Emily Brontë's diary paper for June 26 1837, showing herself and her sister Anne working at the dining room table.

The poems that follow are in the original sequence, with the addition of two poems by Emily which offer comparison with one of Anne's, and underline the strength of her voice, that voice which spoke to Charlotte and led to the creation of the anthology in the first place.

The Bells' Poetry Anthology

A Reminiscence is often linked, rightly or wrongly, with the Rev. William Weightman, one of Patrick Brontë's curates. Weightman, whom the girls nicknamed Celia Amelia, was very popular in the parsonage; he befriended Branwell and once, discovering that the girls had never received a Valentine, sent them one each. He died tragically young, having contracted cholera through diligent visiting of the sick during an outbreak in the village.

Charlotte's mischievous gossip to her intimate friend Ellen Nussey has led to a wide belief that Anne and Weightman found each other more than usually attractive. Certainly *A Reminiscence* is an appropriate 'obituary' poem for a close friend:

THE POOR CURATE.

A REMINISCENCE

Yes, thou art gone! and never more
Thy sunny smile shall gladden me;
But I may pass the old church door,
And pace the floor that covers thee,

May stand upon the cold, damp stone,
And think that, frozen, lies below
The lightest heart that I have known,
The kindest I shall ever know.

Yet, though I cannot see thee more,
'Tis still a comfort to have seen;
And though thy transient life is o'er,
'Tis sweet to think that thou hast been;

To think a soul so near divine,
Within a form, so angel fair,
United to a heart like thine,
Has gladdened once our humble sphere.

Acton

Curates were a constant source of merriment in the Brontë household. Poorly paid, hard-worked and probably in awe of their Irish parson, they were none of them spared the mischievous pens of the three quick-witted girls. It would be pleasant to think that William Weightman, friend to Branwell, visitor of the sick and respected Sunday school teacher, was an exception to Charlotte's rule of censure.

Together with curates and personal familiarity with their foibles went a close knowledge of church matters. It could hardly be otherwise. How could children living in the corner of a graveyard fail to take death and remembrance as the subject for their writing? As Anne's poem reflects upon a buried loved one, so we find the same theme in Emily's *Remembrance*, and at once the difference between Emily's and Anne's writing is plain to see. Anne's composed, careful poem juxtaposes Emily's impassioned evocation of landscape, season and deeply felt, precious sentiments. The common subject, springing from similar experiences of moor, church and winter, gives rise to a strikingly different work.

REMEMBRANCE

Cold in the earth – and the deep snow piled above
      thee,
Far, far, removed, cold in the dreary grave!
Have I forgot, my only Love, to love thee,
Severed at last by Time's all-severing wave?

Now, when alone, do my thoughts no longer hover
Over the mountains, on that northern shore,
Resting their wings where heath and fern-leaves
      cover
Thy noble heart for ever, ever more?

Cold in the earth – and fifteen wild Decembers,
From those brown hills, have melted into spring:
Faithful, indeed, is the spirit that remembers
After such years of change and suffering!

Sweet Love of youth, forgive, if I forget thee,
While the world's tide is bearing me along;
Other desires and other hopes beset me,
Hopes which obscure, but cannot do thee wrong!

No later light has lightened up my heaven,
No second morn has ever shone for me;
All my life's bliss from thy dear life was given,
All my life's bliss is in the grave with thee.

But, when the days of golden dreams had perished,
And even Despair was powerless to destroy;
Then did I learn how existence could be cherished,
Strengthened, and fed without the aid of joy.

Then did I check the tears of useless passion –
Weaned my young soul from yearning after thine;
Sternly denied its burning wish to hasten
Down to that tomb already more than mine.

And, even yet, I dare not let it languish,
Dare not indulge in memory's rapturous pain;
Once drinking deep of that divinest anguish,
How could I seek the empty world again?

Ellis

The Bells' Poetry Anthology

Most of the longer poems in the anthology are by Charlotte, in the narrative mode derived from her reading of Byron and of the tales of travellers and adventurers printed in newspapers and magazines such as *Blackwoods* and *John Bull*. *Frances* is typical of such poems. The following extracts indicate the romantic, almost Gothic emphasis in her writing, with its sensuous overtones. The poem complements the rich watercolours that Charlotte painted and which were to fill Jane Eyre's portfolio. The third extract from the poem, although written earlier, is often linked with Charlotte's own distress after her return from Brussels where she had unwisely formed an attachment to her married teacher M. Heger. She knew the sadness of longing for letters from Heger which were never to be written:

The parsonage under snow.

'Unloved – I love; unwept – I weep;
Grief I restrain – hope I repress:
Vain is this anguish – fixed and deep;
Vainer, desires and dreams of bliss.

My love awakes no love again,
My tears collect, and fall unfelt;
My sorrow touches none with pain,
My humble hopes to nothing melt.

For me the universe is dumb,
Stone-deaf, and blank, and wholly blind;
Life I must bound, existence sum
In the strait limits of one mind;

That mind my own. Oh! narrow cell;
Dark – imageless – a living tomb!
There must I sleep, there wake and dwell
Content, with palsy, pain, and gloom.'

Again she paused; a moan of pain,
A stifled sob, alone was heard;
Long silence followed – then again,
Her voice the stagnant midnight stirred.

Oh! Love was all a thin illusion;
Joy, but the desert's flying stream;
And, glancing back on long delusion
My memory grasps a hollow dream.

Signed watercolour by Charlotte Brontë, probably a copy from an engraving.

Sketch of Roe Head School, Mirfield, attributed to Anne Brontë.

Ye', whence that wondrous change of feeling,
I never knew, and cannot learn,
Nor why my lover's eye, congealing,
Grew cold, and clouded, proud, and stern.

Nor wherefore, friendship's forms forgetting,
He careless left, and cool withdrew;
Nor spoke of grief, nor fond regretting,
Nor even one glance of comfort threw.

And neither word nor token sending,
Of kindness, since the parting day,
His course, for distant regions bending,
Went, self-contained and calm, away.

Currer

Letters played an important part in the Brontës' lives, helping to offset the comparative isolation of their moorland home. When away, at school or elsewhere, letters continually passed back and forth. At Roe Head school in 1836, Charlotte, a 20-year-old teacher, writes to Branwell 'because I cannot help it' and expresses her impatience, seeking escape from the humdrum life through imagination, composition and the sharing of ideas with her loved brother and sisters.

The opening stanzas of *The Letter* demonstrates Charlotte's remarkable ability to let her fancy transform a familiar ordinary event, to begin with a carefully observed situation and sustain an imaginative flow of narrative:

What is she writing? Watch her now,
    How fast her fingers move!
How eagerly her youthful brow
    Is bent in thought above!
Her long curls, drooping, shade the light,
    She puts them quick aside,
Nor knows, that band of crystals bright,
    Her hasty touch untied.
It slips adown her silken dress,
    Falls glittering at her feet;
Unmarked it falls, for she no less
    Pursues her labour sweet.

The very loveliest hour that shines,
    Is in that deep blue sky;
The golden sun of June declines,
    It has not caught her eye.
The cheerful lawn, and unclosed gate,
    The white road, far away,
In vain for her light footsteps wait,
    She comes not forth to-day.
There is an open door of glass
    Close by that lady's chair,
From thence, to slopes of mossy grass,
    Descends a marble stair.

                          Currer.

Emily Brontë's writing desk.

Charlotte's fear that she might, while away from Haworth, have lost 'the divine, silent, unseen land of thought' is answered by Emily's poem *To Imagination*. Emily strikes an almost Wordsworthian note as she celebrates the attribute that she and her sisters enjoyed in such abundance:

TO IMAGINATION

When weary with the long day's care,
    And earthly change from pain to pain,
And lost and ready to despair,
    Thy kind voice calls me back again:
Oh, my true friend! I am not lone,
While thou canst speak with such a tone!

So hopeless is the world without;
    The world within I doubly prize;
Thy world, where guile, and hate, and doubt,
    And cold suspicion never rise;
Where thou, and I, and Liberty,
Have undisputed sovereignty.

What matters it, that, all around,
    Danger, and guilt, and darkness lie,
If but within our bosom's bound
    We hold a bright, untroubled sky,
Warm with ten thousand mingled rays
Of suns that know no winter days?

Reason, indeed, may oft complain
    For Nature's sad reality,
And tell the suffering heart, how vain
    Its cherished dreams must always be;
And Truth may rudely trample down
The flowers of Fancy, newly-blown:

But, thou art ever there, to bring
    The hovering vision back, and breathe
New glories o'er the blighted spring,
    And call a lovelier Life from Death,
And whisper, with a voice divine,
Of real worlds, as bright as thine.

I trust not to thy phantom bliss,
    Yet, still, in evening's quiet hour,
With never-failing thankfulness,
    I welcome thee, Benignant Power;
Sure solacer of human cares,
And sweeter hope, when hope despairs!

Ellis

Engraving of a studious
schoolboy, 19th century.

All three sisters were at one time or another teachers, either in school or with private families as governesses. On one occasion they even set about establishing their own school in the parsonage – another venture doomed to fail, like the poetry anthology. It is hardly surprising, therefore, to find so many references to teaching and evocations of classrooms in both their verse and prose. To all of them the parsonage offered a unique refuge:

'My home is humble and unattractive to strangers, but to me it contains what I shall find nowhere else in the world – the profound, and intense affection which brothers and sisters feel for each other when their minds are cast in the same mould, their ideas drawn from the same source – when they have clung to each other from childhood, and when disputes have never sprung up to divide them.'
Charlotte Brontë. Letter to Henry Nussey, 9 May 1841

The Teacher's Monologue is a characteristic piece, the fourth stanza typifying the homesickness that Charlotte and her sisters felt for Haworth:

The room is quiet, thoughts alone
People its mute tranquillity;
The yoke put off, the long task done, —
I am, as it is bliss to be,
Still and untroubled. Now, I see,
For the first time, how soft the day
O'er waveless water, stirless tree,
Silent and sunny, wings its way.
Now, as I watch that distant hill,
So faint, so blue, so far removed,
Sweet dreams of home my heart may fill,
That home where I am known and loved:
It lies beyond; yon azure brow
Parts me from all Earth holds for me;
And, morn and eve, my yearnings flow
Thitherward tending, changelessly.
My happiest hours, aye! all the time,
I love to keep in memory,
Lapsed among moors, ere life's first prime
Decayed to dark anxiety.

Currer

Waterfall known as the Brontë Falls. After heavy rain or melting snow, the streams of the moors can become spectacular. It was while walking up to see such a sight that Charlotte caught a chill from which she never recovered.

Beyond the security of the parsonage fireside lay the wilderness of the moors. A constant presence was the driving wind that blusters its way across from the Irish Sea and batters the great stone slabs that form the low-pitched roofs of Haworth. Anne linked her memories of this wind with her later love of the sea at Scarborough:

LINES COMPOSED IN A WOOD ON A
WINDY DAY

My soul is awakened, my spirit is soaring
And carried aloft on the wings of the breeze;
For above and around me the wild wind is roaring,
Arousing to rapture the earth and the seas.

The long withered grass in the sunshine is glancing,
The bare trees are tossing their branches on high;
The dead leaves, beneath them, are merrily dancing,
The white clouds are scudding across the blue sky.

I wish I could see how the ocean is lashing
The foam of its billows to whirlwinds of spray;
I wish I could see how its proud waves are dashing,
And hear the wild roar of their thunder to-day!

Acton

A shared response to nature and the elements is matched in early writing by common themes or explorations. One such example, deriving perhaps from a teasing exercise where each submitted a version of a particular scene or situation, is provided by *The Captive Dove* written by Anne, with its counterpart in Emily's *The Caged Bird* (not published in the Bell anthology). Such a comparison enables us to hear the distinctive voice and to appreciate the individual strength of each poet's thought:

THE CAPTIVE DOVE

Poor restless dove, I pity thee;
And when I hear thy plaintive moan,
I mourn for thy captivity,
And in thy woes forget mine own.

To see thee stand prepared to fly,
And flap those useless wings of thine,
And gaze into the distant sky,
Would melt a harder heart than mine.

In vain — in vain! Thou canst not rise:
Thy prison roof confines thee there;
Its slender wires delude thine eyes,
And quench thy longings with despair.

Oh, thou wert made to wander free
In sunny mead and shady grove,
And, far beyond the rolling sea,
In distant climes, at will to rove!

Yet, hadst thou but one gentle mate
Thy little drooping heart to cheer,
And share with thee thy captive state,
Thou couldst be happy even there.

Yes, even there, if, listening by,
One faithful dear companion stood,
While gazing on her full bright eye,
Thou mightst forget thy native wood.

But thou, poor solitary dove,
Must make, unheard, thy joyless moan;
The heart, that Nature formed to love,
Must pine, neglected, and alone.

Acton

The Bells' Poetry Anthology

THE CAGED BIRD

And like myself lone, wholly lone,
It sees the day's long sunshine glow;
And like myself it makes its moan
In unexhausted woe.

Give we the hills our equal prayer:
Earth's breezy hills and heaven's blue sea;
We ask for nothing further here
But our own hearts and liberty.

Ah! could my hand unlock its chain,
How gladly would I watch it soar,
And ne'er regret and ne'er complain
To see its shining eyes no more.

But let me think that if to-day
It pines in cold captivity,
To-morrow both shall soar away
Eternally, entirely Free.

Ellis

Emily is considered to be the finest poet of the Brontë family. It seems that Charlotte's own response to Emily's poems was right: 'a deep conviction that these were not common affusions . . . to my ear they had also a peculiar music'. A lyric to be found in an 1844 manuscript but which was not included in the Bell anthology testifies unequivocally to Emily's artistic power:

LOVE AND FRIENDSHIP

Love is like the wild rose-briar,
Friendship like the holly-tree —
The holly is dark when the rose-briar blooms
But which will bloom most constantly?

The wild rose-briar is sweet in spring,
Its summer blossoms scent the air;
Yet wait till winter comes again,
And who will call the wild-briar fair?

Then, scorn the silly rose-wreath now
And deck thee with the holly's sheen,
That when December blights thy brow
He still may leave thy garland green.

Ellis

Right A page of a manuscript poem by Charlotte Brontë, evidence of the habit of scribbled drawings shared by all the Brontë children.

Below Pencil drawing of a tree, attributed to Emily Brontë.

The Bells' anthology, although a complete failure at the time of publication, is of paramount interest today. Events that followed — the triumph of Currer's *Jane Eyre*, the controversy over the violent nature of *Wuthering Heights* by Ellis, and the success of Acton's second novel, *The Tenant of Wildfell Hall*, brought the Bells notoriety and later fame. Once the other works had established Charlotte, Emily and Anne as writers, the anthology was bought by Charlotte's publisher, Smith Elder, who reissued the book in 1848. Since then copies of the first Aylott and Jones edition have become very rare collectors' items.

The little book of poems is emphatically a woman's anthology and in no way limited by that fact. The poems centre upon shared family experiences at home, not dwelling, however, on the menial and necessary tasks of the household but concerned with the interplay of sisterly relationships, the processes of maturing and the yearning for love, comfort and affection.

The romantic, imaginative element of the poems is true to the companionship from which it derived, echoing the shared reading and excitement over Byron and the *Arabian Nights* stories. The poems honestly record the feelings, interests and hopes of the young women: and whatever else its authors may have published, the book stands secure with its own integrity.

The book's failure in 1847 must have been a blow to Charlotte's pride as the organizer of the venture; it did not, however, deter any of the sisters from further writing. Without waiting to know how their poetry had fared, each had been engaged in completing a novel. The manuscripts of *Wuthering Heights*, *Agnes Grey* and *The Professor* would shortly begin to go the round of London publishers.

IV
JANE EYRE

'I wish you had not sent me Jane Eyre. It interested me so much that I have lost (or won if you like) a whole day reading it . . .'
William Thackeray. Letter to W. S. Williams of Smith Elder. 23 October 1847.

In July 1845 Charlotte sent a parcel of three manuscripts to a London publisher. They were her own *The Professor*, based on her experiences of teaching in Brussels, Anne's *Agnes Grey*, in turn modelled upon the author's time as governess in Mirfield and Thorp Green near York, and Emily's *Wuthering Heights*, which did not take teaching as a subject, finding its inspiration in the wild countryside surrounding the sisters' home.

Charlotte had already advised the publisher of the poetry anthology that the Messrs Bell were preparing novels:

'Gentleman – C, E and A Bell are now preparing for the press a work of fiction, consisting of three distinct and unconnected tales, which may be published either together, as a work of three volumes . . . or separately as single volumes . . .'
Charlotte Brontë to Aylott and Jones, 6 April 1846

Aylott and Jones did not publish novels but gave Charlotte a list of houses that might be approached. So in July of that year the parcel of novels began its round of publishers. Thomas Newby, a twelvemonth later, agreed to publish *Wuthering Heights* and *Agnes Grey*, at their author's expense, but rejected Charlotte's manuscript. Faced with the likelihood that her sisters would overtake her in the race to be printed, Charlotte resolutely relabelled her parcel and sent her lone manuscript off to other publishers.

All this was done under the guise of the masculine pen-names. Charlotte, until this time, had written above her real name 'on behalf of Currer Bell'; now she signed letters *Mr* Currer Bell, thus abandoning any pretence of ambiguity in the disguise.

Newby delayed publishing *Wuthering Heights* and *Agnes Grey* until

Opposite Wycoller Dene, with the ruins of Wycoller Hall believed to have suggested Ferndean to Charlotte.

Jane Eyre

December 1847, a decision that was to allow Charlotte to lead her sisters into print, in an unexpected and, for her, most satisfying manner.

The much-travelled manuscript of *The Professor* eventually reached George Smith's publishing house. W. S. Williams, a reader for the firm, discerned ability in the novel and took the trouble to couch his rejection of it in encouraging words.

Charlotte described the nature of this latest rejection:

'There came a letter which he opened in dreary anticipation of finding two hard, hopeless lines, intimating that "Messrs Smith, Elder & Co were not disposed to publish the MS", and instead, he took out of the envelope a letter of two pages. He read it trembling. It declined, indeed, to publish that tale for business reasons, but it discussed its merits and demerits so courteously, so considerately, in a spirit so rational, with a discrimination so enlightened, that this very refusal cheered the author better than a vulgarly expressed acceptance would have done. It was added that a work in three volumes would meet with careful attention.'
Memoir of Ellis and Acton Bell. Smith, Elder, 1850

Portrait of William Makepeace Thackeray (1811–63), the celebrated novelist, to whom Charlotte dedicated the second edition of *Jane Eyre*, by S. Laurence.

Charlotte had already been working on *Jane Eyre* and was quick to assure Smith, Elder that this new work would have 'a more vivid interest than belongs to *The Professor*'. She received the courteous rejection early in August, and the completed *Jane Eyre* was in George Smith's hands by the end of the same month. Smith was so taken with the new manuscript that he agreed, with similar alacrity, to publish it at once. The book came out two months later, in October 1847, to become an immediate success. Thus Charlotte, no longer with cause for dejection, was able to put *The Professor* on a shelf and see her newest work in print while Newby lumbered towards publication of her sisters' works.

Charlotte's confidence that her new work would impart 'a more vivid interest than belongs to *The Professor*' is a considerable understatement, for it tends to diminish the extraordinary difference between the two novels and the single most significant development in Charlotte's writing. In *The Professor*, she adopts a masculine narrator and makes him the hero of the story, whilst keeping the narrative within sober, realistic bounds. In *Jane Eyre* the subject of the story is female and she tells the tale herself. At a stroke Charlotte found her own voice and the confidence to express her intimate feelings. The orphan teacher, who appears but palely in *The Professor* as eventual companion to its hero, now takes the centre of the stage. In *Jane Eyre* Charlotte's own schooldays, her fears, her loves, her anger and delight are all given full measure. The result is a book that Thackeray, like so many others after him, was quite unable to put down until he had reached the end.

Jane Eyre perhaps has more immediate biographical material in its narrative than any of the other Brontë novels, a fact that was to cause not a little discussion and unease in later years. Charlotte reached back to her earliest memories and, in telling the story of an orphan child, used settings and situations that she and her sisters knew well. The most striking instance, resulting in the harshest words when her own biography was published by Mrs Gaskell, was her use of the School for the Daughters of Poor Clergy at Cowan Bridge as a model for the novel's Lowood, and of its founder, Rev. William Carus Wilson, as the original for Mr Brocklehurst.

Left Drawing by Charlotte Brontë, believed to be of Mr Brocklehurst in *Jane Eyre* who is based on her memories of Rev. Carus Wilson.

Right Rev. W. Carus Wilson, founder of The Clergy Daughter's School at Cowan Bridge, the model for Lowood in *Jane Eyre*.

The very opening of the novel, however, signals Charlotte's intention to make use of her own experiences and interests, and those of her family, in her fiction. Throughout her work it is the shared life of the parsonage that provides the detail of setting and incident. The books mentioned in the novels are those the children knew and loved, the paintings and drawings those they had studied, discussed and copied. Bewick's *History of British Birds*, Aesop's *Fables*, Bunyan's *Pilgrim's Progress*, Walter Scott's novels, Byron, Shakespeare, Ossian and the *Arabian Nights*, events in local newspapers – all were used as source material for theme, setting and style. Little wonder that the orphan Jane, sitting with her book in the window seat, is so real a figure.

Little Jane Eyre, at the outset of the novel bearing her name, indulges in a typical Brontë habit: hiding with a book. The book is special, one the family owned and knew well: Thomas Bewick's *History of British Birds*. Like Jane, the Brontë children had marvelled at the scenes of

Jane Eyre

arctic waste; moreover, they had painstakingly copied the miniatures from the book – the birds, the scenes with moral tales and the tiny landscapes. Every picture that Jane describes can be found in Bewick. Yet there is more to it than a simple shared interest of author and heroine in little drawings. The windswept scenes, the deserted beach, the marooned mariner alone on a rock, all reflect Jane's dilemma. The movement, in symbolic terms, of the novel will be from isolation and the frozen wastes towards the warmth of loving relationships and shelter. At the crux of the novel, when Rochester seeks to make Jane his mistress, Charlotte gives him words that come from page one:

'"You have as good as said that I am a married man – as a married man you will shun me . . . just now you have refused to kiss me . . . you will say 'That man had nearly made me his mistress: I must be ice and rock to him;' and ice and rock you will accordingly become."'
Chapter 27

In 1824 the Brontë girls, Maria (aged 10½), Elizabeth (9), Charlotte (8) and Emily (6½), were all sent as boarders to the newly opened school for the Daughters of Poor Clergy at Cowan Bridge. The school was highly recommended and there was little call to suspect how tragic this step towards providing an education for the girls would prove in a matter of months. A combination of a harsh regime and weak constitutions caused the two older girls, Maria and Elizabeth, to fall ill. Their father was sent for, only to bring them home too late, for both died of consumption within a short time. Charlotte and Emily were immediately taken away from the school. When she came to use it in *Jane Eyre*, Charlotte described the school precisely as it was; and she also drew upon her friends and teachers there for characters in her narrative. Her own sister served as the model for Helen Burns, the saintly little girl in the novel, as is confirmed by a letter to Mr Williams, George Smith's perceptive and encouraging reader:

'You are right in having faith in the reality of Helen Burns; she was real enough. I have exaggerated nothing there. I abstained from recording much that I remember respecting her, lest the narrative should sound incredible. Knowing this, I could not but smile at the quiet self-complacent dogmatism with which one of the journals lays it down that "such creations as Helen Burns are very beautiful but very untrue." '

The Brontës: Their Lives, Friendships and Correspondence. *Wise & Symington*.

In later life, Charlotte maintained that she had of course drawn upon her childhood memory of the school, but that in essence Lowood was indeed Cowan Bridge. Certainly the real walk from Cowan Bridge to the church at Tunstall became the fictional walk from Lowood to Brocklebridge:

'During January, February, and part of March, the deep snows, and after their melting, the almost impassable roads, prevented our stirring beyond the garden walls, except to go to church, but within these limits we had to pass an hour every day in the open air. Our clothing was insufficient to protect us from the severe cold; we had no boots, the snow got into our shoes, and melted there; our ungloved hands became numbed and covered with chilblains, as were our feet. I remember well the distracting irritation I endured from this cause every evening, when my feet inflamed, and the torture of thrusting the swelled, raw, and stiff toes into my shoes in the morning. Then the scanty supply of food was distressing: with the keen appetites of growing children, we had scarcely

Sickness and Health by Thomas Webster.

Jane Eyre

sufficient to keep alive a delicate invalid. From this deficiency of nourishment resulted an abuse which pressed hardly on the younger pupils: whenever the famished great girls had an opportunity they would coax or menace the little ones out of their portion. Many a time I have shared between two claimants the precious morsel of brown bread distributed at teatime, and after relinquishing to a third half the contents of my mug of coffee, I have swallowed the remainder with an accompaniment of secret tears, forced from me by the exigency of hunger.

Sundays were dreary days in that wintry season. We had to walk two miles to Brocklebridge Church, where our patron officiated. We set out cold, we arrived at church colder: during the morning service we became almost paralyzed. It was too far to return to dinner, and an allowance of cold meat and bread, in the same penurious proportion observed in our ordinary meals, was served round between the services.

At the close of the afternoon service we returned by an exposed and hilly road, where the bitter winter wind, blowing over a range of snowy summits to the north, almost flayed the skin from our faces.

I can remember Miss Temple walking lightly and rapidly along our drooping line, her plaid cloak which the frosty wind fluttered, gathered close about her, and encouraging us, by precept, and example, to keep up our spirits, and march forward, as she said, "like stalwart soldiers". The other teachers, poor things, were generally themselves too much dejected to attempt the task of cheering others.

Lowood, the school in *Jane Eyre*. An illustration from the 1872 edition by E. M. Wimperis who was commissioned by the publishers to visit and draw the locations described in the novels.

How we longed for the light and heat of a blazing fire when we got back! But, to the little ones at least, this was denied: each hearth in the school-room was immediately surrounded by a double row of great girls, and behind them the younger children crouched in groups, wrapping their starved arms in their pinafores.

A little solace came at tea-time, in the shape of a double ration of bread – a whole, instead of a half, slice – with the delicious addition of a thin scrape of butter: it was the hebdomadal treat to which we all looked forward from Sabbath to Sabbath. I generally contrived to reserve a moiety of this bounteous repast for myself; but the remainder I was invariably obliged to part with.

Chapter 7

Whether or not Carus Wilson was Brocklehurst in *Jane Eyre*, there is no doubt that the punishment inflicted on little Jane by Brocklehurst tallies with the treatment recommended on almost every page of Carus Wilson's *The Children's Friend* – a journal filled with cautionary stories and the threats of a fierce and vengeful deity. It was a style of religious teaching for children that was far removed from anything the Brontë children had experienced with their own clergyman father:

'"Fetch that stool," said Mr Brocklehurst, pointing to a very high one from which a monitor had just risen: it was brought.

"Place the child upon it."

And I was placed there, by whom I don't know. I was in no condition to note particulars. I was only aware that they had hoisted me up to the height of Mr Brocklehurst's nose, that he was within a yard of me, and that a spread of shot orange and purple silk pelisses, and a cloud of silvery plumage extended and waved below me.

Tunstall Church, the original for Brocklebridge Church in *Jane Eyre*. The room over the porch is where the schoolgirls remained to eat their lunch before the long walk back to the school in all weathers.

Jane Eyre

Mr Brocklehurst hemmed.

"Ladies," said he, turning to his family; "Miss Temple, teachers, and children, you all see this girl?"

Of course they did; for I felt their eyes directed like burning-glasses against my scorched skin.

"You see she is yet young; you observe she possesses the ordinary form of childhood; God has graciously given her the shape that He has given to all of us; no single deformity points her out as a marked character. Who would think that the Evil One had already found a servant and agent in her? Yet such, I grieve to say, is the case."

A pause – in which I began to study the palsy of my nerves, and to feel that the Rubicon was passed, and that the trial, no longer to be shirked, must be firmly sustained.

"My dear children," pursued the black marble clergyman with pathos, "this is a sad, a melancholy occasion; for it becomes my duty to warn you that this girl, who might be one of God's own lambs, is a little castaway – not a member of the true flock, but evidently an interloper and an alien. You must be on your guard against her; you must shun her example – if necessary, avoid her company, exclude her from your sports, and shut her out from your converse. Teachers, you must watch her; keep your eyes on her movements, weigh well her words, scrutinize her actions, punish her body to save her soul – if, indeed, such salvation be possible, for (my tongue falters while I tell it) this girl, this child, the native of a Christian land, worse than many a little heathen who says its prayers to Brahma and kneels before Juggernaut – this girl is – a liar!"'

Chapter 7

Cowan Bridge School as the Brontë girls knew it.

The burning memory of such childhood embarrassment, one we all share, became the fuel for Charlotte Brontë's artistic energy. Time and again early experiences are recalled in vividly descriptive scenes. Jane's youthful indignation matures in the novel to become, in a later chapter, an early defence of a woman's need for identity and consideration:

'It is in vain to say human beings ought to be satisfied with tranquillity: they must have action; and they will make it if they cannot find it. Millions are condemned to a stiller doom than mine, and millions are in silent revolt against their lot. Nobody knows how many rebellions besides political rebellions ferment in the masses of life which people earth. Women are supposed to be very calm generally: but women feel just as men feel; they need exercise for their faculties, and a field for their efforts as much as their brothers do; they suffer from too rigid a restraint, too absolute a stagnation, precisely as men would suffer; and it is narrow-minded in their more privileged fellow-creatures to say that they ought to confine themselves to making puddings and knitting stockings, to playing on the piano and embroidering bags. It is thoughtless to condemn them, or laugh at them, if they seek to do more or learn more than custom has pronounced necessary for their sex.'
Chapter 12

It is not hard to hear Charlotte's voice behind that of Jane; and this paragraph is pre-dated and pre-figured by her correspondence with Southey, the Poet Laureate:

Southey to Charlotte Brontë
'Literature cannot be the business of a woman's life, and it ought not to be. The more she is engaged in her proper duties, the less leisure she will have for it, even as an accomplishment and a recreation.'
Keswick, March 1837

Charlotte to Southey
'Following my father's advice . . . I have endeavoured . . . to observe all the duties a woman ought to fulfil . . . I don't always succeed, for sometimes when I'm teaching or sewing, I would rather be reading or writing; but I try to deny myself; and my father's approbation amply rewarded me for the privation.'
Roe Head, March 1837

How thankful we should be that the 21-year-old Charlotte stood up to Southey; and how interesting it is to note her unwavering insistence on a woman's need to think. Had she heeded Southey's warning that her 'daydreams (were) likely to induce a distempered state of mind', Jane Eyre might never have first met Rochester in such interesting circum-stances.
Jane Eyre's first meeting with the man she will eventually marry relates to Charlotte's life at the parsonage. The novel's Bessie, with her tales of the Gytrash, clearly has much in common with Tabbie, the

housekeeper who shared the parsonage kitchen with the growing children, regaling them with local fairy tales and yarns of the ghosts up on the moors behind the house. Jane's 'governessing' also derives from Charlotte's own experience as in her first meeting with Rochester after walking to post a letter.

'This lane inclined uphill all the way to Hay; having reached the middle, I sat down on a stile which led thence into a field. Gathering my mantle about me, and sheltering my hands in my muff, I did not feel the cold, though it froze keenly; as was attested by a sheet of ice covering the causeway, where a little brooklet, now congealed, had overflowed after a rapid thaw some days since. From my seat I could look down on Thornfield: the grey and battlemented hall was the principal object in the vale below me; its woods and dark rookery arose against the west. I lingered till the sun went down amongst the trees, and sank crimson and clear behind them. I then turned eastward.

On the hill-top above me sat the rising moon; pale, yet as a cloud but brightening momently; she looked over Hay, which, half lost in trees, sent up a blue smoke from its few chimneys; it was yet a mile distant, but in the absolute hush I could hear plainly its thin murmurs of life. My ear, too, felt the flow of currents; in what dales and depths I could not tell: but there were many hills beyond Hay, and doubtless many becks threading their passes. That evening calm betrayed alike the tinkle of the nearest streams, the sough of the most remote.

A rude noise broke out on these fine ripplings and whisperings, at once so far away and so clear: a positive tramp, tramp, a metallic clatter, which effaced the soft wave-wanderings; as, in a picture, the solid mass of a crag, or the rough boles of a great oak, drawn in dark and strong in the foreground, efface the aerial distance of azure hill, sunny horizon, and blended clouds, where tint melts into tint.

The din was on the causeway: a horse was coming; the windings of the lane yet hid it, but it approached. I was just leaving the stile; yet as the path was narrow, I sat still to let it go by. In those days I was young, and all sorts of fancies bright and dark tenanted my mind: the memories of nursery stories were there amongst other rubbish; and when they recurred, maturing youth added to them a vigour and vividness beyond what childhood could give. As this horse approached, and as I watched for it to appear through the dusk, I remembered certain of Bessie's tales, wherein figured a North-of-England spirit, called a "Gytrash"; which, in the form of horse, mule, or large dog, haunted solitary ways, and sometimes came upon belated travellers, as this horse was now coming upon me.

It was very near, but not yet in sight; when, in addition to the tramp, tramp, I heard a rush under the hedge, and close down by the hazel stems glided a great dog, whose black and white colour made him a distinct object against the trees. It was exactly one mask of Bessie's Gytrash – a lion-like creature with long hair and a huge head; it passed me, however, quietly enough; not staying to look up, with strange pretercanine eyes, in my face, as I half expected it would. The horse followed – a tall steed, and on its back a rider. The man, the human

Opposite Robert Southey, the Poet Laureate, who advised Charlotte that writing was no profession for a woman.

being, broke the spell at once. Nothing ever rode the Gytrash; it was always alone; and goblins, to my notions, though they might tenant the dumb carcasses of beasts, could scarce covet shelter in the commonplace human form. No Gytrash was this – only a traveller taking a short cut to Millcote. He passed, and went on; a few steps, and I turned; a sliding sound and an exclamation of "What the deuce is to do now?" and a clattering tumble, arrested my attention. Man and horse were down; they had slipped on the sheet of ice which glazed the causeway. The dog came bounding back, and seeing his master in a predicament, and hearing the horse groan, barked till the evening hills echoed the sound, which was deep in proportion to his magnitude. He sniffed round the prostrate group, and then he ran up to me; it was all he could do – there was no other help at hand to summon. I obeyed him, and walked down to the traveller, by this time struggling himself free of his steed. His efforts were so vigorous, I thought he could not be much hurt; but I asked him the question –

"Are you injured, sir?"

I think he was swearing, but I am not certain; however, he was pronouncing some formula which prevented him from replying to me directly.

"Can I do anything?" I asked again.

"You must just stand on one side," he answered as he rose, first to his knees, and then to his feet. I did; whereupon began a heaving, stamping, clattering process, accompanied by a barking and baying which removed me effectually some yards distance; but I would not be driven quite away till I saw the event. This was finally fortunate; the horse was re-established, and the dog was silenced with a "Down Pilot!" The traveller now, stooping, felt his foot and leg, as if trying whether they were sound; apparently something ailed them, for he halted to the stile whence I had just risen, and sat down.

I was in the mood for being useful, or at least officious, I think, for I now drew near him again.

"If you are hurt, and want help, sir, I can fetch some one either from Thornfield Hall or from Hay."

"Thank you; I shall do: I have no broken bones – only a sprain"; and again he stood up and tried his foot, but the result extorted an involuntary "Ugh!"'
Chapter 12

Few protagonists can have had a more dramatic or unexpected entrance than Rochester. Here we encounter Charlotte's originality. With her plain Jane for heroine, she deliberately introduces her 'hero' in a comic scene that dispels any hint of romance, skilfully implying all the potential discomfort and unease that the encounter will bring.

Having introduced her hero falling off a horse, Charlotte continues her description of Rochester in the same vein. All the Brontë sisters showed unusual originality as writers in the men that they invented. Scorning stereotyped romantic heroes, their descriptions are of real, recognizable people. This strength at creating male characters is apparent here:

Opposite The first meeting of Jane Eyre and Rochester. Painting by Thomas Davidson.

Jane Eyre

'Something of daylight still lingered, and the moon was waxing bright; I could see him plainly. His figure was enveloped in a riding cloak, fur collared and steel clasped; its details were not apparent, but I traced the general points of middle height, and considerable breadth of chest. He had a dark face, with stern features and a heavy brow; his eyes and gathered eyebrows looked ireful and thwarted just now; he was past youth, but had not reached middle age; perhaps he might be thirty-five. I felt no fear of him, and but little shyness. Had he been a handsome, heroic-looking young gentleman, I should not have dared to stand thus questioning him against his will, and offering my services unasked. I had hardly ever seen a handsome youth; never in my life spoken to one. I had a theoretical reverence and homage for beauty, elegance, gallantry, fascination; but had I met those qualities incarnate in masculine shape, I should have known instinctively that they neither had nor could have sympathy with anything in me, and should have shunned them as one would fire, lightning, or anything else that is bright but antipathetic.

If even this stranger had smiled and been good-humoured to me when I addressed him; if he had put off my offer of assistance gaily and with thanks, I should have gone on my way and not felt any vocation to renew inquiries: but the frown, the roughness of the traveller set me at my ease: I retained my station when he waved to me to go, and announced –

"I cannot think of leaving you, sir, at so late an hour, in this solitary lane, till I see you are fit to mount your horse."

He looked at me when I said this: he had hardly turned his eyes in my direction before.

Engraving from Thomas Bewick's *History of British Birds*, one of the pictures that the little Jane Eyre is looking at in Chapter 1.

"I should think you ought to be at home yourself," said he, "if you have a home in this neighbourhood."'
Chapter 12

The complete disregard for convention, the singleness of imagination, are both clear in the quick, sure depiction of an intriguing man. Once again the early images of cold and ice are juxtaposed by the mention of 'fire' and 'lightning' – hints of what is in store for Jane and the reader.

The appeal of Jane Eyre is the ease with which the reader identifies with her. The modesty and clearsighted appraisal of herself as a person of little beauty and less worth – echoing Charlotte Brontë's painful assessment of her own image – bespeak a character we can all take to our hearts. The author soliloquizes upon the contrast of a traditional 'beauty' and a plain governess after her heroine has allowed herself, unwisely, to imagine that Mr Rochester, her employer, may notice her:

'When once more alone, I reviewed the information I had got; looked into my heart, examined its thoughts and feelings, and endeavoured to bring back with a strict hand such as had been straying through imagination's boundless and trackless waste, into the safe fold of common sense.

Illustration by E.M. Wimperis from the 1872 edition showing Thornfield Hall, Mr Rochester's residence.

Jane Eyre

Arraigned at my own bar, Memory having given her evidence of the hopes, wishes, sentiments I had been cherishing since last night — of the general state of mind in which I had indulged for nearly a fortnight past; Reason having come forward and told, in her own quiet way, a plain, unvarnished tale, showing how I had rejected the real, and rapidly devoured the ideal; — I pronounced judgement to this effect:

That a greater fool than Jane Eyre had never breathed the breath of life: that a more fantastic idiot had never surfeited herself on sweet lies, and swallowed poison as if it were nectar.

"You," I said, "a favourite with Mr Rochester? *You* gifted with the power of pleasing him? *You* of importance to him in any way? Go! your folly sickens me. And you have derived pleasure from occasional tokens of preference — equivocal tokens shown by a gentleman of family and a man of the world to a dependant and a novice. How dared you? Poor stupid dupe! — Could not even self-interest make you wiser? You repeated to yourself this morning the brief scene of last night? — Cover your face and be ashamed! He said something in praise of your eyes, did he? Blind puppy! Open their bleared lids and look on your own accursed senselessness! It does good to no woman to be flattered by her superior, who cannot possibly intend to marry her; and it is madness in all women to let a secret love kindle within them, which, if unreturned and unknown, must devour the life that feeds it; and, if discovered and responded to, must lead *ignis-fatuus*-like, into miry wilds whence there is no extrication.

Detail from the foot of a letter written by Charlotte, showing herself as the ugly-duckling she believed herself to be.

"Listen, then, Jane Eyre, to your sentence: to-morrow, place the glass before you, and draw in chalk your own picture, faithfully, without softening one defect; omit no harsh line, smooth away no displeasing irregularity, write under it, 'Portrait of a Governess, disconnected, poor, and plain'.

"Afterwards take a piece of smooth ivory — you have one prepared in your drawing box: take your palette; mix your freshest, finest, clearest tints; choose your most delicate camel-hair pencils; delineate carefully the loveliest face you can imagine; paint it in your softest shades and sweetest hues, according to the description given by Mrs Fairfax of Blanche Ingram: remember the raven ringlets, the oriental eye; — What! you revert to Mr Rochester as a model! Order! No snivel! — no sentiment! — no regret! I will endure only sense and resolution. Recall the august yet harmonious lineaments, the Grecian neck and bust; let the round and dazzling arm be visible, and the delicate hand; omit neither diamond ring nor gold bracelet; portray faithfully the attire, aerial lace and glistening satin, graceful scarf and golden rose: call it, 'Blanche, an accomplished lady of rank'.

"Whenever in future you should chance to fancy Mr Rochester thinks well of you, take out these two pictures and compare them: say, 'Mr Rochester might probably win that noble lady's love, if he chose to strive for it; is it likely he would waste a serious thought on this indigent and insignificant plebeian?'"

One of the most striking watercolours attributed to Charlotte Brontë. This 'beauty' is in marked contrast to the plainness of the self-portrait opposite.

"I'll do it," I resolved: and having framed this determination, I grew calmer, and fell asleep.

I kept my word. An hour or two sufficed to sketch my own portrait in crayons; and in less than a fortnight I had completed an ivory miniature of an imaginary Blanche Ingram. It looked a lovely face enough, and when compared with the real head in chalk, the contrast was as great as self-control could desire. I derived benefit from the task: it had kept my head and hands employed, and had given force and fixedness to the new impressions I wished to stamp indelibly on my heart.'
Chapter 16

Jane's portrait has many parallels in the drawings we find today preserved in Haworth parsonage. Charlotte often indulged in the exercise of comparison, always finding herself to be plain if not an ugly duckling.

Jane Eyre

A constant theme among young women growing up is marriage, and the Brontë sisters were no exception. Their poems and early juvenile prose tales are of lovers, of husbands and wives; their mature published novels deal with marriage, courtship and the plight of the single woman. A crux in *Jane Eyre* occurs in the chapter of the interrupted wedding. Here the sense of drama, skill with dialogue and sound knowledge of church ceremony, which Charlotte shared with her sisters, lend power to the episode.

This is perhaps the most celebrated scene in the novel. Rochester is on the point of marrying Jane Eyre, the governess he employs. Miss Eyre does not allow herself to imagine being called Mrs Rochester, perhaps with good cause:

'We entered the quiet and humble temple; the priest waited in his white surplice at the lowly altar, the clerk beside him. All was still: two shadows only moved in a remote corner. My conjecture had been correct: the strangers had slipped in before us, and they now stood by the vault of the Rochesters, their backs towards us, viewing through the rails the old time-stained marble tomb, where a kneeling angel guarded the remains of Damer de Rochester, slain at Marston Moor, in the time of the civil wars, and of Elizabeth, his wife.

Our place was taken at the communion rails. Hearing a cautious step behind me, I glanced over my shoulder: one of the strangers – a gentleman, evidently – was advancing up the chapel. The service began. The explanation of the intent of matrimony was gone through; and then the clergyman came a step farther forward, and, bending slightly towards Mr Rochester, went on:

"I require and charge you both (as ye will answer at the dreadful Day of Judgement when the secrets of all hearts shall be disclosed), that if either of you know any impediment why ye may not lawfully be joined together in matrimony, ye do now confess it; for be ye well assured that so many as are coupled together otherwise than God's word doth allow, are not joined together by God, neither is their matrimony lawful."

He paused, as the custom is. When is the pause after that sentence ever broken by reply? Not perhaps, once in a hundred years. And the clergyman, who had not lifted his eyes from his book, and had held his breath but for a moment, was proceeding: his hand was already stretched towards Mr Rochester, as his lips unclosed to ask, "Wilt thou have this woman for thy wedded wife?" – when a distinct and near voice said –

"The marriage cannot go on: I declare the existence of an impediment."

The clergyman looked up at the speaker and stood mute; the clerk did the same; Mr Rochester moved slightly, as if an earthquake had rolled under his feet: taking a firmer footing, and not turning his head or eyes, he said, "Proceed."

Profound silence fell when he uttered that word, with deep but low intonation. Presently Mr Wood said –

"I cannot proceed without some investigation into what has been asserted, and evidence of its truth or falsehood."

"The ceremony is quite broken off," subjoined the voice behind us.

"I am in a condition to prove my allegation: an insuperable impediment to this marriage exists."

Mr Rochester heard, but heeded not: he stood stubborn and rigid, making no movement but to possess himself of my hand. What a hot and strong grasp he had! and how like quarried marble was his pale, firm, massive front at this moment. How his eyes shone, still watchful, and yet wild beneath!

Mr Wood seemed at a loss. "What is the nature of the impediment?" he asked. "Perhaps it may be got over – explained away?"

"Hardly," was the answer. "I have called it insuperable, and I speak advisedly."

The speaker came forward and leaned on the rails. He continued, uttering each word distinctly, calmly, steadily, but not loudly –

"It simply consists in the existence of a previous marriage. Mr Rochester has a wife now living."

My nerves vibrated to those low-spoken words as they had never vibrated to thunder – my blood felt their subtle violence as it had never felt frost or fire; but I was collected, and in no danger of swooning. I looked at Mr Rochester; I made him look at me. His whole face was colourless rock; his eye was both spark and flint. He disavowed nothing: he seemed as if he would defy all things. Without speaking, without smiling, without seeming to recognize in me a human being, he only twined my waist with his arm and riveted me to his side.'
Chapter 26

Bigamous marriage and the potential for adultery were lively subjects for a mid-19th-century audience to accept. *Jane Eyre* was an immediate commercial success, but its reception was more than a little controversial. Some readers suggested that its author was a depraved man, and that it was a thoroughly unpleasant book. For a while Charlotte Brontë was grateful that she could hide behind Currer Bell.

While herself a governess for the Sidgwick family at Stone Gappe in Lothersdale, Yorkshire, Charlotte experienced much that she was to narrate in the life of Jane Eyre:

Gateshead Hall, home of the Reed family, where the orphaned Jane Eyre lived as a child. Wimperis illustration.

Jane Eyre

'I see now more clearly than I have ever done before that a private governess has no existence, is not considered as a living and rational being except as connected with the wearisome duties she has to fulfil.'
Charlotte Brontë to Ellen Nussey. 8 June 1839

While serving with the Sidgwick family, however, Charlotte accompanied them on a visit to a relative who rented Norton Conyers, an old, elegant and impressive house near the city of Ripon. Here she might have heard the tale of a woman locked in an attic: the attic is there to this day, a room tucked under eaves near fake battlements that seem to claim notice as possible locations for Bertha Rochester's prison, arson, and fall to her death.

In the novel the interrupted wedding is followed swiftly by the visit to Bertha Rochester's room. The reason for the halting of the ceremony is disclosed:

'He lifted the hangings from the wall, uncovering the second door: this, too, he opened. In a room without a window, there burnt a fire, guarded by a high and strong fender, and a lamp suspended from the ceiling by a chain. Grace Poole bent over the fire, apparently cooking something in a saucepan. In the deep shade, at the farther end of the room, a figure ran backwards and forwards. What it was, whether beast or human being, one could not, at first sight tell: it grovelled, seemingly, on all fours; it snatched and growled like some strange wild animal: but it was covered with clothing, and a quantity of dark, grizzled hair, wild as a mane, hid its head and face.

"Good-morrow, Mrs Poole!" said Mr Rochester. "How are you? and how is your charge to-day?"

"We're tolerable, sir, I thank you," replied Grace, lifting the boiling mess carefully on to the hob: "rather snappish, but not 'rageous."

A fierce cry seemed to give the lie to her favourable report: the clothed hyena rose up, and stood tall on its hind-feet.

"Ah! sir, she sees you!" exclaimed Grace: "you'd better not stay."

"Only a few moments, Grace: you must allow me a few moments."

"Take care, then, sir! – for God's sake, take care!"

The maniac bellowed: she parted her shaggy locks from her visage, and gazed wildly at her visitors. I recognized well that purple face – those bloated features. Mrs Poole advanced.

"Keep out of the way," said Mr Rochester, thrusting her aside: "she has no knife now, I suppose? and I'm on my guard."

"One never knows what she has, sir: she is so cunning: it is not in mortal discretion to fathom her craft."

"We had better leave her," whispered Mason.

"Go to the devil!" was his brother-in-law's recommendation.

"'Ware!" cried Grace. The three gentlemen retreated simultaneously. Mr Rochester flung me behind him: the lunatic sprang and grappled his throat viciously, and laid her teeth to his cheek: they struggled. She was a big woman, in stature almost equalling her husband, and corpulent besides: she showed virile force in the contest – more than once she

Opposite The attic room at Norton Conyers where it is said a mad woman was once locked-up. Charlotte visited this house and may well have first heard the story of such an imprisonment here.

Jane Eyre

almost throttled him, athletic as he was. He could have settled her with a well-planted blow; but he would not strike: he would only wrestle. At last he mastered her arms; Grace Poole gave him a cord, and he pinioned them behind her: with more rope, which was at hand, he bound her to a chair. The operation was performed amidst the fiercest yells and the most convulsive plunges. Mr. Rochester then turned to the spectators: he looked at them with a smile both acrid and desolate.

"That is *my wife*," said he. "Such is the sole conjugal embrace I am ever to know – such are the endearments which are to solace my leisure hours! And *this* is what I wished to have" (laying his hand on my shoulder) "this young girl, who stands so grave and quiet at the mouth of hell, looking collectedly at the gambols of a demon. I wanted her just as a change after that fierce ragout. Wood and Briggs, look at the difference! Compare these clear eyes with the red balls yonder – this face with that mask – this form with that bulk; then judge me, priest of the gospel and man of the law, and remember with what judgement ye judge ye shall be judged! Off with you now. I must shut up my prize."'
Chapter 26

Jane ponders her situation and the author draws together the imagery of the book, from Bewick's Norwegian wastes to the charge of 'liar' inflicted upon a little girl at school:

'Jane Eyre, who had been an ardent, expectant woman – almost a bride, was a cold, solitary girl again: her life was pale; her prospects were desolate. A Christmas frost had come at midsummer; a white December storm had whirled over June; ice glazed the ripe apples, drifts crushed the blowing roses; on hayfield and cornfield lay a frozen shroud; lanes which last night blushed full of flowers, to-day were pathless with untrodden snow; and the woods, which twelve hours since waved leafy and fragrant as groves between the tropics, now spread, waste, wild, and white as pine-forests in wintry Norway. My hopes were all dead – struck with a subtle doom, such as, in one night, fell on all the first-born in the land of Egypt. I looked on my cherished wishes, yesterday so blooming and glowing: they lay stark, chill, livid corpses that could never revive. I looked at my love – that feeling which was my master's, which he had created: it shivered in my heart, like a suffering child in a cold cradle; sickness and anguish had seized it; it could not seek Mr Rochester's arms – it could not derive warmth from his breast. Oh, never more could it turn to him; for faith was blighted – confidence destroyed! Mr Rochester was not to me what he had been, for he was not what I had thought him. I would not ascribe vice to him; I would not say he had betrayed me; but the attributes of stainless truth was gone from his idea.'
Chapter 26

'Stainless truth' was a most precious attribute in Charlotte Brontë's evaluation of a person. That Rochester is proven a liar is harsh but just:

he will not escape punishment in the working-out of the author's moral scheme. Rochester's blinding and maiming by fire, a punishment for his intended bigamy and unrepentant hyprocrisy, continues a theme introduced at the very start of the novel. Brocklehurst, with his real-life counterpart Carus Wilson, was the kind of clergyman who believed that God in his *mercy* would set fire to children in order to teach them not to tell lies. Charlotte uses such attitudes in her story. The maimed Rochester is a chastened man. Such extremes, a mad wife locked in an attic, the blinding of the hero, are what Charlotte Brontë, in notes jotted down in an exercise book, called 'certain remarkable occurrences'. It was such occurrences that *The Professor* had lacked.

Haworth parsonage, which nurtured imaginations vivid enough to create Heathcliff and the mad Bertha Rochester, also abounded in curates. Charlotte in particular scorned them — until she eventually married one. In *Jane Eyre*, however, she gives a brisk portrait of a clergyman as a potential rival to Rochester for Jane Eyre's hand. St John Rivers is as cold and unloving a person as one can imagine, offering a marriage of duty in contrast to one of potential warmth and love. Jane is about to accept his chilly offer when she hears Rochester calling her from miles away — perhaps the most remarkable occurrence in the book:

'"My prayers are heard!" ejaculated St John. He pressed his hand firmer on my head, as if he claimed me: he surrounded me with his arm, *almost* as if he loved me (I say *almost* – I knew the difference – for I had felt what it was to be loved; but, like him, I had now put love out of the question, and thought only of duty). I contended with my inward dimness of vision, before which clouds yet rolled. I sincerely, deeply, fervently longed to do what was right; and only that. "Show me, show me the path!" I entreated of Heaven. I was excited more than I had ever been; and whether what followed was the effect of excitement the reader shall judge.

All the house was still; for I believe all, except St John and myself, were now retired to rest. The one candle was dying out: the room was full of moonlight. My heart beat fast and thick: I heard its throb. Suddenly it stood still to an inexpressible feeling that thrilled it through, and passed at once to my head and extremities. The feeling was not like an electric shock, but it was quite as sharp, as strange, as startling: it acted on my senses as if their utmost activity hitherto had been but torpor, from which they were now summoned and forced to wake. They rose expectant: eye and ear waited while the flesh quivered on my bones.

"What have you heard? What do you see?" asked St John. I saw nothing, but I heard a voice somewhere cry –

"Jane! Jane! Jane!" – nothing more.

"O God! what is it?" I gasped.

I might have said, "Where is it?" for it did not seem in the room, nor in the house, nor in the garden; it did not come out of the air, nor from under the earth, nor from overhead. I had heard it – where, or whence, for ever impossible to know! And it was the voice of a human being – a known, loved, well-remembered voice – that of Edward Fairfax

Jane Eyre

Rochester; and it spoke in pain and woe, wildly, eerily, urgently.

"I am coming!" I cried. "Wait for me! Oh, I will come!" I flew to the door and looked into the passage: it was dark. I ran out into the garden: it was void.

"Where are you?" I exclaimed.

The hills beyond March Glen sent the answer faintly back, "Where are you!" I listened. The wind sighed low in the firs: all was moorland loneliness and midnight hush.

"Down superstition!" I commented, as that spectre rose up black by the black yew at the gate. "This is not thy deception, nor thy witchcraft: it is the work of nature. She was roused, and did – no miracle – but her best.'"

Chapter 35

The Apostles Cupboard that Jane Eyre saw by flickering candlelight.

After the reconciliation with Rochester, we hear his version of the same strange event:

'"You will think me superstitious — some superstition I have in my blood, and always had: nevertheless, this is true — true at least it is that I heard what I now relate.

"As I exclaimed, 'Jane! Jane! Jane!' a voice — I cannot tell whence the voice came, but I know whose voice it was — replied, 'I am coming; wait for me'; and a moment after, went whispering on the wind the words, 'Where are you?'

"I tell you, if I can, the idea, the picture these words opened to my mind: yet it is difficult to express what I want to express. Ferndean is buried, as you see, in a heavy wood, where sound falls dull, and dies unreverberating. 'Where are you?' seemed spoken amongst mountains, for I heard a hill-sent echo repeat the words. Cooler and fresher at the moment the gale seemed to visit my brow: I could have deemed that in some wild, lone scene, I and Jane were meeting. In spirit, I believe, we must have met. You no doubt were, at that hour, in unconscious sleep, Jane: perhaps your soul wandered from its cell to comfort mine; for those were your accents — as certain as I live — they were yours!"

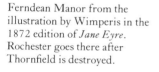

Ferndean Manor from the illustration by Wimperis in the 1872 edition of *Jane Eyre*. Rochester goes there after Thornfield is destroyed.

Reader, it was on Monday night — near midnight — that I too had received the mysterious summons: those were the very words by which I replied to it. I listened to Mr Rochester's narrative, but made no

Jane Eyre

disclosure in return. The coincidence struck me as too awful and inexplicable to be communicated or discussed. If I told anything, my tale would be such as must necessarily make a profound impression on the mind of my hearer: and that mind, yet from its sufferings too prone to gloom, needed not the deeper shade of the supernatural. I kept these things then, and pondered them in my heart.'
Chapter 37

Once Jane Eyre is reunited with Rochester, the resolution is simply told: 'Reader I married him.' The fire started by Rochester's mad wife having consumed her and but maimed him, there is no longer any moral impediment to their marriage. Jane's happiness is complete and the language with which she extols married life echoes Charlotte Brontë's father's advice to a couple about to be married at the end of his tale *The Maid of Killarney* (published 1818), a predecessor of *Jane Eyre* by some thirty years:

'Now my children, in two months hence . . . you shall be married; and I hope that your lot will be as good as can be expected in this uncertain and sinful world. But do not look forward to an uninterrupted flow of happiness. This is not the portion of mortals on this side eternity. Make up your minds for some difficulties, that when they come, you may rather meet them as the common lot, than struggle under them with impatience. When the young fancy is warm, it sees nothing but a gay prospect before it. But sage experience removes the delusion, and teaches more moderate expectations. Let me advise you both, then, whether in prosperous or adverse circumstances, to be fully resigned to the Divine will, constantly preserving a tranquil equanimity. Let each look upon the other as the best earthly friend. And be not blind to faults on either side, but cover them with a mantle of charity. Either never let your minds be ruffled at all, or be not angry at the same instant; let not the sun go down upon your wrath.'
The Maid of Killarney. *Chapter 11*

Charlotte's Jane seems to have heard Patrick Brontë's comfortable words, for the novel closes in much the same way as his *Maid of Killarney*:

'My tale draws to its close: one word respecting my experience of married life, and one brief glance at the fortunes of those whose names have most frequently recurred in this narrative, and I have done.
I have now been married ten years. I know what it is to live entirely for and with what I love best on earth. I hold myself supremely blest — blest beyond what language can express; because I am my husband's life as fully as he is mine. No woman was ever nearer to her mate than I am: ever more absolutely bone of his bone and flesh of his flesh. I know no weariness of my Edward's society: he knows none of mine, any more than we each do of the pulsation of the heart that beats in our separate bosoms; consequently, we are ever together. To be together is for us to be at once as free as in solitude, as gay as in company. We talk, I believe, all day long: to talk to each other is but a more animated and an

Photograph presumed to be of
Charlotte Brontë at the time of
her marriage in 1854.

audible thinking. All my confidence is bestowed on him, all his
confidence is devoted to me; we are precisely suited in character. . .'
Chapter 38

In *Jane Eyre* Charlotte drew upon her own schooldays, her life as a
governess, her yearning for love and affection; she also used her
knowledge of painting, music and literature in her novel, which has
much in common with the works that her sisters were busy getting into
print in 1847. The 'plainness' of her heroine, her common sense and her
implacable sense of duty were to become hallmarks of her later writing.

The man that Charlotte Brontë married in 1854 was the fourth to
propose to her. None of her three previous rejections caused her distress
or regret, although it is clear from her letters and fiction that she craved
affection and love. It is interesting to read the account of the rejection of
her first proposal for the bearing it has on Jane Eyre's behaviour.

Seven years before writing *Jane Eyre*, the sentiments expressed in a

Jane Eyre

letter to the sister of a man she had rejected are markedly similar to those of her heroine. The suitor was Henry Nussey, a clergyman and the brother of Charlotte's closest school friend and companion of her mature years. Many believe that he is the model for St John Rivers in *Jane Eyre*:

'Now, my dear Ellen, there were in this proposal some things which might have proved a strong temptation. I thought if I were to marry Henry Nussey, his sister could live with me, and how happy should I be. But again I asked myself two questions: Do I love him as much as a woman ought to love the man she marries? Am I the person best qualified to make him happy? Alas! Ellen, my conscience answered *no* to both these questions. I felt that though I esteemed, though I had a kindly leaning towards him, because he is an amiable and well-disposed man, yet I had not, and could not have, that intense attachment which would make me willingly to die for him; and, if ever I marry, it must be in that light of adoration that I will regard my husband.'
Letter to Ellen Nussey, 12 March 1839

Detail of the doorway of Norton Conyers.

Jane Eyre's rejection of St John Rivers is couched in similar terms and derives from the same ideal of passionate love. Charlotte Brontë, through her heroine, leaves us in no doubt about the difference between true love and convenience:

'I looked at his features, beautiful in their harmony, but strangely formidable in their still severity; at his brow, commanding but not open; at his eyes, bright and deep and searching, but never soft; at his tall imposing figure – and fancied myself in idea *his wife*. Oh! it would never do! As his curate, his comrade, all would be right: I would cross oceans with him in that capacity; toil under Eastern suns, in Asian deserts with him in that office; admire and emulate his courage and devotion and vigour; accommodate quietly to his masterhood; smile undisturbed at his ineradicable ambition; discriminate the Christian from the man – profoundly esteem the one, and freely forgive the other. I should suffer often, no doubt, attached to him only in this capacity: my body would be under rather a stringent yoke, but my heart and mind would be free. I should still have my unblighted self to turn to – my natural unenslaved feelings with which to communicate in moments of loneliness. There would be recesses in my mind which would be only mine, to which he never came, and sentiments growing there fresh and sheltered which his austerity could never blight, nor his measured warrior-march trample down: but as his wife – at his side always, and always restrained, and always checked – forced to keep the fire of my nature continually low, to compel it to burn inwardly and never utter a cry, though the imprisoned flame consumed vital after vital – *this* would be undendurable.'

"St John!" I exclaimed, when I had got so far in my meditation.

"Well?" he answered icily.

"I repeat I freely consent to go with you as your fellow-missionary, but not as your wife; I cannot marry you and become part of you."

"It is what I want," he said, speaking to himself; "it is just what I want. And there are obstacles in the way: they must be hewn down. Jane, you would not repent marrying me – be certain of that; we *must* be married. I repeat it: there is no other way; and undoubtedly enough of love would follow upon marriage to render the union right even in your eyes."

"I scorn your idea of love," I could not help saying, as I rose up and stood before him, leaning my back against the rock. "I scorn the counterfeit sentiment you offer: yes, St John, and I scorn you when you offer it."'

Chapter 34

Norton Conyers, near Ripon, the house Charlotte visited while working as a governess for the Sidgwick family.

V

WUTHERING HEIGHTS

'Whether it is right or advisable to create things like Heathcliff, I do not know. I scarcely think it is.'
Charlotte Brontë, Preface to Wuthering Heights, 1850.

Of the three manuscripts despatched to publishers in 1847, one surpasses the others in its evocation of landscape and its deep-rooted attachment to a particular location: Emily Brontë's sole novel *Wuthering Heights*. Throughout the world her name evokes images of moorland, blustering wind, storm and tempest. In fair weather and foul, people of all nationalities walk the moors above the parsonage at Haworth to experience for themselves the setting and inspiration for one of literature's most loved works.

No detail of her home, its immediate and distant surroundings escaped Emily's eye or pen. The fireside, the graveyard view through the window, the distant hills – all provided material for reflection:

'I SEE AROUND ME TOMBSTONES GREY'

I see around me tombstones grey
Stretching their shadows far away.
Beneath the turf my footsteps tread
Lie low and lone the silent dead;
Beneath the turf, beneath the mould –
Forever dark, forever cold,
And my eyes cannot hold the tears
Thay memory hoards from vanished years;
For Time and Death and Mortal pain
Give wounds that will not heal again.

Opposite View of the moors above Haworth.

The sombre mood evoked by the graveyard is dispelled by Emily's celebration of freedom on the moors, as in this verse from *Stanzas*:

Wuthering Heights

> 'I'll walk where my own nature would be leading:
>   It vexes me to choose another guide:
> Where the grey flocks in ferny glens are feeding;
>   Where the wild wind blows on the mountainside.

It is, however, at the hearthside and the writing table that we find the true Emily Brontë. Here she invokes her muse and summons up the extraordinary visions that give paramount quality to her poetry and her single novel. She alone of the sisters comes near to explaining the mystery and power of their shared achievement, derived from their reading, their inventive games and their zeal for literature:

THE VISIONARY

Silent is the house: all are laid asleep;
One, alone, looks out o'er the snow-wreaths deep;
Watching every cloud, dreading every breeze
That whirls the wildering drift, and bends the groaning
    trees.

Cheerful is the hearth, soft the matted floor;
Not one shivering gust creeps through pane or door;
The little lamp burns straight, its rays shoot strong and
    far;
I trim it well to be the Wanderer's guiding-star.

Frown, my haughty sire; chide, my angry dame;
Set your slaves to spy, threaten me with shame:
But neither sire nor dame, nor prying serf shall know
What angel nightly tracks that waste of frozen snow.

What I love shall come like visitant of air,
Safe in secret power from lurking human snare;
Who loves me, no word of mine shall e'er betray,
Thou for faith unstained my life must forfeit pay.

Burn then, little lamp; glimmer straight and clear –
Hush! a rustling wing stirs, methinks, the air:
He for whom I wait, thus ever comes to me;
Strange Power! I trust thy might; trust thou my
    constancy.

Opposite Fragment of a portrait. Emily Brontë by her brother Patrick Branwell Brontë.

Below Streams are hidden in the folds of the high moorland above Haworth. The forbidding prospect has secret valleys found only by those who walk the moors as did the Brontë children.

Of the three girls, Emily felt the most attachment to home, thriving when there, languishing whenever away. Yet her brief sorties laid down rich store for her writing. Like her sisters, she grew up with the moor as her playground; unlike them, she made it her special world:

'One long ramble . . . was far over the moors to a spot familiar to Emily and Anne, which they called "The meeting of the Waters". It was a small oasis of emerald green turf, broken here and there by small clear

Wuthering Heights

springs: a few large stones serving as resting-places; seated here, we were hidden from all the world, nothing appearing in view but miles and miles of heather, a glorious blue sky, and brightening sun. A fresh breeze wafted on us its exhilarating influence. . . .'
Ellen Nussey. Reminiscences

Beyond the moors, Emily recalled houses visited or seen, tales told of their inhabitants and the history of families and estates. Her novel blends the real with the imagined so skilfully that to this day no one can be sure of the actual location of farmhouse or parkland; nor, try as we may, can we match the real map to the topography of her world.

Emily, like her sisters, tried to earn a living by teaching. At Law Hill, above Halifax, her long hours of work evoked Charlotte's pity:

'My sister Emily is gone into a situation as teacher in a large school of near forty pupils, near Halifax. I have had one letter from her since her departure; it gives an appalling account of her duties – hard labour from six in the morning until near eleven at night, with only one half-hour of exercise between, this is slavery. I fear she will never stand it.'
Charlotte Brontë. Letter to Ellen Nussey, 2 October 1837

Halifax was a cultural and trading centre in the 18th and early 19th centuries. Only the rapid growth of Bradford and Leeds as industrial centres in the mid-19th century diminished its importance in the area.

The brief extract from Charlotte's letter is all we know of Emily's stay at Law Hill. There is even confusion as to how long she was there, suggestions ranging from a minimum of three months to a maximum of eighteen months.

Whatever doubt there may be about duration, there is wide agreement that what Emily saw and heard during her stay at Law Hill served her well in the composition of *Wuthering Heights*. Much has been made of a tale of malpractice and illegitimacy in a local family as a source for her narrative, and houses have been mentioned that appear to match the homes of the Earnshaws and the Lintons. Admittedly certain similarities and suggestions of features can be culled from the pages of the novel. However, the book remains a work of the imagination, all the stronger in its impact because it is not obliged to follow either the strictures of verisimilitude or the requirements of precise geographical location.

Wuthering Heights opens with its first narrator, Mr Lockwood, congratulating himself on the isolation of the house he has just rented. At once we taste what Emily knew so well. The inhospitable landscape breeds inhospitable householders; both are drawn directly from life on the high moorland:

'1801 – I have just returned from a visit to my landlord – the solitary neighbour that I shall be troubled with. This is certainly, a beautiful country! In all England, I do not believe that I could have fixed on a situation so completely removed from the stir of society. A perfect misanthropist's Heaven – and Mr Heathcliff and I are such a suitable pair to divide the desolation between us. A capital fellow! He little imagined how my heart warmed towards him when I beheld his black eyes withdraw so suspiciously under their brows, as I rode up, and when

Law Hill, the building that housed Miss Patchet's school, where Emily spent some time as a teacher.

his fingers sheltered themselves, with a jealous resolution, still further in his waistcoat, as I announced my name.

"Mr Heathcliff?" I said.

A nod was the answer.

"Mr Lockwood, your new tenant, sir. I do myself the honour of calling as soon as possible, after my arrival, to express the hope that I have not inconvenienced you by my perseverance in soliciting the occupation of Thrushcross Grange: I heard, yesterday, you had had some thoughts – "

"Thrushcross Grange is my own, sir," he interrupted wincing, "I should not allow any one to inconvenience me, if I could hinder it – walk in!"

The "walk in" was uttered with closed teeth, and expressed the sentiment, "Go to the Deuce"; even the gate over which he leant manifested no sympathizing movement to the words; and I think that circumstances determined me to accept the invitation: I felt interested in

Wuthering Heights

a man who seemed more exaggeratedly reserved than myself.'
Chapter 1

The scattered and isolated farmhouses of the moors above Haworth are still strange and inhospitable places nowadays for the occasional visitor. Chained dogs growl at the caller and to southern ears the welcome sounds forbiddingly gruff.

The poised opening to the novel, with a male narrator at once involving us in an unusual encounter, establishes the atmosphere and intrigue that is to follow. Astonishingly, it also challenges the reader to beware of identification with characters. Lockwood, our guide, is verbose and self-adulatory, rather like an 18th-century survivor in the harsher 19th-century world. His over-courteous manner receives, and perhaps merits, a curt response. Lockwood's southern airs are hardly a match for Heathcliff's northern rejoinders.

After the laboured welcome comes Emily Brontë's description of the house known as Wuthering Heights, and the first of her brisk sketches that capture the precise quality of its surroundings and windswept setting. The interior of the house is that of a typical yeoman farmer of the area:

'Wuthering Heights is the name of Mr Heathcliff's dwelling. "Wuthering" being a significant provincial adjective, descriptive of the atmospheric tumult to which its station is exposed in stormy weather. Pure, bracing ventilation they must have up there at all times, indeed: one may guess the power of the north wind, blowing over the edge, by

Pencil sketch by Branwell Brontë of farm buildings which resemble Top Withins, the popular setting of *Wuthering Heights*.

P. B. Brontë

July 2? 1833

the excessive slant of a few stunted firs at the end of the house; and by a range of gaunt thorns all stretching their limbs one way, as if craving alms of the sun. Happily, the architect had foresight to build it strong: the narrow windows are deeply set in the wall, and the corners defended with large jutting stones.

Before passing the threshold, I paused to admire a quantity of grotesque carving lavished over the front, and especially about the principal door, above which, among a wilderness of crumbling griffins, and shameless little boys, I detected the date "1500," and the name "Hareton Earnshaw." I would have made a few comments, and requested a short history of the place, from the surly owner, but his attitude at the door appeared to demand my speedy entrance, or complete departure, and I had no desire to aggravate his impatience, previous to inspecting the penetralium.

One step brought us into the family sitting-room, without any introductory lobby, or passage: they call it here "the house" pre-eminently. It includes kitchen, and parlour, generally, but I believe at Wuthering Heights the kitchen is forced to retreat altogether into another quarter, at least I distinguished a chatter of tongues, and a clatter of culinary utensils, deep within; and I observed no signs of roasting, boiling, or baking, about the huge fire-place; nor any glitter of copper saucepans and tin cullenders on the walls. One end, indeed, reflected splendidly both light and heat, from ranks of immense pewter dishes, interspersed with silver jugs and tankards, towering row after row, in a vast oak dresser, to the very roof. The latter had never been underdrawn, its entire anatomy laid bare to an inquiring eye, except

High Sunderland Hall, now demolished, a house near to Law Hill School that may have been in Emily's mind when she invented the houses of *Wuthering Heights*.

where a frame of wood laden with oatcakes, and clusters of legs of beef, mutton, and ham, concealed it. Above the chimney were sundry villainous old guns, and a couple of horse-pistols, and, by way of ornament, three gaudily painted canisters disposed along its ledge. The floor was of smooth, white stone: the chairs, high-backed, primitive structures, painted green: one or two heavy black ones lurking in the shade. In an arch, under the dresser, reposed a huge, liver-coloured bitch pointer surrounded by a swarm of squealing puppies; and other dogs haunted other recesses.'
Chapter 1

The Haworth parsonage was never short of animals. A roll-call at any time would have included more than one dog and an assortment of cats and kittens, plus, at one stage, a merlin hawk and two geese called Victoria and Adelaide. All the sisters use animals in their novels: cats, dogs, birds and wild game. The animals in the books are accurately observed, never sentimentalized, and often used skilfully for comic effect.

In this early passage of *Wuthering Heights* the effect is comic but there is also a hint of real danger and threat. Shortly afterwards, an attack by dogs so injures Lockwood that he is forced to spend the night at Wuthering Heights. Dogs were as much part of a remote homestead as was the blunderbuss over the fireplace or the massive bolts on the heavy doors. Lockwood's encounter with the dogs at the Heights emphasizes his southern unease and reminds the reader that he is an intruder:

'I took a seat at the end of the hearthstone opposite that towards which my landlord advanced, and filled up an interval of silence by attempting to caress the canine mother, who had left her nursery, and was sneaking wolfishly to the back of my leg, her lip curled up, and her white teeth watering for a snatch.

My caress provoked a long, guttural snarl.

"You'd better let the dog alone," growled Mr Heathcliff, in unison, checking fiercer demonstrations with a punch of his foot. "She's not accustomed to be spoiled – not kept for a pet."

Then, striding to a side door, he shouted again.

"Joseph!"

Joseph mumbled indistinctly in the depths of the cellar, but gave no intimation of ascending; so, his master dived down to him, leaving me *vis-à-vis* the ruffianly bitch, and a pair of grim, shaggy sheep dogs, who shared with her a jealous guardianship over all my movements.

Not anxious to come in contact with their fangs, I sat still; but, imagining they would scarcely understand tacit insults, I unfortunately indulged in winking and making faces at the trio, and some turn of my physiognomy so irritated madam, that she suddenly broke into a fury and leapt on my knees. I flung her back, and hastened to interpose the table between us. This proceeding aroused the whole hive. Half-a-dozen four-footed fiends, of various sizes, and ages, issued from hidden dens to the common centre. I felt my heels and coat-laps peculiar subjects of assault; and, parrying off the larger combatants, as effectually as I could, with the poker, I was constrained to demand, aloud, assistance from some of the household, in reestablishing peace.

Mr Heathcliff and his man climbed the cellar steps with vexatious phlegm. I don't think they moved one second faster than usual, though the hearth was an absolute tempest of worrying and yelping.

Happily, an inhabitant of the kitchen made more dispatch; a lusty dame, with tucked-up gown, bare arms, and fire-flushed cheeks, rushed into the midst of us flourishing a frying-pan; and used that weapon, and her tongue, to such purpose, that the storm subsided magically, and she only remained, heaving like a sea after a high wind, when her master entered on the scene.

"What the devil is the matter?" he asked, eyeing me in a manner I could ill endure after this inhospitable treatment.

"What the devil indeed!" I muttered. "The herd of possessed swine could have had no worse spirits in them than those animals of yours, sir. You might as well leave a stranger with a brood of tigers!"

"They won't meddle with persons who touch nothing," he remarked, putting the bottle before me, and restoring the displaced table. "The dogs do right to be vigilant. Take a glass of wine?"'
Chapter 1

The unfortunate and unexpected reception that Lockwood receives from Heathcliff's dogs suggests the abnormality of behaviour in a remote part of England. Emily's account was undoubtedly based on direct observation. In warning Mrs Gaskell about the nature of Haworth, Charlotte was to endorse Emily's fictional view:

'When you come to Haworth, you must do it in the spirit which might sustain you in case you were setting out on a brief trip to the backwoods of America, leaving behind you, husband, children and civilization, you must come out to barbarism, loneliness, and liberty.'

Rev. Patrick Brontë confirmed this attitude in a letter about the Haworth Sunday School:

'I have resided in Yorkshire above 30 years and have preached and visited in different parishes ... and from my reading, personal observation and experience I do not hesitate to say that the populace in general, are either ignorant, or wicked, and in most cases where they have a little learning it is either of a skismatical, vainly philosophical or treacherously political nature.'
4 August 1843

Clearly the discomfort that Lockwood, a stranger to the north, feels when visiting his landlord has some foundation in fact. Haworth was a challenging place and the normal courtesies of cultured life were at a premium.

The story of *Wuthering Heights* unfolds in a series of puzzles. The reader shares Lockwood's perplexity as his visit turns to nightmare, both

Wuthering Heights

sleeping and waking; real nightmares give way to nightmare reality, as in the scene of the casement-window. In a fitful sleep Lockwood dreams of hearing a hell-fire sermon that culminates in loud rapping sounds which, awakening, he records as taps on the window of his room:

'And what was it that had suggested the tremendous tumult? . . . Merely, the branch of a fir-tree that touched my lattice, as the blast wailed by, and rattled its dry cones against the panes!

Nineteenth-century engraving. During the Brontës' childhood, body-snatchers were active in Yorkshire.

I listened doubtingly an instant; detected the disturber, then turned and dozed, and dreamt again; if possible, still more disagreeably than before.

This time, I remembered I was lying in the oak closet, and I heard distinctly the gusty wind, and the driving of the snow; I heard, also, the fir-bough repeat its teasing sound, and ascribed it to the right cause; but it annoyed me so much, that I resolved to silence it, if possible; and, I thought, I rose and endeavoured to unhasp the casement. The hook was soldered into the staple, a circumstance observed by me when awake, but forgotten.

"I must stop it, nevertheless!" I muttered, knocking my knuckles through the glass, and stretching an arm out to seize the importunate branch: instead of which, my fingers closed on the fingers of a little, ice-cold hand!

The intense horror of nightmare came over me; I tried to draw back my arm, but the hand clung to it, and a most melancholy voice sobbed,

"Let me in – let me in!"

"Who are you?" I asked, struggling, meanwhile, to disengage myself.

"Catherine Linton," it replied shiveringly (why did I think of *Linton*? I had read *Earnshaw* twenty times for Linton), "I'm come home, I'd lost my way on the moor!"

As it spoke, I discerned, obscurely, a child's face looking through the window – terror made me cruel; and, finding it useless to attempt shaking the creature off, I pulled its wrist on to the broken pane, and rubbed it to and fro till the blood ran down and soaked the bedclothes: still it wailed, "Let me in!" and maintained its tenacious gripe, almost maddening me with fear.

"How can I!" I said at length. "Let *me* go, if you want me to let you in!"

The fingers relaxed, I snatched mine through the hole, hurriedly piled the books up in a pyramid against it, and stopped my ears to exclude the lamentable prayer.

I seemed to keep them closed above a quarter of an hour, yet, the instant I listened, again, there was the doleful cry moaning on!

"Begone!" I shouted, "I'll never let you in, not if you beg for twenty years."

"It's twenty years," mourned the voice, "twenty years, I've been a waif for twenty years!"

Thereat began a feeble scratching outside, and the pile of books moved as if thrust forward.

I tried to jump up, but could not stir a limb; and so yelled aloud, in a frenzy of fright.'
Chapter 3

It is hardly surprising that the Brontë children should enjoy and make use of ghost stories. Living in the corner of a graveyard at a time when body-snatchers were at work, their active minds would have much to feed on. This preoccupation shows in their juvenile writings with frequent tales of creatures rising from graves and knocking at windows and doors. In both *Jane Eyre* and *Wuthering Heights* important scenes similarly draw upon the supernatural. Little Jane Eyre, shut in the red room where her uncle died, fears the approach of someone from the grave:

The churchyard in Haworth, where in ten years there were 1,344 burials, cast more than a melancholy gloom over the village. In 1850, a public health inspector declared it a positive threat to the health of the parish.

Wuthering Heights

'A singular notion dawned upon me. I doubted not – never doubted – that if Mr Reed had been alive he would have treated me kindly; and now, as I sat looking at the white bed and overshadowed walls – occasionally also turning a fascinated eye towards the dimly-gleaming mirror – I began to recall what I had heard of dead men, troubled in their graves by the violation of their last wishes, revisiting the earth to punish the perjured and avenge the oppressed; and I thought Mr Reed's spirit, harassed by the wrongs of his sister's child, might quit its abode – whether in the church vault or in the unknown world of the departed – and rise before me in this chamber. I wiped my tears and hushed my sobs, fearful lest any sign of violent grief might waken a preternatural voice to comfort me, or elicit from the gloom some haloed face, bending over me with strange pity. This idea, consolatory in theory, I felt would be terrible if realized: with all my might I endeavoured to stifle it – I endeavoured to be firm. Shaking my hair from my eyes, I lifted my head and tried to look boldly round the dark room; at this moment a light gleamed on the wall. Was it, I asked myself, a ray from the moon penetrating some aperture in the blind? No; moonlight was still, and this stirred; while I gazed, it glided up to the ceiling and quivered over my head. I can now conjecture readily that this streak of light was, in all likelihood, a gleam from a lantern carried by some one across the lawn: but then, prepared as my mind was for horror, shaken as my nerves were by agitation, I thought the swift darting beam was a herald of some coming vision from another world. My heart beat thick, my head grew hot; a sound filled my ears, which I deemed the rushing of wings; something seemed near me; I was oppressed, suffocated: endurance broke down; I rushed to the door and shook the lock in desperate effort. Steps came running along the outer passage; the key turned, Bessie and Abbot entered.

"Miss Eyre, are you ill?" said Bessie.

"What a dreadful noise! it went quite through me!" exclaimed Abbot.

"Take me out! Let me go into the nursery!" was my cry.

"What for? Are you hurt? Have you seen something?" again demanded Bessie.

"Oh! I saw a light, and I thought a ghost would come." I had now got hold of Bessie's hand, and she did not snatch it from me.'
Jane Eyre. *Chapter 2*

Here is ample evidence that the Brontë sisters revelled in spine-chilling tales, probably by oil or candlelight in the drawing-room where they sat up writing late at night. Charlotte's school friends relate how she had young girls in hysterics when she told them ghost stories. Emily's ghoulish scene when the long-dead Catherine grips Lockwood's hand is one of the most startling in literature, and worthy of the graveyard children's delight in tension and suspense.

This scene in *Wuthering Heights* links Heathcliff and Catherine for the first time. Lockwood's landlord, disturbed by his guest's cry in the night, sends him to another part of the house, but not before he himself is observed behaving strangely:

'. . . I stood still, and was witness, involuntarily, to a piece of superstition on the part of my landlord, which belied, oddly, his apparent sense.

He got onto the bed, and wrenched open the lattice, bursting, as he pulled at it, into an uncontrollable passion of tears.

"Come in! come in!" he sobbed. "Cathy, do come. Oh do – *once* more! Oh! my heart's darling! hear me *this* time – Catherine, at last!"

The spectre showed a spectre's ordinary caprice; it gave no sign of being; but the snow and wind whirled wildly through, even reaching my station, and blowing out the light.

There was such anguish in the gush of grief that accompanied this raving, that my compassion made me overlook its folly, and I drew off, half angry to have listened at all, and vexed at having related my ridiculous nightmare, since it produced that agony; though *why*, was beyond my comprehension.'
Chapter 3

Lockwood's questioning is also the reader's. Swiftly Emily Brontë has spun a web of possibilities that we are keen to unravel.

Lockwood returns to his rented house, Thrushcross Grange, after a snowstorm. Emily's fictional description of conditions on Haworth moor in winter could have been written today:

The Worth valley lies at the foot of Haworth village, with mills lining the banks of the river.

'I declined joining their breakfast, and, at the first gleam of dawn, took an opportunity of escaping into the free air, now clear, and still, and cold as impalpable ice.

My landlord hallooed for me to stop ere I reached the bottom of the garden, and offered to accompany me across the moor. It was well he did, for the whole hill-back was one billowy, white ocean; the swells and falls not indicating corresponding rises and depressions in the ground – many pits, at least, were filled to a level; and entire ranges of mounds, the refuse of the quarries, blotted out from the chart which my yesterday's walk left pictured in my mind.

I had remarked on one side of the road, at intervals of six or seven yards, a line of upright stones, continued through the whole length of the barren: these were erected, and daubed with lime on purpose to serve as guides in the dark, and also, when a fall, like the present, confounded the deep swamps on either hand with the firmer path: but, excepting a dirty dot pointing up, here and there, all traces of their existence had vanished; and my companion found it necessary to warn me frequently to steer to the right, or left, when I imagined I was following, correctly, the windings of the road.

We exchanged little conversation, and he halted at the entrance of Thrushcross park, saying I could make no error there. Our adieux were limited to a hasty bow, and then I pushed forward, trusting to my own resources, for the porter's lodge is untenanted as yet.

The distance from the gate to the Grange is two miles: I believe I managed to make it four, what with losing myself among the trees, and sinking up to the neck in snow, a predicament which only those who have

Wuthering Heights

experienced it can appreciate. At any rate, whatever were my wanderings, the clock chimed twelve as I entered the house; and that gave exactly
an hour for every mile of the usual way from Wuthering Heights.'
Chapter 3

Thrushcross Grange, in contrast to the bleak exposed farmhouse on
the Heights, is set in parkland with none of the grim features of
Heathcliff's home. Both owe something to halls and houses Emily
knew, though none can be identified with certainty as originals for
either. Thrushcross Grange serves Emily as a foil or counterbalance to
the barbarity of Wuthering Heights.

Each house comes to represent a particular set of values held together
in a tension of opposites as the story unfolds. The Brontë sisters were
always aware of the contrast between the relative seclusion of Haworth
and the outside world. This isolation characterizes all aspects of their
life, their hopes and their interests. Despite a voracious appetite for
books, magazines and newspapers, their ideas always lagged somewhat
behind those of their contemporaries, not only southerners but also
northern town-dwellers. Culture in the form of fashion, familiarity with
developments in the arts and awareness of political events, had to be
imported, initially from Bradford or Leeds to the nearby town of
Keighley, then to Haworth and the parsonage. The double force of
deprivation and appetite, of isolation and intellectual curiosity, seems to
have enlivened the family's imaginative powers rather than blunting or
diminishing them. Nevertheless, the tension between refined society and
the everyday existence of Haworth is never far removed. The crudeness
of life in remote hill farms is set against more civilized standards of
behaviour. Such tension in real life is transformed into fiction where the
implications of seclusion and barbarism can be explored.

Just as Tabitha, the Brontë's servant, kept the family abreast of local
gossip in the township of Haworth, so Lockwood's housekeeper Ellen
Dean tells him the tale of Heathcliff and the strange events at
Wuthering Heights. Ellen Dean becomes the narrator of the story, and,
as former servant in both houses, her account has the ring of
authenticity.

She begins by telling of the unexpected arrival of Heathcliff, a
foundling, at what was then the Earnshaw's farmhouse:

'One fine summer morning – it was the beginning of harvest, I
remember – Mr Earnshaw, the old master, came down stairs, dressed
for a journey; and, after he had told Joseph what was to be done during
the day, he turned to Hindley and Cathy, and me – for I sat eating my
porridge with them – and he said, speaking to his son, "Now, my bonny
man, I'm going to Liverpool today, what shall I bring you? You may
choose what you like; only let it be little, for I shall walk there and back;
sixty miles each way, that is a long spell!"

Hindley named a fiddle, and then he asked Miss Cathy; she was
hardly six years old, but she could ride any horse in the stable, and she
chose a whip.

Opposite Top Withins, the ruin
of a farmhouse long associated
with *Wuthering Heights*. Rightly
or wrongly, it is the scene most
often envisaged as the
Earnshaw's farm.

He did not forget me; for he had a kind heart, though he was rather severe, sometimes. He promised to bring me a pocketful of apples and pears, and then he kissed his children good-bye, and set off.

It seemed a long while to us all – the three days of his absence – and often did little Cathy ask when he would be home. Mrs Earnshaw expected him by supper-time, on the third evening; and she put off the meal hour after hour; there were no signs of his coming, however, and at last the children got tired of running down to the gate to look – Then it grew dark, she would have had them to bed, but they begged sadly to be allowed to stay up; and, just about eleven o'clock, the door-latch was raised quietly and in stepped the master. He threw himself into a chair, laughing and groaning, and bid them all stand off, for he was nearly killed – he would not have another such walk for the three kingdoms.

"And at the end of it, to be flighted to death!" he said, opening his great coat, which he held bundled up in his arms. "See here, wife; I was never so beaten with anything in my life; but you must e'en take it as a gift of God; though it's as dark almost as if it came from the devil."

We crowded round, and, over Miss Cathy's head, I had a peep at a dirty, ragged, black-haired child; big enough both to walk and talk – indeed, its face looked older than Catherine's – yet, when it was set on its feet, it only stared round, and repeated over and over again some gibberish that nobody could understand. I was frightened, and Mrs Earnshaw was ready to fling it out of doors: she did fly up – asking how he could fashion to bring that gipsy brat into the house, when they had their own bairns to feed, and fend for? What he meant to do with it, and whether he were mad?

The master tried to explain the matter; but he was really half dead with fatigue, and all that I could make out, amongst her scolding, was a tale of his seeing it starving, and houseless, and as good as dumb in the streets of Liverpool where he picked it up and inquired for its owner – Not a soul knew to whom it belonged, he said, and his money and time, being both limited, he thought it better to take it home with him, at once, than run into vain expenses there; because he was determined he would not leave it as he found it.

Well, the conclusion was that my mistress grumbled herself calm; and Mr Earnshaw told me to wash it, and give it clean things, and let it sleep with the children.'

Chapter 4

The taking-in of foundlings was by no means unusual in Yorkshire in the early 19th century. Indeed, Keighley, the town situated near a gap in the Pennine Hills only four miles from Haworth, seems always to have had an immigrant population as people moved from north to south and east to west. There was much public concern about the welfare and upbringing of such children, reflected to some degree in the work of Dickens. Heathcliff's ancestry is purposely vague.

Taken into the family, Heathcliff finds a soulmate in Catherine, the daughter of the house who is almost his own age. Their childhood scrambling over the moors is described in idyllic scenes, and they are always depicted as wild untamed creatures at home among the elements. It is Ponden Kirk, an outcrop of rock on the moor above Haworth, the 'Penistone Crags' of the novel, that is particularly associated with their moorland wanderings.

Catherine and Heathcliff's last escapade together after his benefactor has died is a night jaunt to spy on the inmates of Thrushcross Grange. This inquisitiveness must have been a Brontë game for, as we shall see later, the hero of Anne's *The Tenant of Wildfell Hall* eavesdrops in a similar manner. Here the 'barbaric' children of the moor venture to the edge of the more civilized world:

'"Cathy and I escaped from the wash-house to have a ramble at liberty, and getting a glimpse of the Grange lights, we thought we would just go and see whether the Lintons passed their Sunday evenings standing shivering in corners, while their father and mother sat eating and drinking, and singing and laughing, and burning their eyes out before the fire. ... We ran from the top of the Heights to the park, without stopping – Catherine completely beaten in the race, because she was barefoot. You'll have to seek for her shoes in the bog tomorrow. We crept through a broken hedge, groped our way up the path, and planted ourselves on a flower-pot under the drawing-room window. The light came from thence; they had not put up the shutters, and the curtains were only half closed. Both of us were able to look in by standing on the basement, and clinging to the ledge, and we saw – ah! it was beautiful – a splendid place carpeted with crimson, and crimson-covered chairs and tables, and a pure white ceiling bordered by gold, a shower of glass-drops hanging in silver chains from the centre, and shimmering with little soft tapers. Old Mr and Mrs Linton were not there. Edgar and his sister had it entirely to themselves; shouldn't they have been happy? We should have thought ourselves in heaven! And now, guess what your good children were doing? Isabella – I believe she is eleven, a year younger than Cathy – lay screaming at the farther end of the room, shrieking as if witches were running red-hot needles into her. Edgar stood on the hearth weeping silently, and in the middle of the table sat a little dog shaking its paw and yelping, which, from their mutual accusations, we understood they had nearly pulled in two between them. The idiots! That was their pleasure! to quarrel who should hold a heap of warm hair, and each begin to cry because both, after struggling to get it, refused to take it. We laughed outright at the petted things, we did despise them!"'
Chapter 6

How often the Brontë girls found themselves on the outside looking in at another world, like a trio of Cinderellas, is a matter of conjecture. We can be sure, however, that their acute shyness in company, combined with their poverty, set them apart from contemporaries. Later events in their lives testify to the sense of loneliness that the awkward girls must often have felt. A visit to Covent Garden Opera House with their publisher George Smith underlines their situation. Charlotte and Anne, in plain everyday dresses, were escorted by Smith in full evening dress, and his jewel-bedecked sister. Yet such experiences, though intimidating, failed to crush the girls' spirits. Short in stature, unfashionably dressed, they shrank from exposure but when it happened they gave as good as they got. Charlotte's comments on that evening's Rossini opera convey no hint of their embarrassment; she merely finds the opera not as good as it should have been.

The Brontë sisters look at events without flinching and there is a toughness about their writing. Emily's legendary control of her bull-mastiff Keeper haunts Heathcliff's description of the dog Skulker in the eavesdropping scene at Thrushcross Grange:

"'I told you we laughed," he answered. "The Lintons heard us, and with one accord, they shot like arrows to the door; there was silence, and then a cry, 'Oh, mamma, mamma! Oh, papa, Oh, mamma, come here. Oh, papa, oh!' They really did howl out, something in that way. We made frightful noises to terrify them still more, and then we dropped off the ledge, because somebody was drawing the bars, and we felt we had better flee. I had Cathy by the hand, and was urging her on, when all at once she fell down.

"'Run, Heathcliff, run!' she whispered. 'They have let the bull-dog loose, and he holds me!'

"The devil had seized her ankle, Nelly; I heard his abominable snorting. She did not yell out – no! She would have scorned to do it, if she had been spitted on the horns of a mad cow. I did, though, I vociferated curses enough to annihilate any fiend in Christendom, and I got a stone and thrust it between his jaws, and tried with all my might to

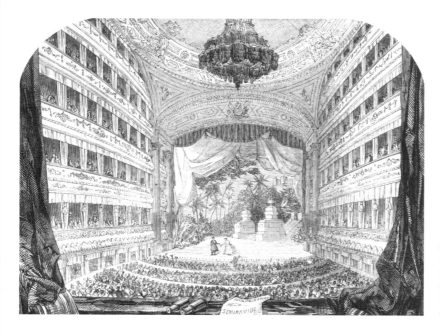

Covent Garden Opera House to which Charlotte and Anne Brontë were taken by their publisher. Charlotte was not very impressed by the Rossini opera performed there.

Emily Brontë's watercolour of her dog, Keeper.

cram it down his throat. A beast of a servant came up with a lantern, at last, shouting –

"'Keep fast, Skulker, keep fast!'

"He changed his note, however, when he saw Skulker's game. The dog was throttled off, his huge, purple tongue hanging half a foot out of his mouth, and his pendant lips streaming with bloody slaver.

"The man took Cathy up; she was sick; not from fear, I'm certain, but from pain. He carried her in; I followed, grumbling execrations and vengeance.

"'What prey, Robert?' hallooed Linton from the entrance.

"'Skulker has caught a little girl, sir,' he replied; 'and there's a lad here,' he added, making a clutch at me, 'who looks an out-and-outer! . . .'

"While they examined me, Cathy came round; she heard the last speech, and laughed. Edgar Linton, after an inquisitive stare, collected sufficient wit to recognize her. They see us at church, you know, though we seldom meet them elsewhere.

"'That's Miss Earnshaw!' he whispered to his mother, 'and look how Skulker has bitten her – how her foot bleeds!'

"'Miss Earnshaw? Nonsense!' cried the dame. 'Miss Earnshaw scouring the country with a gipsy! And yet, my dear, the child is in mourning – surely it is – and she may be lamed for life!'

"'What culpable carelessness in her brother!' exclaimed Mr Linton, turning from me to Catherine. 'I've understood from Shielders'" (that was the curate, sir) "'that he lets her grow up in absolute heathenism. But who is this? Where did she pick up this companion? Oho! I declare he is that strange acquisition my late neighbour made, in his journey to Liverpool – a little Lascar, or an American or Spanish castaway.'""

Chapter 6

Catherine is taken into the Linton household while Heathcliff is sent packing. The barbarian is banished and thus begins Heathcliff's estrangement from Catherine which leads to his unrelenting plan of vengeance. His very name is redolent of the open moorland and it is no surprise that he can scarcely be contained inside a civilized home.

When Catherine returns to Wuthering Heights, it is clear that she is attracted by the more refined, Linton style of life. Heathcliff is increasingly alienated. In due course Edgar Linton calls upon Catherine at the Heights.

Courtship, possibly because they had little experience of it, is often taken as a topic in the sisters' fiction. Edgar's first visit to court Catherine at Wuthering Heights is a hilarious parody of all that such encounters should be, as seen through the eyes of a romantic girl. Behind the episode we can detect a devastating comic cynicism:

'"I'm not come too soon, am I?" he said, casting a look at me. I had begun to wipe the plate, and tidy some drawers at the far end in the dresser.

"No," answered Catherine. "What are you doing there, Nelly?"

"My work, Miss," I replied. (Mr Hindley had given me directions to make a third party in any private visits Linton chose to pay.)

She stepped behind me and whispered crossly, "Take yourself and your dusters off! when company are in the house, servants don't commence scouring and cleaning in the room where they are!"

"It's a good opportunity, now that master is away," I answered aloud. "He hates me to be fidgeting over these things in his presence. I'm sure Mr Edgar will excuse me."

"I hate you to be fidgeting in *my* presence," exclaimed the young lady imperiously, not allowing her guest time to speak — she had failed to recover her equanimity since the little dispute with Heathcliff.

"I'm sorry for it, Miss Catherine!" was my response; and I proceeded assiduously with my occupation.

She, supposing Edgar could not see her, snatched the cloth from my hand, and pinched me, with a prolonged wrench, very spitefully on the arm.

I've said I did not love her, and rather relished mortifying her vanity now and then; besides, she hurt me extremely, so I started up from my knees, and screamed out,

"Oh, Miss, that's a nasty trick! You have no right to nip me, and I'm not going to bear it!"

"I didn't touch you, you lying creature!" cried she, her fingers tingling to repeat the act, and her ears red with rage. She never had power to conceal her passion, it always set her whole complexion in a blaze.

"What's that, then?" I retorted, showing a decided purple witness to refute her.

She stamped her foot, wavered a moment, and then, irresistibly impelled by the naughty spirit within her, slapped me on the cheek a stinging blow that filled both eyes with water.

Opposite Relatively few of Emily Brontë's drawings have survived. This typical example of detailed copying is of St Simon Stylites. Charlotte Brontë believed the analysis required for copying a composition a fine discipline.

"Catherine, love! Catherine!" interposed Linton, greatly shocked at the double fault of falsehood and violence which his idol had committed.

"Leave the room, Ellen!" she repeated, trembling all over.

Little Hareton, who followed me everywhere, and was sitting near me on the floor, at seeing my tears commenced crying himself, and sobbed out complaints against "wicked aunt Cathy," which drew her fury on to his unlucky head: she seized his shoulders, and shook him till the poor child waxed livid, and Edgar thoughtlessly laid hold of her hands to deliver him. In an instant one was wrung free, and the astonished young man felt it applied over his own ear in a way that could not be mistaken for jest.'

Chapter 8

From smiles to face-slapping, the descent is briskly accomplished, providing a telling satire of daydream romance. It is not hard to sense the sisters' irony in their joint observation of such episodes.

There is, however, no precedent for the description of Heathcliff's behaviour at the death of Catherine, who had become Edgar Linton's wife. This scene, in its strength and passion, epitomizes the singular vision of Emily Brontë. Even Charlotte found it difficult to explain where Emily found such a character and doubted whether her sister had been right to release him into the world. Characteristically, Heathcliff had been waiting outside the grange through the night in which Catherine had died:

'I wished yet feared to find him. I felt the terrible news must be told, and I longed to get it over, but *how* to do it, I did not know.

He was there – at least a few yards further in the park; leant against an old ash tree, his hat off, and his hair soaked with the dew that had gathered on the budded branches, and fell pattering round him. He had been standing a long time in that position, for I saw a pair of ousels passing and repassing, scarcely three feet from him, busy in building their nest, and regarding his proximity no more than that of a piece of timber. They flew off at my approach, and he raised his eyes and spoke:

"She's dead!" he said; "I've not waited for you to learn that. Put your handkerchief away – don't snivel before me. Damn you all! she wants none of *your* tears!"

I was weeping as much for him as her: we do sometimes pity creatures that have none of the feeling either for themselves or others; and when I first looked into his face, I perceived that he had got intelligence of the catastrophe; and a foolish notion struck me that his heart was quelled, and he prayed, because his lips moved, and his gaze was bent on the ground.

"Yes, she's dead!" I answered, checking my sobs, and drying my cheeks. "Gone to heaven, I hope, where we may, every one, join her, if we take due warning, and leave our evil ways to follow good!"

"Did *she* take due warning, then?" asked Heathcliff, attempting a sneer. "Did she die like a saint? Come, give me a true history of the event. How did – "

Opposite Haworth Churchyard.

He endeavoured to pronounce the name, but could not manage it; and compressing his mouth, he held a silent combat with his inward agony, defying, meanwhile, my sympathy with an unflinching, ferocious stare.

"How did she die?" he resumed, at last — fain, notwithstanding his hardihood, to have a support behind him, for, after the struggle, he trembled, in spite of himself, to his very finger-ends.

"Poor wretch!" I thought; "you have a heart and nerves the same as your brother men! Why should you be anxious to conceal them? your pride cannot blind God! You tempt him to wring them, till he forces a cry of humiliation!"

"Quietly as a lamb!" I answered, aloud, "She drew a sigh, and stretched herself, like a child reviving, and sinking again to sleep; and five minutes after I felt one little pulse at her heart, and nothing more!"

"And — did she ever mention me?" he asked, hesitating, as if he dreaded the answer to his question would introduce details that he could not bear to hear.

"Her senses never returned — she recognized nobody from the time you left her," I said. "She lies with a sweet smile on her face; and her latest ideas wandered back to pleasant early days. Her life closed in a gentle dream — may she wake as kindly in the other world!"

"May she wake in torment!" he cried, with frightful vehemence, stamping his foot, and groaning in a sudden paroxysm of ungovernable passion. "Why, she's a liar to the end! Where is she? Not *there* — not in heaven — not perished — where? Oh! you said you cared nothing for my sufferings! And I pray one prayer — I repeat it till my tongue stiffens — Catherine Earnshaw, may you not rest, as long as I am living! You said I killed you — haunt me then! The murdered *do* haunt their murderers. I believe — I know that ghosts *have* wandered on earth. Be with me always — take any form — drive me mad! only *do* not leave me in this abyss, where I cannot find you! Oh God! it is unutterable! I *cannot* live without my life! I *cannot* live without my soul!"

He dashed his head against the knotted trunk; and, lifting up his eyes, howled, not like a man, but like a savage beast getting goaded to death with knives and spears.'
Chapter 16

Heathcliff's terrible curse is all too effective and his fate for the rest of the novel is torment. He only finds peace after getting the sexton to open Catherine's coffin seven years after her burial. Once more we are in a graveyard:

'"I'll tell you what I did yesterday! I got the sexton, who was digging Linton's grave, to remove the earth off her coffin lid, and I opened it. I thought, once, I would have stayed there, when I saw her face again — it is hers yet — he had hard work to stir me; but he said it would change, if the air blew on it, and so I struck one side of the coffin loose — and covered it up — not Linton's side, damn him! I wish he'd been soldered in lead — and I bribed the sexton to pull it away, when I'm laid there, and slide mine out too. I'll have it made so, and then, by the time Linton gets to us, he'll not know which is which!"

"You were very wicked, Mr Heathcliff!" I exclaimed; "were you not ashamed to disturb the dead?"

"I disturbed nobody, Nelly," he replied; "and I gave some ease to myself. I shall be a great deal more comfortable now; and you'll have a better chance of keeping me underground, when I get there. Disturbed her? No! she has disturbed me, night and day, through eighteen years — incessantly — remorselessly — till yesternight — and yesternight, I was tranquil. I dreamt I was sleeping the last sleep, by that sleeper, with my heart stopped, and my cheek frozen against hers."

"And if she had been dissolved into earth, or worse, what would you have dreamt of then?" I said.

"Of dissolving with her, and being more happy still!" he answered. "Do you suppose I dread any change of that sort? I expected such a transformation on raising the lid, but I'm better pleased that it should not commence till I share it. Besides, unless I had received a distinct impression of her passionless features, that strange feeling would hardly have been removed. It began oddly. You know, I was wild after she died, and eternally, from dawn to dawn, praying her to return to me — her spirit — I have a strong faith in ghosts; I have a conviction that they can, and do exist, among us!

The day she was buried there came a fall of snow. In the evening I went to the churchyard. It blew bleak as winter — all round was solitary: I didn't fear that her fool of a husband would wander up the den so late — and no one else had business to bring them there.

Being alone, and conscious two yards of loose earth was the sole barrier between us, I said to myself —

'I'll have her in my arms again! If she be cold, I'll think it is this north wind that chills me; and if she be motionless, it is sleep.'

"I got a spade from the toolhouse, and began to delve with all my might — it scraped the coffin; I fell to work with my hands; the wood commenced cracking about the screws, I was on the point of attaining my object, when it seemed that I heard a sigh from some one above, close at the edge of the grave, and bending down. 'If I can only get this off,' I muttered, 'I wish they may shovel in the earth over us both!' and I wrenched more desperately still. There was another sigh, close at my ear. I appeared to feel the warm breath of it displacing the sleet-laden wind. I knew no living thing in flesh and blood was by — but as certainly as you perceive the approach to some substantial body in the dark, though it cannot be discerned, so certainly I felt that Cathy was there, not under me, but on the earth.

A sudden sense of relief flowed, from my heart, through every limb. I relinquished my labour of agony, and turned consoled at once, unspeakably consoled. Her presence was with me; it remained while I re-filled the grave, and led me home. You may laugh, if you will, but I was sure I should see her there. I was sure she was with me, and I could not help talking to her.'"

Chapter 29

Wuthering Heights

Only with his death is any peace restored in *Wuthering Heights*. In the room where Lockwood had his nightmare at the beginning of the story, Heathcliff's yearning for reunion with Catherine reaches its end:

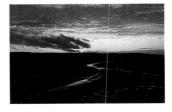

Penistone Hill, the setting for scenes of Heathcliff and Catherine's childhood scrambles in *Wuthering Heights*.

'The following evening was very wet; indeed, it poured down, till day-dawn; and, as I took my morning walk round the house, I observed the master's window swinging open, and the rain driving straight in.

"He cannot be in bed," I thought, "those showers would drench him through! He must either be up, or out. But I'll make no more ado, I'll go boldly, and look!"

Having succeeded in obtaining entrance with another key, I ran to unclose the panels, for the chamber was vacant – quickly pushing them aside, I peeped in. Mr Heathcliff was there – laid on his back. His eyes met mine so keen, and fierce, I started; and then, he seemed to smile.

I could not think him dead – but his face and throat were washed with rain; the bed-clothes dripped, and he was perfectly still. The lattice, flapping to and fro, had grazed one hand that rested on the sill – no blood trickled from the broken skin, and when I put my fingers to it, I could doubt no more – he was dead and stark!

I hasped the window; I combed his black long hair from his forehead; I tried to close his eyes – to extinguish, if possible, that frightful, life-like gaze of exultation, before any one else beheld it. They would not shut – they seemed to sneer at my attempts, and his parted lips, and sharp, white teeth sneered too! Taken with another fit of cowardice, I cried for Joseph. Joseph shuffled up, and made a noise, but resolutely refused to meddle with him.

"Th' divil's harried off his soul," he cried, "and he muh hev his carcass intuh t' bargain, for ow't Aw care! Ech! what a wicked un he looks girning at death!" and the old sinner grinned in mockery.

I thought he intended to cut a caper round the bed; but suddenly composing himself, he fell on his knees, and raised his hands, and returned thanks that the lawful master and the ancient stock were restored to their rights.

I felt stunned by the awful event; and my memory unavoidably recurred to former times with a sort of oppressive sadness. But poor Hareton, the most wronged, was the only one that really suffered much. He sat by the corpse all night, weeping in bitter earnest. He pressed its hand, and kissed the sarcastic, savage face that every one else shrank from contemplating; and bemoaned him with that strong grief which springs naturally from a generous heart, though it be tough as tempered steel.

Kenneth was perplexed to pronounce of what disorder the master died. I concealed the fact of his having swallowed nothing for four days, fearing it might lead to trouble, and then, I am persuaded he did not abstain on purpose; it was the consequence of his strange illness, not the cause.

We buried him, to the scandal of the whole neighbourhood, as he had wished. Earnshaw, and I, the sexton and six men to carry the coffin, comprehended the whole attendance.'
Chapter 34

There is a deep pessimism in *Wuthering Heights*. In setting characters against the elements it seems to deny any value in relationships. There is a cruelty in the plot as Heathcliff relentlessly pursues his revenge. Any re-establishment of a normal world in the second generation of the younger Catherine and Hareton seems an anticlimax; the true sequel to the story seems, indeed, to be the sighting of Heathcliff and Catherine's spirits on the moors.

Be that as it may, there can be little doubt that the novel fittingly commemorates the environment that Emily Brontë knew well in all its moods, and evokes for the reader the terrible loneliness that such an exposed place can inflict on those who live there. The novel does not reconcile the harshness of northern ways with southern manners, and the flower garden that is established in a corner of the space in front of Wuthering Heights seems a very fragile and tenuous decoration.

Ponden Hall, possible original for the houses in *Wuthering Heights*. Home of the Heaton family whose extensive library was well known by the Brontë family.

VI

Agnes Grey

'Anne's nothing, absolutely nothing'
Charlotte Brontë. My Angria and the Angrians

Of the first group of three novels sent from Haworth parsonage to publishers, *Agnes Grey* tends to be somewhat overlooked, lying as it does in the shadow of *Wuthering Heights* and the subsequent success of *Jane Eyre* – not one of the original three. Anne, more than her sisters, has suffered by being one of a trio of writers, it being all too easy to dismiss her as the youngest child of the family who emulated her elder sisters in most things, including writing. If we can separate her voice and her work from theirs, and trace the individual course of her life both in and away from Haworth, the superficial alignment of her nature and talent with that of Emily and Charlotte immediately appears over-simplified.

As with her sister Emily, the lack of real evidence about Anne – evidence, that is, which is not percolated through other interested parties – permits Charlotte's partial portrayal to stand virtually unchallenged. The extent of this partiality and the complexity of its nature is apparent in a piece of writing by Charlotte at eighteen in which she lampoons her brother Patrick Branwell, in the guise of Patrick Benjamin Wiggins, and has him descant on his sister's deficiencies:

'"... in a way, I may be said to have no relations ... I've some people who call themselves akin to me in the shape of three girls. They are honoured by possessing me as a brother, but I deny that they are my sisters ..."
"What are your sisters' names?"
"Charlotte Wiggins, Jane Wiggins, and Anne Wiggins."
"Are they as queer as you?"
"Oh, they are miserable, silly creatures, not worth talking about. Charlotte's eighteen years old, a broad dumpy thing, whose head does not come higher than my elbow. Emily's sixteen, lean and scant, with a face about the size of a penny, and Anne's nothing, absolutely nothing."
"What! Is she an idiot?"
"Next door to it."'
Charlotte Brontë. My Angria and the Angrians

The complex device of Charlotte offering self-criticism through an

Opposite View of Scarborough as Anne Brontë knew it, showing, above the bathing machines, the building where she rented accommodation during her final illness. The Grand Hotel now occupies this site.

Agnes Grey

invented version of Branwell should not be taken too seriously. Yet the echoes to be found in *Agnes Grey*, which is clearly autobiographical, provide intriguing evidence of the subtlety of family typecasting.

At the outset of the novel Anne Brontë describes a younger sister seeking to leave home and earn a living:

"'I wish *I* could do something,' said I.

'You Agnes! well, who knows? You draw pretty well too: if you choose some simple piece for your subject, I dare say you will be able to produce something we shall all be proud to exhibit.'

'But I have another scheme in my head, mamma, and have had long, only I did not like to mention it.'

'Indeed! pray tell us what it is.'

'I should like to be a governess.'

My mother uttered an exclamation of surprise, and laughed. My sister dropped her work in astonishment, exclaiming, '*You* a governess, Agnes! What *can* you be dreaming of?'

'Well! I don't see anything so *very* extraordinary in it. I do not pretend to be able to instruct great girls; but surely, I could teach little

The Governess, painting by Richard Redgrave that points up the contrast between the governess of no status and the young ladies in her charge.

ones: and I should like it *so* much: I am so fond of children. Do let me, mamma!"

"But, my love, you have not learned to take care of *yourself* yet: and young children require more judgement and experience to manage than elder ones."

"But, mamma, I am above eighteen, and quite able to take care of myself, and others, too. You do not know half the wisdom and prudence I possess, because I have never been tried."

"Only think," said Mary, "what would you do in a house full of strangers, without me or mamma to speak and act for you – with a parcel of children, besides yourself, to attend to; and no one to look to for advice? You would not even know what clothes to put on."

"You think, because I always do as you bid me, I have no judgement of my own: but only try me – that is all I ask – and you shall see what I can do."

At that moment my father entered, and the subject of our discussion was explained to him.

"What, my little Agnes, a governess!" cried he, and, in spite of his dejection, he laughed at the idea.'
Chapter 1

Even earlier, when Agnes tries to help her mother in the house, she receives the youngest child's rebuff:

'"Help me you cannot, Agnes; and I cannot go out with *you* – I have far too much to do."

"Then let me help you."

"You cannot, indeed, dear child. Go and practise your music, or play with the kitten."'
Chapter 1

The parallels are too beguiling. A poor clergy household where young women are trying to find ways of earning a living without much education or any recourse to rich relatives or influential people suggests a close similarity to much of Anne's life at Haworth. Was she often sent off to practise her music or play with the kitten?

Several of Anne's poems included in the Bells' anthology gently suggest a privacy and depth of feeling that biographers more readily associate with Emily than with the youngest sister, as displayed, for instance, in this extract from *Self Congratulation*:

Last night, as we sat round the fire
    Conversing merrily,
We heard, without, approaching steps
    Of one well known to me!

There was no trembling in my voice,
　　No blush upon my cheek,
No lustrous sparkle in my eyes,
　　Of hope, or joy, to speak;
But, oh! my spirit burned within,
　　My heart beat full and fast!
He came not nigh – he went away –
　　And then my joy was passed.

And yet my comrades marked it not:
　　My voice was still the same;
They saw me smile, and o'er my face
　　No signs of sadness came.
They little knew my hidden thoughts;
　　And they will *never* know
The aching anguish of my heart,
　　The bitter burning woe!

From the very opening *Agnes Grey* displays a confidence and ease with prose that indicates how much writing must have preceded it. Thinking her own thoughts and going her own way – we should never forget that she alone of the family worked effectively and lived happily away from Haworth – Anne succeeded in polishing her own style and found her own voice. Could it be that her stubborn demand to be taken to Scarborough when she knew she was dying was her final act of self-assertion: a blunt refusal to die after the pattern of her brother and sister whose recent deaths so troubled her mind? Anne had her wish and lies buried in the churchyard on the steep hill at Scarborough that is the setting for one of the happiest chapters she ever wrote. While the rest of the family are buried at Haworth, she alone is elsewhere, in a place where she created and maintained her own life.

Anne Brontë was a moralist, her understanding of fiction avowedly didactic:

'All true histories contain instruction; though, in some, the treasure may be hard to find, and when found, so trivial in quantity, that the dry, shrivelled kernel scarcely compensates for the trouble of cracking the nut. Whether this be the case with my history or not, I am hardly competent to judge. I sometimes think it might prove useful to some, and entertaining to others; but the world may judge for itself. Shielded by my own obscurity, and by the lapse of years, and a few fictitious names, I do not fear to venture; and will candidly lay before the public what I would not disclose to the most intimate friend.'
Chapter 1

Anne Brontë's theme and the obvious reference to her own background are quickly established:

'My father was a clergyman of the north of England, who was

deservedly respected by all who knew him; and, in his younger days, lived pretty comfortably on the joint income of a small incumbency and a snug little property of his own. My mother, who married him against the wishes of her friends, was a squire's daughter, and a woman of spirit. In vain it was represented to her, that if she became the poor parson's wife, she must relinquish her carriage and her lady's-maid, and all the luxuries and elegancies of affluence; which to her were little less than the necessaries of life. A carriage and a lady's-maid were great conveniences; but, thank Heaven, she had feet to carry her, and hands to minister to her own necessities. An elegant house and spacious grounds were not to be despised; but she would rather live in a cottage with Richard Grey than in a palace with any other man in the world.'
Chapter 1

The headstone of Anne Brontë's grave in the old churchyard high on the cliffs at Scarborough. The age shown is incorrect, Charlotte spoke of having it changed, but never did. Anne was twenty nine when she died in 1849.

Effective, happy relationships within families; relationships based upon mutual respect and concern – these are the precepts that her novels seek to illustrate.

Agnes Grey is a *governess* novel, and Agnes Grey, like her creator, a governess – like Jane Eyre, we might be tempted to add – but mistakenly, for *Agnes Grey* was written first.

Agnes Grey

Anne's experience as a governess belongs to two households, both providing models for *Agnes Grey*. The first was her appointment at Blake Hall, Mirfield with the Ingham family in 1839; the second, and longer, with the Robinson's at Thorp Green near York in 1840. Her battles with children of various ages gave her the opportunity to set fanciful ideas of teaching against realities:

'How delightful it would be to be a governess! To go out into the world; to enter upon a new life; to act for myself; to exercise my unused faculties; to try my unknown powers; to earn my own maintenance, and something to comfort and help my father, mother, and sister, besides exonerating them from the provision of my food and clothing; to show papa what his little Agnes could do; to convince mamma and Mary that I was not quite the helpless, thoughtless being they supposed. And then, how charming to be entrusted with the care and education of children!'
Chapter 1

Almost at once Agnes Grey learns what it is to be in charge of children, spoiled by their mother, ignored by their father, and encouraged to consider their governess as of no consequence:

'The Governess of No Consequence', a 19th-century engraving depicting the 'invisible' nature of a governess.

A lock of Anne Brontë's hair set in a gold brooch.

'I particularly remember one wild, snowy afternoon, soon after my return in January; the children had all come up from dinner, loudly declaring that they meant "to be naughty"; and they had well kept their resolution, though I had talked myself hoarse, and wearied every muscle in my throat, in the vain attempt to reason them out of it. I had got Tom pinned up in a corner, whence, I told him, he should not escape till he had done his appointed task. Meantime, Fanny had possessed herself of my work-bag, and was rifling its contents – and spitting into it besides. I told her to let it alone, but to no purpose, of course. "Burn it, Fanny!" cried Tom: and *this* command she hastened to obey. I sprang to snatch it from the fire, and Tom darted to the door. "Mary Ann, throw her desk out of the window!" cried he: and my precious desk, containing my letters and papers, my small amount of cash, and all my valuables, was about to be precipitated from the three-storey window. I flew to rescue it. Meanwhile Tom had left the room, and was rushing down the stairs, followed by Fanny. Having secured my desk, I ran to catch them, and Mary Ann came scampering after. All three escaped me, and ran out of the house into the garden, where they plunged about in the snow, shouting and screaming in exultant glee.

What must I do? If I followed them, I should probably be unable to capture one, and only drive them farther away, if I did not, how was I to get them in? and what would their parents think of me, if they saw or heard the children rioting, hatless, bonnetless, gloveless, and bootless, in the deep, soft snow? While I stood in this perplexity, just without the door, trying by grim looks and angry words, to awe them into subjection, I heard a voice behind me, in harshly piercing tones, exclaiming, –

"Miss Grey! Is it possible! What, in the devil's name, can you be thinking about?"

"I can't get them in, sir," said I, turning round, and beholding Mr Bloomfield, with his hair on end, and his pale blue eyes bolting from their sockets.

"But I INSIST upon their being got in!" cried he, approaching nearer, and looking perfectly ferocious.

"Then, sir, you must call them yourself, if you please, for they won't listen to me," I replied, stepping back.

"Come in with you, you filthy brats; or I'll horse-whip you every one!" roared he; and the children instantly obeyed. "There, you see! they come at the first word!"'
Chapter 4

The humour in *Agnes Grey* is not confined to the observation of children. Agnes's arrival after a cold journey on the outside of a coach leaves her chilled and at a disadvantage for her first meeting with the wife of her employer:

'I was somewhat dismayed at my appearance on looking in the glass: the cold wind had swelled and reddened my hands, uncurled and entangled my hair, and dyed my face of a pale purple; add to this my collar was horribly crumpled, my frock splashed with mud, my feet clad in stout new boots, and as the trunks were not brought up, there was no remedy; so having smoothed my hair as well as I could, and repeatedly twitched my obdurate collar, I proceeded to clomp down the two flights of stairs, philosophizing as I went; and with some difficulty found my way into the room where Mrs Bloomfield awaited me.

She led me into the dining-room, where the family luncheon had been laid out. Some beefsteaks and half-cold potatoes were set before me; and while I dined upon these, she sat opposite, watching me (as I thought) and endeavouring to sustain something like a conversation — consisting chiefly of a succession of commonplace remarks, expressed with frigid formality: but this might be more my fault than hers, for I really *could* not converse. In fact, my attention was almost wholly absorbed in my dinner: not from ravenous appetite, but from distress at the toughness of the beefsteaks, and the numbness of my hands, almost palsied by their five hours' exposure to the bitter wind. I would gladly have eaten the potatoes and let the meat alone, but having got a large piece of the latter on to my plate, I could not be so impolite as to leave it; so, after many awkward and unsuccessful attempts to cut it with the knife, or tear it with the fork, or pull it asunder between them, sensible that the awful lady was a spectator to the whole transaction, I at last desperately grasped the knife and fork in my fists, like a child of two years old, and fell to work with all the little strength I possessed. But this needed some apology — with a feeble attempt at a laugh, I said, "My hands are so benumbed with the cold that I can scarcely handle my knife and fork."

"I dare say you would find it cold," replied she with a cool, immutable gravity that did not serve to reassure me.'
Chapter 2

A famous episode in the novel is that of the fledglings. Tom, the wayward, spoiled son of the family, is of a particularly unpleasant disposition, and has already made his intentions clear in an earlier encounter:
'Sometimes I give them (fledglings) to the cat; sometimes I cut them in pieces with my penknife; but the next I mean to roast alive.'
Chapter 2

In this longer passage Anne Brontë's description is unsentimental:

'. . . Tom, who had been with his uncle into the neighbouring plantation, came running in high glee into the garden, with a brood of little callow nestlings in his hands. Mary Ann and Fanny, whom I was just bringing out, ran to admire his spoils, and to beg each a bird for themselves. "No, not one!" cried Tom. "They're all mine: uncle Robson gave them to me — one, two, three, four, five — you shan't touch one of them! no, not one, for your lives!" continued he, exultingly; laying the nest on the ground, and standing over it with his legs wide apart, his hands thrust into his breeches-pockets, his body bent forward, and his face twisted into all manner of contortions in the ecstasy of his delight.

"But you shall see me fettle 'em off. My word, but I *will* wallop 'em!

See if I don't now. By gum! but there's rare sport for me in that nest."

"But, Tom," said I, "I shall not allow you to torture those birds. They must either be killed at once or carried back to the place you took them from, that the old birds may continue to feed them."

"But you don't know where that is, madam: it's only me and uncle Robson that knows that."

"But if you don't tell me, I shall kill them myself – much as I hate it."

"You daren't. You daren't touch them for your life! because you know papa and mamma, and uncle Robson, would be angry. Ha, ha! I've caught you there, Miss!"

"I shall do what I think right in a case of this sort without consulting any one. If your papa and mamma don't happen to approve of it, I shall be sorry to offend them; but your uncle Robson's opinions, of course, are nothing to me."

So saying – urged by a sense of duty – at the risk of both making myself sick and incurring the wrath of my employers – I got a large flat stone, that had been reared up for a mouse-trap by the gardener, then, having once more vainly endeavoured to persuade the little tyrant to let the birds be carried back, I asked what he intended to do with them. With fiendish glee he commenced a list of torments; and while he was busied in the relation, I dropped the stone upon his intended victims and crushed them flat beneath it. Loud were the outcries, terrible the execrations, consequent upon this daring outrage; uncle Robson had been coming up the walk with his gun, and was just then pausing to kick his dog. Tom flew towards him, vowing he would make him kick me instead of Juno. Mr Robson leant upon his gun, and laughed excessively at the violence of his nephew's passion, and the bitter maledictions and

A Home for Aged Governesses set up in 1849 to provide for those 'whose high sense of private duty deprived them of a self-provided home'. This action was borne out of recognition that governesses in general had no means of saving their meagre earnings to support themselves in old age.

THE ASYLUM FOR AGED GOVERNESSES
WILL BE OPENED BY H.R.H. THE DUKE OF CAMBRIDGE IN PERSON,
ON THE 12TH JUNE, 1849;
And on that and the following day the FANCY SALE commenced at Chelsea, will be continued under the same Royal patronage.

opprobrious epithets he heaped upon me. "Well, you *are* a good 'un!" exclaimed he, at length, taking up his weapon and proceeding towards the house. "Damme, but the lad has some spunk in him, too. Curse me, if ever I saw a nobler little scoundrel than that. He's beyond petticoat government already: by God! he defies mother, granny, governess, and all! Ha, ha, ha! Never mind, Tom, I'll get you another brood tomorrow."

"If you do, Mr Robson, I shall kill them too," said I.'
Chapter 5

Agnes Grey leaves her first post and takes up the second at Horton Lodge, clearly based upon Thorp Green. The description of the journey, again in the cold, is finer than any comparable passage in either of her sisters' works:

'. . . it was dark some hours before I reached my journey's end, and that a most bewildering storm came on at last, which made the few miles space between O—— and Horton Lodge a long and formidable passage. I sat resigned, with the cold, sharp snow drifting through my veil and filling my lap, seeing nothing, and wondering how the unfortunate horse and driver could make their way even as well as they did: and indeed it was but a toilsome, creeping style of progression to say the best of it. At length we paused; and, at the call of the driver, some one unlatched and rolled back upon their creaking hinges what appeared to be the park gates. Then we proceeded along a smoother road, whence, occasionally, I perceived some huge hoary mass gleaming through the darkness, which I took to be a portion of a snow-clad tree. After a considerable time we paused again, before the stately portico of a large house with long windows descending to the ground.

Cottage interior painted by William Mulready (1786–1863), who was a highly successful Victorian genre painter.

I rose with some difficulty from under the super-incumbent snow-drift, and alighted from the carriage. . . .'
Chapter 7

Arriving *under* a snowdrift must often have been the lot of winter travellers.

The two young ladies that the governess was to teach were little better than those left at the Bloomfields:

'Miss Murray, otherwise Rosalie . . . had never been perfectly taught the distinction between right and wrong; she had, like her brothers and sisters, been suffered, from infancy to tyrannize over nurses, governesses, and servants; she had not been taught to moderate her desires, to control her temper or bridle her will. . . .

Miss Matilda Murray was a veritable hoyden . . . As an animal Matilda was all right, full of life, vigour and activity; as an intelligent being, she was barbarously ignorant, indocile, careless and irrational. . . .'
Chapter 7

Agnes's charges, as they grew up, found delight in asserting their superiority over the poor of the parish and of anyone, curates and clergymen included, whom they considered to be beneath their station in life. The description of the Misses Murray visiting the poor is explicit:

'They would watch the poor creatures at their meals, making uncivil remarks about their food, and their manner of eating; they would laugh at their simple notions and provincial expressions, till some of them scarcely durst venture to speak; they would call the grave elderly men and women old fools and silly old blockheads to their faces; and all this without meaning to offend. I could see that the people were often hurt and annoyed by such conduct, though their fear of the "grand ladies" prevented them from testifying any resentment; but *they* never perceived it. They thought that, as these cottagers were poor and untaught, they must be stupid and brutish; and as long as they, their superiors, condescended to talk to them, and to give them shillings and half-crowns, or articles of clothing, they had a right to amuse themselves, even at their expense; and the people must adore them as angels of light, condescending to minister to their necessities, and enlighten their humble dwellings.'
Chapter 11

The hurtful treatment of the cottagers is condemned by Anne Brontë as much as the tormenting of nestlings; yet the clear social comment is neither shrill nor harsh. Kicking cats, setting hounds on them, giving pet dogs to ratcatchers notorious for treating them cruelly — all find censure. A vicar who calls an old parishioner a 'canting old fool' in her hearing is contrasted with a curate — the young man that Agnes is eventually to marry — who is never too busy to sit by the fireside of the cottager or forget Agnes's delight in bluebells. The tirade of the old

Agnes Grey

cottager, Nancy Brown, against the unfeeling parson is delivered as a well-sustained piece of gossipy talk:

"'Well, my rheumatiz got better – I know not whether wi' going to church or not, but one frosty Sunday I got this cold i' my eyes. Th' inflammation didn't come on all at once like, but bit by bit – but I wasn't going to tell you about my eyes, I was talking about my trouble o' mind; – and to tell the truth, Miss Grey, I don't think it was anyways eased by coming to church – nought to speak on, at least: I like got my health better; but that didn't mend my soul. I hearkened and hearkened the ministers, and read an' read at my prayer-book; but it was all like sounding brass, and a tinkling cymbal: the sermons I couldn't understand, an' the' prayer-book only served to show me how wicked I was, that I could read such good words an' never be no better for it, and oftens feel it a sore labour an' a heavy task beside, instead of a blessing and a privilege as·all good Christians does. It seemed like as all were barren an' dark to me. And then, them dreadful words, 'Many shall seek to enter in, and shall not be able.' They like as they fair dried up my sperrit.

"But one Sunday, when Maister Hatfield gave out about the sacrament, I noticed where he said, 'If there be any of you that cannot quiet his own conscience, but requireth further comfort or counsel, let him come to me, or some other discreet and learned minister of God's word, and open his grief!' So, next Sunday morning, afore service, I just looked into the vestry, an' began a talking to th' Rector again. I hardly could fashion to take such a liberty, but I thought when my soul was at stake I shouldn't stick at a trifle. But he said he hadn't time to attend to me then.

"'And, indeed,' says he, 'I've nothing to say to you but what I've said before. Take the sacrament, of course, and go on doing your duty; and if that won't serve you, nothing will. So don't bother me any more.'

"So then, I went away. But I heard Maister Weston – Maister Weston was there, Miss – this was his first Sunday at Horton, you know, an' he was i' th' vestry in his surplice, helping th' Rector on with his gown – "

"Yes, Nancy."

"And I heard him ask Maister Hatfield who I was; an' he says, 'Oh, she's a canting old fool.'

"And I was very ill grieved, Miss Grey; but I went to my seat, and I tried to do my duty as aforetime: but I like got no peace. An' I even took the sacrament; but I felt as though I were eating and drinking to my own damnation all th' time. So I went home, sorely troubled.'

Chapter 11

Anne's robust Christianity, derived from her father, is warmly human and rare in writing of her time. Her theme is compassion and the need for people to care for one another. Agnes visits the 'canting old fool' ignored by the vicar, and even helps the rheumatic old soul with her sewing. Her compassion leads to a meeting with Mr Weston, the curate she will later marry:

'Nancy's eyes were better, but still far from well: she had been trying to make a Sunday shirt for her son, but told me she could only bear to do a little bit at it now and then, so that it progressed but slowly, though the poor lad wanted it sadly. So I proposed to help her a little, after I had read to her, for I had plenty of time that evening, and need not return till dusk. She thankfully accepted the offer. "An' you'll be a bit o' company for me too, miss," said she; "I like as I feel lonesome without my cat." But when I had finished reading, and done the half of a seam, with Nancy's capacious brass thimble fitted on to my finger by means of a roll of paper, I was disturbed by the entrance of Mr Weston, with the identical cat in his arms. I now saw that he could smile, and very pleasantly too.

"I've done you a piece of good service, Nancy," he began: then seeing me, he acknowledged my presence by a slight bow. I should have been invisible to Hatfield, or any other gentleman of those parts. "I've delivered your cat," he continued, "from the hands, or rather the gun, of Mr Murray's gamekeeper."

"God bless you, sir!" cried the grateful old woman, ready to weep for joy as she received her favourite from his arms.

This picture of young ladies engaged in charitable visiting well illustrates that activity in *Agnes Grey*, Chapter 11, The Cottagers.

Agnes Grey

"Take care of it," said he, "and don't let it go near the rabbit warren, for the gamekeeper swears he'll shoot it if he sees it there again: he would have done so to-day, if I had not been in time to stop him. I believe it is raining, Miss Grey," added he, more quietly, observing that I had put aside my work, and was preparing to depart. "Don't let me disturb you – I shan't stay two minutes."

"You'll *both* stay while this shower gets owered," said Nancy, as she stirred the fire, and placed another chair beside it; "what! there's room for all."'
Chapter 12

The *invisibility* of governesses is Anne's theme and the novel describes the tormenting of Agnes by the flighty girls she is hired to teach. Their flirting, even to the lengths of pretending that they fancy Mr Weston, and deliberately keeping their governess away from him, leaves Agnes dejected and forced to hide her true feelings. The heroine, like her creator, takes refuge in literature, on this occasion poetry, and Anne Brontë is eloquent about the use to which this can be put:

'When we are harassed by sorrows or anxieties, or long oppressed by any powerful feelings which we must keep to ourselves, for which we can obtain and seek no sympathy from any living creature, and which yet we cannot, or will not wholly crush, we often naturally seek relief in poetry

The Clergyman's Visit by Frederick Daniel Hardy (1826–1911).

– and often find it, too – whether in the effusions of others, which seem to harmonize with out existing case, or in our own attempts to give utterance to those thoughts and feelings in strains less musical, perchance, but more appropriate, and therefore more penetrating and sympathetic, and, for the time, more soothing, or more powerful to rouse and to unburden the oppressed and swollen heart. Before this time, at Wellwood House and here, when suffering from home-sick melancholy, I had sought relief twice or thrice at this secret source of consolation; and now I flew to it again, with greater avidity than ever, because I seemed to need it more. I still preserve those relics of past sufferings and experience, like pillars of witness set up in travelling through the vale of life, to mark particular occurrences. The footsteps are obliterated now; the face of the country may be changed; but the pillar is still there, to remind me how all things were when it was reared. Lest the reader should be curious to see any of these effusions, I will favour him with one short specimen: cold and languid as the lines may seem, it was almost a passion of grief to which they owed their being.

> O, they have robbed me of the hope
>   My spirit held so dear,
> They will not let me hear that voice
>   My soul delights to hear.
>
> They will not let me see that face
>   I so delight to see;
> And they have taken all thy smiles,
>   And all thy love from me.
>
> Well, let them seize on all they can; –
>   One treasure still is mine, –
> A heart that loves to think on thee,
>   And feels the worth of thine.

Yes, at least, they could not deprive me of that: I could think of him day and night; and I could feel that he was worthy to be thought of. Nobody knew him as I did; nobody could appreciate him as I did; nobody could love him as I – could. . . .'
Chapter 17

Later, when Weston has left for a parish of his own, and one of her charges, now married to a lord, is Lady Ashby, Agnes's life has become Grey indeed. Visiting her former pupil, who is by no means happy, Miss Grey sits before a window of the great house:

'As I was not rich enough to possess a watch, I could not tell how time was passing, except by observing the slowly lengthening shadows from the window; which presented a side view, including a corner of the park, a clump of trees, whose topmost branches had been colonized by

an innumerable company of noisy rooks, and a high wall with a massive wooden gate: no doubt communicating with the stable-yard, as a broad carriage-road swept up to it from the park. The shadow of this wall soon took possession of the whole of the ground as far as I could see, forcing the golden sunlight to retreat inch by inch, and at last take refuge in the very tops of the trees. Ere long, even they were left in shadow – the shadow of the distant hills, or of the earth itself; and, in sympathy for the busy citizens of the rookery, I regretted to see their habitation, so lately bathed in glorious light, reduced to the sombre, work-a-day hue of the lower world, or of my own world within. For a moment, such birds as soared above the rest might still receive the lustre on their wings, which imparted to their sable plumage the hue and brilliance of deep red gold; at last, that too departed. Twilight came stealing on; the rooks became more quiet; I became more weary, and wished I were going home to-morrow.'
Chapter 22

The most bitter scene in the novel comes when Agnes Grey hears from home that her father is dangerously ill:

'But our wishes are like tinder: the flint and steel of circumstances are continually striking out sparks, which vanish immediately, unless they chance to fall upon the tinder of our wishes; then, they instantly ignite, and the flame of hope is kindled in a moment.

But alas! that very morning, my flickering flame of hope was dismally quenched by a letter from my mother, which spoke so seriously of my father's increasing illness, that I feared there was little or no chance of his recovery; and, close at hand as the holidays were, I almost trembled lest they should come too late for me to meet him in this world. Two days after, a letter from Mary told me his life was despaired of, and his end seemed fast approaching. Then, immediately, I sought permission to anticipate the vacation, and go without delay. Mrs Murray stared, and wondered at the unwonted energy and boldness with which I urged the request, and thought there was no occasion to hurry; but finally gave me leave: stating, however, that there was "no need to be in such agitation about the matter – it might prove a false alarm after all; and if not – why, it was only in the common course of nature: we must all die some time; and I was not to suppose myself the only afflicted person in the world"; and concluding with saying I might have the phaeton to take me to O——. "And instead of *repining*, Miss Grey, be thankful for the *privileges* you enjoy. There's many a poor clergyman whose family would be plunged into ruin by the event of his death; but *you*, you see, have influential friends ready to continue their patronage, and to show you every consideration."

I thanked her for her "consideration," and flew to my room to make some hurried preparations for my departure. My bonnet and shawl being on, and a few things hastily crammed into my largest trunk, I descended. But I might have done the work more leisurely, for no one else was in a hurry; and I had still a considerable time to wait for the phaeton. At length it came to the door, and I was off: but, oh, what a dreary journey was that! how utterly different from my former passages homewards! Being too late for the last coach to ———, I had to hire a cab for ten miles, and then a car to take me over the rugged hills. It was half-past ten before I reached home. They were not in bed.

My mother and sister both met me in the passage – sad – silent – pale! I was so much shocked and terror-stricken that I could not speak, to ask the information I so much longed yet dreaded to obtain.

"Agnes!" said my mother, struggling to repress some strong emotion.

"Oh, Agnes!" cried Mary, and burst into tears.

"How is he?" I asked, gasping for the answer.

"Dead!"

It was the reply I had anticipated: but the shock seemed none the less tremendous.'

Chapter 18

Anne Brontë uses none of the coincidental tricks or supernatural events of her sisters' novels. In her work people, in the manner of Shakespeare's characters, earn their fate. Nowhere is this more plain than in the closing chapters of *Agnes Grey*. At her father's death, Agnes gives up her work to set up a school with her mother – the school is in a town that is clearly, without any attempt at disguise, Scarborough, Anne's favourite place.

Agnes takes an early walk, by a route so carefully detailed that it can be followed today:

'I awoke early on the third morning after my return from Ashby Park – the sun was shining through the blind, and I thought how pleasant it would be to pass through the quiet town and take a solitary ramble on the sands while half the world was in bed. I was not long in forming the resolution, nor slow to act upon it. Of course I would not disturb my mother, so I stole noiselessly downstairs, and quietly unfastened the door. I was dressed and out, when the church clock struck a quarter to six. There was a feeling of freshness and vigour in the very streets; and when I got free of the town, when my foot was on the sands and my face towards the broad, bright bay, no language can describe the effect of the deep, clear azure of the sky and ocean, the bright morning sunshine on the semicircular barrier of craggy cliffs surmounted by green swelling hills, and on the smooth, wide sands, and the low rocks out at sea – looking, with their clothing of weeds and moss, like little grass-grown islands – and above all, on the brilliant, sparkling waves. And then, the unspeakable purity and freshness of the air! there was just enough heat to enhance the value of the breeze, and just enough wind to keep the whole sea in motion, to make the waves come bounding to the shore, foaming and sparkling, as if wild with glee. Nothing else was stirring – no living creature was visible besides myself. My footsteps were the first to press the firm, unbroken sands; – nothing before had trampled them since last night's flowing tide had obliterated the deepest marks of yesterday, and left it fair and even, except where the subsiding water had left behind it

Agnes Grey

the traces of dimpled pools and little running streams.

Refreshed, delighted, invigorated, I walked along, forgetting all my cares, feeling as if I had wings to my feet, and could go at least forty miles without fatigue, and experiencing a sense of exhilaration to which I had been an entire stranger since the days of early youth. About half-past six, however, the grooms began to come down to air their master's horses – first one, and then another, till there were some dozen horses and five or six riders: but that need not trouble me, for they would not come as far as the low rocks which I was now approaching. When I had reached these, and walked over the moist, slippery seaweed (at the risk of floundering into one of the numerous pools of clear, salt water that lay between them), to a little mossy promontory with the sea splashing round it, I looked back again to see who next was stirring. Still, there were only the early grooms with their horses, and one gentleman with a little dark speck of a dog running before him, and one water-cart coming out of the town to get water for the baths. In another minute or two, the distant bathing machines would begin to move, and then the elderly gentlemen of regular habits, and sober quaker ladies would be coming to take their salutary morning walks. But however interesting such a scene might be, I could not wait to witness it, for the sun and the sea so dazzled my eyes in that direction, that I could but afford one glance; and then I turned again to delight myself with the sight and the sound of the sea dashing against my promontory – with no prodigious

Opposite Charlotte Brontë's watercolour miniature portrait of her sister Anne Brontë.

Below Scarborough by J.M.W. Turner (1775–1851), which was the setting for the last chapters of *Agnes Grey*.

force, for the swell was broken by the tangled seaweed and the unseen rocks beneath; otherwise I should soon have been deluged with spray. But the tide was coming in; the water was rising; the gulfs and lakes were filling; the straits were widening, it was time to seek some safer footing; so I walked, skipped, and stumbled back to the smooth, wide sands, and resolved to proceed to a certain bold projection in the cliffs, and then return.

Presently, I heard a snuffling sound behind me, and then a dog came frisking and wriggling to my feet. It was my own Snap – the little, dark, wire-haired terrier! When I spoke his name, he leapt up in my face and yelled for joy. Almost as much delighted as himself, I caught the little creature in my arms, and kissed him repeatedly. But how came he to be there? He could not have dropped from the sky, or come all that way alone: it must be either his master, the rat-catcher, or somebody else that had brought him; so, repressing my extravagant caresses, and endeavouring to repress his likewise, I looked round, and beheld – Mr Weston!'
Chapter 24

One further walk completes the tale:

'Mr Weston would have me to take his arm: he said little during our passage through the crowded streets, but walked very fast, and appeared grave and abstracted. I wondered what was the matter, and felt an indefinite dread that something unpleasant was on his mind; and vague surmises, concerning what it might be, troubled me not a little, and made me grave and silent enough. But these fantasies vanished upon reaching the quiet outskirts of the town; for as soon as we came within sight of the venerable old church, and the —— hill, with the deep blue sea beyond it, I found my companion was cheerful enough.

"I'm afraid I've been walking too fast for you, Agnes," said he: "in my impatience to be rid of the town, I forgot to consult your convenience; but now, we'll walk as slowly as you please. I see, by those light clouds in the west, there will be a brilliant sunset, and we shall be in time to witness its effect upon the sea, at the most moderate rate of progression."

When we had got about half-way up the hill, we fell into silence again; which, as usual, he was the first to break.

"My house is desolate yet, Miss Grey," he smilingly observed, "and I am acquainted now with all the ladies in my parish, and several in this town too; and many others I know by sight and by report; but not one of them will suit me for a companion: in fact, there is only one person in the world that will; and that is yourself; and I want to know your decision?"

"Are you in earnest, Mr Weston?"

"In earnest! How could you think I should jest on such a subject?"

He laid his hand on mine that rested on his arm: he must have felt it tremble – but it was no great matter now.

"I hope I have not been too precipitate," he said, in a serious tone.

"You must have known it was not my way to flatter and talk soft nonsense, or even to speak the admiration that I felt; and that a single word or glance of mine meant more than the honeyed phrases and fervent protestations of most other men."

I said something about not liking to leave my mother, and doing nothing without her consent.

"I settled everything with Mrs Grey, while you were putting on your bonnet," replied he. "She said I might have her consent, if I could obtain yours; and I asked her, in case I should be so happy, to come and live with us – for I was sure you would like it better. But she refused, saying she could now afford to employ an assistant, and would continue the school till she could purchase an annuity sufficient to maintain her in comfortable lodgings; and, meantime, she would spend her vacations alternately with us and your sister, and should be quite contented if you were happy. And so now I have overruled your objections on her account. Have you any other?"

"No – none."

"You love me then?" said he, fervently pressing my hand.

"Yes."

Here I pause. My Diary, from which I have compiled these pages, goes but little further. I could go on for years; but I will content myself with adding, that I shall never forget that glorious summer evening, and always remember with delight that steep hill, and the edge of the precipice where we stood together, watching the splendid sunset mirrored in the restless world of waters at our feet – with hearts filled with gratitude to heaven, and happiness, and love – almost too full for speech.

A few weeks after that, when my mother had supplied herself with an assistant, I became the wife of Edward Weston; and never have found cause to repent it, and am certain that I never shall. We have had trials, and we know that we must have them again; but we bear them well together, and endeavour to fortify ourselves and each other against the final separation – that greatest of all afflictions to the survivor. . . .'
Chapter 25

Ann Brontë's drawing of a sunset, probably a copy.

VII
THE TENANT OF WILDFELL HALL

'My object in writing the following pages was not simply to amuse the Reader, neither was it to gratify my own taste . . . I wished to tell the truth, for truth always contains its own moral to those who are able to receive it.' Anne Brontë. Preface to the second edition of *The Tenant of Wildfell Hall*.

The publication of Anne's book, less than a year after the appearance of *Agnes Grey*, must have caused a stir in the parsonage at Haworth. For here was the youngest member of the family with two novels in print. Acton had overtaken not only Ellis, but also Currer who had so patronizingly included her *simple* poems in the poetry anthology. The point would be forced home with the need for a second edition of *The Tenant of Wildfell Hall* in the year of its publication. The younger sister in *Agnes Grey*, whom we can surely assume to be Anne Brontë, has clearly done more than play with the cat or do her piano practice.

Anne, more than her sisters, draws on her own experiences, and her artistic gaze is steady and unsentimental. *Agnes Grey*, her tale of a governess, is sober and realistic, avoiding extremes of passion, as in Emily's work, or reliance on remarkable events, as in Charlotte's. Perhaps this is what she had in mind when she claimed that in her writing she sought 'to tell the truth'. The truth in *The Tenant of Wildfell Hall* is a harsh one, for it is the story of the disintegration of a man through drunkenness and the consequent destruction of a marriage. Anne had much experience of the former in her dealings with her brother Branwell; and her womanly instincts enabled her to predict the latter and envisage a possible story. Only Anne, of the three sisters, could have taken her theme from so close to home and yet create an artistic whole. The book is not a disguised biography of her brother, nor is it a temperance tract, though both lend something to its subject.

Charlotte, in the Preface to the 1850 edition of *Wuthering Heights* and *Agnes Grey*, wrote of Anne's second novel: 'The choice of subject was an entire mistake.' Her censure of the book may be the natural reaction of a sister whose brother was a drunkard; but she may also have been somewhat puzzled that the young Anne could be so successful.

Opposite Drawing by Anne Brontë, possibly a copy.

The Tenant of Wildfell Hall

It is part of the Brontë legend that Emily took particular care of Branwell during his drinking bouts; that she would leave the door unlocked at night and a lamp in a window to guide him home from the ale-house. True or not, there can be no doubt that it was Anne who saw her brother at close quarters in public and private during the period of his greatest single disgrace. She alone of the family lived with him at Thorp Green from where, for whatever reason, he was sacked in the most unpleasant circumstances. A sacking, moreover, that caused Anne to lose a position that she had come to value and to enjoy. Anne's tale of Branwell could be bitter indeed, for he not only destroyed himself by his behaviour but also brought to an end her successful career away from Haworth. It is remarkable how well Anne bore her own disappointment and how well she managed to transform her experience into balanced and compassionate writing.

Charlotte's feeling that her sister had a morbid religious turn of mind should not be taken at face value.

It was in 1840 that Anne took up her post as governess with the Robinson family at Thorp Green near York, and not until she had been there two years that Branwell joined her as tutor to Edmund, the only boy in the family. Anne was governess to three girls. Up to this point Branwell's adult life had been a series of disasters, and it appears that it was Anne's standing with her employer, the Rev. Edmund Robinson, that secured him this latest position. Everyone at Haworth was optimistic when Branwell arrived at Thorp Green Hall in 1843. By 23 January 1844 Charlotte was able to write to her school friend Ellen Nussey: 'Anne and Branwell have just left us to return to York. They are both wonderously valued in their situations.'

Nothing indicated the storm that was to follow and would lead to his dismissal in July 1845. Interestingly, a month afterwards Anne had already resigned her post. There is an irony in Branwell continuing in a post his sister had found for him after she herself had been brought to resign her own.

Although Charlotte at this point could write to Ellen:

'My hopes ebb low indeed about Branwell. I sometimes fear he will never be fit for much. His bad habits seem more deeply rooted than I ever thought. The late blow to his prospects and feelings has quite made him reckless. . . .'

it is Anne who had suffered at first hand the effects of Branwell's behaviour and who had to bear the burden of his disgrace.

Anne's introduction of Branwell into her world of work was a disastrous, if understandable error of judgment. Perhaps having been away from Haworth for two years, with only brief holidays at home, she did not fully understand the nature of her elder brother's wilful self-neglect. Equally, how would a younger sister control a brother two and a half years her senior? Society would expect the man to dominate the woman; a tutor had more standing than a governess. Perhaps without realizing it, Anne would be cancelling out her independence and much

Morbid pen and ink sketch in a letter by Branwell Brontë. In 1838, he set himself up as a portrait painter in Bradford, where the Talbot Inn, featured here, became a favourite haunt.

that she had achieved in her emancipation from being the baby of the family. In the event this is precisely what happened, though the exact reasons for it are vague. Branwell behaved very badly towards the end of his time at Thorp Green, and was instantly dismissed in 1845, but not before, as we have seen, he drove his young sister from a post where she had made a success of her career and found affection and respect.

Life at Thorp Green had given Anne an insight into both the life of a comfortable hunting, ball-going county family and the effects of indulgent behaviour in a young man. She was to make good use of both in her writing.

Anne perceived the wider implications of her brother's behaviour and made good use of what she saw.

It was during the time of Branwell's disgrace (1845–7) that the Brontë sisters laid the foundations of their mature writing for publication. The misery of affairs at home where Branwell drank himself into debt and physical decline seems to have driven the girls to reach out of their present wretchedness into other possible worlds.

In three years, from 1845 and Charlotte's discovery of Emily's poems to 1848 and Branwell's sudden death, the girls had progressed from hope and endeavour against the odds to the publication of four novels. They had moved from private isolation and anonymity to fame that bordered on notoriety.

Anne Brontë's second novel shares common features with Emily's writing. The device of double narrator is similar to *Wuthering Heights*, while the theme of a 'tenant' in a northern hall is also common to both

Unfinished drawing of girl and dog, possibly a self-portrait. The dog resembles Anne's King Charles spaniel, Flossie, and the house could be Thorp Green Hall.

The Tenant of Wildfell Hall

novels. The heroine, however, with her painting and independence, must remind us of Jane in *Jane Eyre*. Little wonder that the reading public believed that there was only one Bell who wrote all the novels of the 'so-called' trio. Similarities, however, are only superficial: Anne has her own voice, her own themes and ways of dealing with them, ways that were not available to her sisters.

Neither Charlotte nor Emily treated scenes of family life as accurately as this:

'"Now take your tea," said she; "and I'll tell you what *I've* been doing. I've been to call on the Wilsons; and it's a *thousand* pities you didn't go with me, Gilbert, for Eliza Millward was there!"

"Well! what of her?"

"Oh nothing! – I'm not going to tell you about her; – only that she's a nice, amusing little thing, when she is in a merry humour, and I shouldn't mind calling her – "

"Hush, hush, my dear! your brother has no such idea!" whispered my mother, earnestly, holding up her finger.

"Well," resumed Rose; "I was going to tell you an important piece of news I heard there – I've been bursting with it ever since. You know it was reported a month ago, that somebody was going to take Wildfell Hall – and – what do you think? It has actually been inhabited above a week! – and we never knew!"

"Impossible!" cried my mother.

Beningborough Hall, a fine house in the neighbourhood of Thorp Green. The Robinson family, for whom Anne worked as a governess, were hunting folk and must have had contact with this great house. Set in the Vale of York, Beningborough and Thorp Green provide a striking contrast to Anne's home in Haworth.

Patrick Branwell Brontë's drawing of a goshawk, probably a copy from Thomas Bewick.

"Preposterous!!!" shrieked Fergus.

"It has indeed! – and by a single lady!"

"Good gracious, my dear! The place is in ruins!"

"She has had two or three rooms made habitable; and there she lives, all alone – except an old woman for a servant!"

"Oh dear! that spoils it – I'd hoped she was a witch," observed Fergus, while carving his inch-thick slice of bread and butter.

"Nonsense, Fergus! But isn't it strange, mamma?"

"Strange! I can hardly believe it."

"But you may believe it; for Jane Wilson has seen her. She went with her mother, who, of course, when she heard of a stranger being in the neighbourhood, would be on pins and needles till she had seen her and got all she could out of her. She is called Mrs Graham, and she is in mourning – not widow's weeds, but slightish mourning – and she is quite young, they say, – not above five or six and twenty, – but so reserved! They tried all they could to find out who she was, and where she came from, and all about her, but neither Mrs Wilson, with her pertinacious and impertinent home thrusts, nor Miss Wilson, with her skilful manoeuvering, could manage to elicit a single satisfactory answer, or even a casual remark, or chance expression calculated to allay their curiosity, or throw the faintest ray of light upon her history, circumstances, or connexions. Moreover, she was barely civil to them, and evidently better pleased to say "goodbye," than "how do you do." But Eliza Millward says her father intends to call upon her soon, to offer some pastoral advice, which he fears she needs, as though she is known to have entered the neighbourhood early last week, she did not make her appearance at church on Sunday; and she – Eliza, that is – will beg to accompany him, and is sure *she* can succeed in wheedling something out of her – you know, Gilbert, *she* can do anything. And we should call sometime, mamma; it's only proper, you know."

"Of course, my dear. Poor thing! how lonely she must feel!"

"And pray be quick about it; and mind you bring me word how much sugar she puts in her tea, and what sort of caps and aprons she wears, and all about it; for I don't know how I can live till I know," said Fergus, very gravely.

But if he intended the speech to be hailed as a master-stroke of wit, he signally failed, for nobody laughed. However, he was not much disconcerted at that; for when he had taken a mouthful of bread and butter, and was about to swallow a gulp of tea, the humour of the thing burst upon him with such irresistible force, that he was obliged to jump up from the table, and rush snorting and choking from the room; and a minute after, was heard screaming in fearful agony in the garden.'

Chapter 1

In skilfully describing the fate of the woman who became a family drudge, Anne is writing of a problem close to the Brontë sisters' hearts. In Chapter 10 of *Shirley* Charlotte writes of a similar lady:

'"Miss Ainley is not selfish, Fanny: she is always doing good. How devotedly kind she was to her stepmother, as long as the old lady lived;

The Tenant of Wildfell Hall

and now when she is quite alone in the world, without brother or sister, or any one to care for her, how charitable she is to the poor, as far as her means permit! Still nobody thinks much of her, or has pleasure in going to see her: and how gentlemen always sneer at her!"

"They shouldn't, miss; I believe she is a good woman: but gentlemen think only of ladies' looks."

"I'll go and see her," exclaimed Caroline, starting up: "and if she asks me to stay to tea, I'll stay. How wrong it is to neglect people because they are not pretty, and young , and merry!"'

There was always the question at Haworth Parsonage of who should stay at home and look after their ageing father. Implied in both extracts is the fear that whoever devoted herself to the task — it being unthinkable that the son of the family would make such a sacrifice — would end up unloved, alone and of no consequence at the end of the day. The problem became acute when Aunt Branwell, who had lived as housekeeper with her widower brother-in-law, died in 1842. The question was suddenly 'Who shall live at home?' On that occasion Emily agreed to stay. Anne, in her description of Mary, and Charlotte in her creation of Miss Ainley, explored a possibility in their own lives. We should not forget that Charlotte made it a condition of her marriage that she and her husband would live with her father and remain in Haworth. For time had seen to it that Charlotte was to play Mary and Miss Ainley's part in real life; her marriage was an escape from a role that both sisters understood.

The Rev. Patrick Brontë in old age.

Gilbert Markham, the narrator of *The Tenant of Wildfell Hall*, relates how he first visited the new tenant of the ramshackle and long neglected Hall at the edge of his land. Here a mysterious woman, seemingly a widow by her dress and manner, lives with her young son. The landscape is unmistakably that of Haworth, of the isolated halls far from other habitation.

'I think the day I last mentioned was a certain Sunday, the latest in the October of 1827. On the following Tuesday I was out with my dog and gun, in pursuit of such game as I could find within the territory of Linden-Car; but finding none at all, I turned my arms against the hawks and carrion crows, whose depredations, as I suspected, had deprived me of better prey. To this end, I left the more frequented regions, the wooded valleys, the cornfields, and the meadow lands, and proceeded to mount the steep acclivity of Wildfell, the wildest and the loftiest eminence in our neighbourhood, where, as you ascend, the hedges, as well as the trees, become scanty and stunted, the former, at length, giving place to rough stone fences, partly greened over with ivy and moss, the latter to larches and Scotch fir-trees, or isolated blackthorns. The fields, being rough and stony and wholly unfit for the plough, were mostly devoted to the pasturing of sheep and cattle; the soil was thin and poor: bits of grey rock here and there peeped out from the grassy hillocks; bilberry plants and heather — relics of more savage wildness — grew under the walls; and in many of the enclosures, ragweeds and rushes usurped supremacy over the scanty herbage; — but these were not *my* property.

Near the top of this hill, about two miles from Linden-Car, stood Wildfell Hall, a superannuated mansion of the Elizabethan era, built of dark grey stone, – venerable and picturesque to look at, but, doubtless, cold and gloomy enough to inhabit, with its thick stone mullions and little latticed panes, its time-eaten air-holes, and its too lonely, too unsheltered situation, – only shielded from the war of wind and weather by a group of Scotch firs, themselves half blighted with storms, and looking as stern and gloomy as the hall itself. Behind it lay a few desolate fields, and then, the brown, heath-clad summit of the hill; before it (enclosed by stone walls, and entered by an iron gate with large balls of grey granite – similar to those which decorated the roof and gables – surmounting the gate-posts), was a garden, – once, stocked with such hardy plants and flowers as could best brook the soil and climate, and such trees and shrubs as could best endure the gardener's torturing shears, and most readily assume the shapes he chose to give them, – now, having been left so many years, untilled and untrimmed, abandoned to the weeds and the grass, to the frost and the wind, the rain and the drought, it presented a very singular appearance indeed. The close green walls of privet, that had bordered the principal walk, were two thirds withered away, and the rest grown beyond all reasonable bounds; the old boxwood swan, that sat beside the scraper, had lost its neck and half its body; the castellated towers of laurel in the middle of the garden, the gigantic warrior that stood on one side of the gateway, and the lion that guarded the other, were sprouted into such fantastic shapes as resembled nothing either in heaven or earth, or in the waters under the earth; but, to my young imagination, they presented all of them a goblinish appearance, that harmonized well with the ghostly legends and dark traditions our old nurse had told us respecting the haunted hall and its departed occupants.'
Chapter 2

Here we have all the Brontë novel's ingredients: the celebration of the natural landscape in its peculiar and unmistakable barren reality. Wildfell is in every respect the moor beyond Anne's home; she is at one with it, as was her sister Emily. The hall from which the novel takes its title is a typical house of the moors, exposed, old, mullioned, and set in a derelict garden, with its topiary fallen into neglect in such a way that wilderness merges with order to create 'goblinish appearance' and suggest the 'ghostly legends and dark traditions' linked with the hall. Here in abundance is the atmospheric writing that each of the Brontë sisters could command at will. The mixture of natural observation with supernatural and imaginative invention is typical of all three sisters. It is impossible not to see many of the old houses around Haworth as models for Wildfell Hall, not the least Wycoller Hall in its ruinous state and with its many ghost stories.

Anne's portrayal of children would suggest that her work as governess had not all been bitter and miserable. The delight with which she introduces Mrs Graham, the heroine of the story, through her young son illustrates her enjoyment of children:

The Tenant of Wildfell Hall

'While I stood, leaning on my gun, and looking up at the dark gables, sunk in an idle reverie, weaving a tissue of wayward fancies, in which old associations and the fair young hermit, now within those walls, bore a nearly equal part, I heard a slight rustling and scrambling just within the garden; and, glancing in the direction whence the sound proceeded, I beheld a tiny hand elevated above the wall: it clung to the topmost stone, and then another little hand was raised to take a firmer hold, and then appeared a small white forehead, surmounted with wreaths of light brown hair, with a pair of deep blue eyes beneath, and the upper portion of a diminutive ivory nose.

The eyes did not notice me, but sparkled with glee on beholding Sancho, my beautiful black and white setter, that was coursing about the field with its muzzle to the ground. The litte creature raised its face and called aloud to the dog. The good-natured animal paused, looked up, and wagged his tail, but made no further advances. The child (a little boy, apparently about five years old) scrambled up to the top of the wall and called again and again; but finding this of no avail, apparently made up his mind, like Mahomet, to go to the mountain, since the mountain would not come to him, and attempted to get over; but a crabbed old cherry tree, that grew hard by, caught him by the frock in one of its crooked, scraggy arms that stretched over the wall. In attempting to disengage himself, his foot slipped, and down he tumbled – but not to the earth; – the tree still kept him suspended. There was a silent struggle, and then a piercing shriek; – but, in an instant, I had dropped my gun on the grass, and caught the little fellow in my arms.

I wiped his eyes with his frock, told him he was all right, and called Sancho to pacify him. He was just putting his little hand on the dog's neck and beginning to smile through his tears, when I heard, behind me, a click of the iron gate and a rustle of female garments, and lo! Mrs Graham darted upon me, – her neck uncovered, her black locks streaming in the wind.

"Give me the child!" she said, in a voice scarce louder than a whisper, but with a tone of startling vehemence, and, seizing the boy, she snatched him from me, as if some dire contamination were in my touch, and then stood with one hand firmly clasping his, the other on his shoulder, fixing upon me her large, luminous dark eyes – pale, breathless, quivering with agitation.'
Chapter 2

Anne Brontë swiftly establishes the themes of her novel and we miss the point if we look merely at the story of drunken decline, that single aspect which seems to have disconcerted her sister. The novel does indeed chronicle the downfall of an irresponsible charmer, but that is not all. The poignant movement of the main story is the maturing of a young woman of spirit, told against a background of traditional and habitual values. Helen Huntingdon's behaviour as Mrs Graham reveals Anne Brontë's singular and progressive view of the position of women and their claim for a more reasonable and understanding idea of their role. Nowhere is this more apparent than in her views of the way her son

Opposite The Reading Lesson by John Callcot Horsley (1817– 1903).

should be educated. The typical Brontë theme of education is treated in an original way:

'Rose, now, at a hint from my mother, produced a decanter of wine, with accompaniments of glasses and cake, from the cupboard and the oak sideboard, and the refreshment was duly presented to the guests. They both partook of the cake, but obstinately refused the wine, in spite of their hostess's hospitable attempts to force it upon them. Arthur especially shrank from the ruby nectar as if in terror and disgust, and was ready to cry when urged to take it.

"Never mind, Arthur," said his mamma: "Mrs Markham thinks it will do you good, as you were tired with your walk; but she will not oblige you to take it! – I daresay you will do very well without. He detests the very sight of wine," she added, "and the smell of it almost makes him sick. I have been accustomed to make him swallow a little wine or weak spirits-and-water, by way of medicine, when he was sick, in fact, I have done what I could to make him hate them."

Everybody laughed, except the young widow and her son.

"Well, Mrs Graham," said my mother, wiping the tears of merriment from her bright, blue eyes – "well, you surprise me! I really gave you credit for having more sense – The poor child will be the veriest milksop that ever was sopped! Only think what a man you will make of him, if you persist in – "

"I think it a very excellent plan," interrupted Mrs Graham, with imperturbable gravity. "By that means I hope to save him from one degrading vice at least. I wish I could render the incentives to every other equally innoxious in his case."'
Chapter 2

A village schoolmaster.

Drawing by Patrick Branwell
Brontë, possibly a self-portrait.
His heavy drinking gave Anne
Brontë a sad model for the
drinking scenes of *The Tenant of
Wildfell Hall*.

Anne, in common with her sisters, was genuinely puzzled and concerned about the proper way to bring up boys. An education and circumstances that had seemingly served the Brontë girls well was clearly inadequate for Branwell, their brother. The home that suited them in many respects failed him. The debate is offered early in this novel, as Markham's mother criticizes Mrs Graham's care of her son:

"" – and my dear Mrs Graham, let me warn you in good time against the error – the fatal error, I may call it – of taking that boy's education upon yourself. – Because you are clever, in some things, and well informed, you may fancy yourself equal to the task: but indeed you are not; and, if you persist in the attempt, believe me, you will bitterly repent it when the mischief is done."

"I am to send him to school, I suppose, to learn to despise his mother's authority and affection!" said the lady, with a rather bitter smile.

"Oh, *no!* – But if you would have a boy to despise his mother, let her keep him at home, and spend her life in petting him up, and slaving to indulge his follies and caprices."

"I perfectly agree with you, Mrs Markham; but nothing can be further from my principles and practice than such criminal weakness as that."

"Well, but you will treat him like a girl – you'll spoil his spirit, and make a mere Miss Nancy of him – you will indeed, Mrs Graham, whatever you may think – ""
Chapter 3

If the proper upbringing of boys is one theme of the novel, another is the inequality of education and opportunity for girls and adult women. This theme is delicately handled with none of the exaggeration that can so easily attend this cause, humour often making the point with economy and force:

"'It's always so – if there's anything particularly nice at table, mamma winks and nods at me to abstain from it, and if I don't attend to that, she whispers, "Don't eat so much of that, Rose, Gilbert will like it for his supper" – *I'm* nothing at all – in the parlour, it's "Come, Rose, put away your things, and let's have the room nice and tidy against they come in; and keep up a good fire; Gilbert likes a cheerful fire." In the kitchen – "Make that pie a large one, Rose, I dare say the boys'll be hungry; – and don't put so much pepper in, they'll not like it I'm sure" – or, "Rose, don't put so many spices in the pudding, Gilbert likes it plain," – or, "Mind you put plenty of currants in the cake, Fergus likes plenty." If I say, "Well, mamma, *I* don't," I'm told I ought not to think of myself – "You know, Rose, in all household matters, we have only two things to consider, first, what's proper to be done, and secondly, what's most agreeable to the gentlemen of the house – anything will do for the ladies.""

"And very good doctrine too," said my mother. "Gilbert thinks so, I'm sure."

The Tenant of Wildfell Hall

"Very convenient doctrine, for us at all events," said I; "but if you would really study my pleasure, mother, you must consider your own comfort and convenience a little more than you do – as for Rose, I have no doubt she'll take care of herself; and whenever she does make a sacrifice or perform a remarkable act of devotedness, she'll take good care to let me know the extent of it. But for *you*, I might sink into the grossest condition of self-indulgence and carelessness about the wants of others, from the mere habit of being constantly cared for myself, and having all my wants anticipated or immediately supplied, while left in total ignorance of what is done for me, – if Rose did not enlighten me now and then; and I should receive all your kindness as a matter of course, and never know how much I owe you."

"Ah! and you never *will* know, Gilbert, till you're married. Then, when you've got some trifling, self-conceited girl like Eliza Millward, careless of everything but her own immediate pleasure and advantage, or some misguided, obstinate woman like Mrs Graham, ignorant of her principal duties, and clever only in what concerns her least to know – then, you'll find the difference."

"It will do me good, mother; I was not sent into the world merely to exercise the good capacities and good feelings of others – was I? – but to exert my own towards them; and when I marry, I shall expect to find more pleasure in making my wife happy and comfortable, than in being made so by her: I would rather give than receive."

"Oh! that's all nonsense, my dear – It's mere boy's talk that! You'll soon tire of petting and humouring your wife, be she ever so charming, and *then* comes the trial."

"Well, then, we must bear one another's burdens."

"Then, you must fall each into your proper place. You'll do your business, and she, if she's worthy of you, will do hers; but it's your business to please yourself, and hers to please you. I'm sure your poor, dear father was as good a husband as ever lived, and after the first six months or so were over, I should as soon have expected him to fly, as to put himself out of his way to pleasure me. He always said I was a good wife, and did my duty; and he always did his – bless him! – he was steady and punctual, seldom found fault without a reason, always did justice to my good dinners, and hardly ever spoiled my cookery by delay – and that's as much as any woman can expect of any man.'"
Chapter 6

Markham's mother's advice to him: 'it's your business (as a husband) to please yourself, and hers to please you,' establishes one view of women's place in marriage and society – a view that Mrs Graham confronts and challenges in her behaviour. Bringing upon herself the disapprobation of neighbours and the local parson, Mrs Graham, perhaps understandably, intrigues Gilbert Markham, the first narrator of the story. He visits her at Wildfell Hall and a friendship develops; this seems dogged by restraint and hesitation on Mrs Graham's part until one evening, after a visit to the hall, Markham retraces his steps to eavesdrop – with only the best motives, he would have us believe –

Drawing by Anne Brontë, thought by some to be a self-portrait.

and hears and sees more than he bargained for. His window-peering in some ways links the novel again with *Wuthering Heights* and the famous night escapade where Heathcliff and Catherine encounter Skulker.

'I could see the red firelight dimly gleaming from her parlour window. I went up to the garden wall, and stood leaning over it, with my eyes fixed upon the lattice, wondering what she was doing, thinking, or suffering now, and wishing I could speak to her but one word, or even catch one glimpse of her, before I went.

I had not thus looked, and wished, and wondered long, before I vaulted over the barrier, unable to resist the temptation of taking one glance through the window, just to see if she were more composed than when we parted; – and if I found her still in deep distress, perhaps I might venture to attempt a word of comfort – to utter one of the many things I should have said before, instead of aggravating her sufferings by my stupid impetuosity. I looked. Her chair was vacant: so was the room. But at that moment someone opened the outer door, and a voice – *her* voice – said, –

"Come out – I want to see the moon, and breathe the evening air: they will do me good – if anything will."

Here, then, were she and Rachel coming to take a walk in the garden. I wished myself safe back over the wall. I stood, however, in the shadow of the tall holly bush, which, standing between the window and the porch, at present screened me from observation, but did not prevent me from seeing two figures come forth into the moonlight; Mrs Graham followed by another – *not* Rachel, but a young man, slender and rather tall. Oh heavens, how my temples throbbed! Intense anxiety darkened my sight; but I thought – yes, and the voice confirmed it – it was Mr Lawrence.'
Chapter 6

Markham, who at this point in the novel is in love with Mrs Graham, cannot brook the possibility of Lawrence as a rival; neither he nor the reader can imagine Lawrence as anything else. Markham angrily goes home, only returning after some time to Wildfell Hall to accuse Mrs Graham of insincerity and guile. His accusations lead to a crux in the novel. Mrs Graham is so incensed at his recriminations that she offers him proof of her innocence:

'Her cheeks burned and her whole frame trembled, now, with excess of agitation. She did not speak, but flew to her desk, and snatching thence what seemed a thick album or manuscript volume, hastily tore away a few leaves from the end, and thrust the rest into my hand, saying, "You needn't read it all; but take it home with you," – and hurried from the room. But when I had left the house, and was proceeding down the walk, she opened the window and called me back. It was only to say, –

"Bring it back when you have read it; and don't breathe a word of what it tells you to any living being – I trust to your honour."

Before I could answer, she had closed the casement and turned away. I saw her cast herself back in the old oak chair, and cover her face with her hands. Her feelings had been wrought to a pitch that rendered it necessary to seek relief in tears.

Panting with eagerness, and struggling to suppress my hopes, I hurried home and rushed upstairs to my room, – having first provided myself with a candle, though it was scarcely twilight yet, – then, shut and bolted the door, determined to tolerate no interruption, and sitting down before the table, opened out my prize and delivered myself up to its perusal – first, hastily turning over the leaves and snatching a sentence here and there, and then, setting myself steadily to read it through.'

Chapter 15

The diary that Mrs Graham gives to Markham serves several functions. It clears her of the double-dealing of which Markham accuses her, but at the same time it provides the opportunity for a change of narrator. Mrs Graham, we learn from the diary, is really Mrs Helen Huntingdon, the refugee wife of a drunken man still living. Lawrence is her brother. Now we, with Markham, begin to understand things a little more clearly. We realize why Mrs Graham was so alarmed when she saw her son in Markham's arms at the first meeting. The diary takes us back six years, beginning before Helen Lawrence's marriage to Huntingdon, recounting the gradual disintegration of the marriage and the increasing drunkenness of Arthur Huntingdon. The climax and end of the diary is the description of Mrs Huntingdon's flight from her husband and her adopted disguise as Mrs Graham.

Such an action was not only controversial in 1848 when the book was published, it was also illegal. A wife had no legal rights to her children, and her action was both heroic and brave – the kind of action that Anne's father advised women in a similar situation to take.

Interestingly, the year that Helen Huntingdon's diary begins, 1821, is the year that Anne's mother died at Haworth.

Together with the change of narrator, a new theme is introduced, that of marriage:

'June 1st, 1821. – We have just returned to Staningley – that is, we returned some days ago, and I am not yet settled, and feel as if I never should be. We left town sooner than was intended, in consequence of my uncle's indisposition; – I wonder what would have been the result if we had stayed the full time. I am quite ashamed of my new-sprung distaste for country life. All my former occupations seem so tedious and dull, my former amusements so insipid and unprofitable. I cannot enjoy my music, because there is no one to hear it. I cannot enjoy my walks, because there is no one to meet. I cannot enjoy my books, because they have not power to arrest my attention: my head is so haunted with the recollections of the last few weeks, that I cannot attend to them. My drawing suits me best, for I can draw and think at the same time; and if my productions cannot now be seen by any one but myself, and those who do not care about them, they, possibly, may be, hereafter. But, then, there is one face I am always trying to paint or to sketch, and always without success; and that vexes me. As for the owner of that face, I cannot get him out of my mind – and, indeed, I never try. I wonder whether he ever thinks of me; and I wonder whether I shall ever see him again. And then might follow a train of other wonderments – questions for time and fate to answer – concluding with – Supposing all the rest be answered in the affirmative, I wonder whether I shall ever repent it? as my aunt would tell me I should, if she knew what I was thinking about. How distinctly I remember our conversation that evening before our departure for town, when we were sitting together over the fire, my uncle having gone to bed with a slight attack of the gout.

"Helen" said she, after a thoughtful silence, "do you ever think about marriage?"

"Yes, aunt, often."'

Chapter 16

Courtship and marriage were themes never far from the Brontë girls' writing. It could be said that the lack of opportunity they had to meet strangers, even women of their own kind, was a deprivation that altered and limited their lives while possibly enhancing their imaginative scope. To be unmarried, and not courted in the 1830s and 1840s, was to some degree to be in jeopardy. The lot of the single woman, moreover of a *poor* single woman, had little to recommend it. The ventures into governessing were necessary attempts to earn a living or acquire competence, to find some measure of security. One of the consequences of the Brontë sisters' isolation as daughters of the parsonage in a particularly poor and remote village was their idealized view of love and marriage. Whatever their experiences, they each formed a model which they explored in their writing. In crude terms, these models, though never explicit, can be seen as a different emphasis on parts of the Church of England marriage service. Charlotte's view of marriage seems to look for the removal of any just cause or impediment why the lovers may not be married, as in *Jane Eyre*. Emily in *Wuthering Heights* seems not to see any real hope for marriage on earth, her lovers being people inextricably involved beyond convention or rule of society: those whom no man should seek to separate. Anne in *Agnes Grey* and *The Tenant of Wildfell Hall* explores a cool love based upon gentle understanding and love of equals: the prayer book ideal of best earthly comfort.

Privately or jointly, the sisters created ideals of earthly relationships which their heroines and heroes strove to realize. Helen Huntingdon (née Lawrence) is as eloquent on marriage as she was in the early chapters of the novel about the education of children and the need to teach them to abjure alcohol. The heroine of *The Tenant of Wildfell Hall* addresses herself to the problems of marriage, and through her views we learn much of Anne Brontë's advanced ideas. The novel that began from a man's viewpoint now suddenly turns round to offer an opposing

The Tenant of Wildfell Hall

attitude. The device works for it produces convincing argument from both points of view. In addition it offers an ironic standpoint from which earlier ideas expressed by the masculine narrator can be scrutinized by a comparison with similar ideas on the same subject from a female narrator.

The Brontë sisters were never easily pleased with one another nor with friends. No curate entered the house without being ridiculed and it is hard to believe that there was not an equivalent cut-and-thrust between the children themselves. The ambition that drove them each to develop their talents must at times also have led to rivalry. Anne seems to explore families in her novels with an honesty that rings true. Her explorations of marriage proposals in *The Tenant of Wildfell Hall* bear out the humanity and originality of her vision. When the young Helen first refuses a man that her aunt finds most suitable, we have the initial exposition:

'"Do you deny that he is an upright, honourable man?"

"No."

"Do you deny that he is a sensible, sober, respectable?"

"No; he may be all this, but – "

"But, Helen! How many such men do you expect to meet with in the world? Upright, honourable, sensible, sober, respectable! – Is *this* such an everyday character that you should reject the possessor of such noble qualities, without a moment's hesitation? – Yes, *noble* I may call them; for, think of the full meaning of each, and how many inestimable virtues they include (and I might add many more to the list), and consider that all this is laid at your feet: it is in your power to secure this inestimable blessing for life – a worthy and excellent husband, who loves you tenderly, but not too fondly so as to blind him to your faults, and will be your guide throughout life's pilgrimage, and your partner in eternal bliss! Think how – "

"But I hate him, aunt," said I, interrupting this unusual flow of eloquence.

"Hate him, Helen! Is this a Christian spirit? – *you hate him?* – and he so good a man!"

"I don't hate him as a man, but as a husband. As a man, I love him so much, that I wish him a better wife than I – one as good as himself, or better – if you think that possible – provided she could like him; – but I never could, and therefore – "

"But why not? What objection do you find?"

"Firstly, he is, at least, forty years old – considerably more I should think, and I am but eighteen; secondly, he is narrow-minded and bigoted in the extreme; thirdly, his tastes and feelings are wholly dissimilar to mine; fourthly, his looks, voice, and manner are particularly displeasing to me; and finally, I have an aversion to his whole person that I never can surmount."'

Chapter 22

The reasonableness of Helen's replies can be seen as a characteristic of

the Brontë sisters, if not of the parsonage. Compassion and common-sense based upon unbending honesty at whatever cost are the authentic Brontë voice. High standards were set and expected, and in turn possibly led to Branwell's eventual collapse as he strove to reach impossibly high ideals.

Helen's suitor in this episode is the aptly named Mr Boarham. Her refusal of him is spirited:

'I left the room, and went to seek Mr Boarham. He was walking up and down the drawing-room, humming snatches of tunes, and nibbling the end of his cane.

"My dear young lady," said he, bowing and smirking with great complacency. "I have your kind guardian's permission – "

"I know, sir," said I, wishing to shorten the scene as much as possible, "and I am greatly obliged for your preference, but must beg to decline the honour you wish to confer; for, I think, we were not made for each other – as you yourself would shortly discover if the experiment were tried."'

Chapter 22

The brevity of Helen's refusal astonishes the reader almost as much as it does Mr Boarham. In a paragraph or two Anne Brontë shows us a thinking, determined young woman completely in control of a situation:

'"I am certain we were not made for each other."'

"You really think so?"

"I do."

"But you don't know me – you wish for a further acquaintance – a longer time to – "

"No, I don't. I know you as well as I ever shall, and better than you know me, or you would never dream of uniting yourself to one so incongruous – so utterly unsuitable to you in every way."

"But my dear young lady, I don't look for perfection, I can excuse – "

"Thank you, Mr Boarham, but I won't trespass upon your goodness. You may save your indulgence and consideration for some more worthy object, that won't tax them so heavily."'

Chapter 22

And that is that. So instead of marrying Mr Boarham, a predictable, secure but dull man, Helen marries Mr Huntingdon; not a man that her aunt approves of, nor one to offer a boring married life.

Almost as soon as she is married, Mrs Huntingdon regrets her marriage. Nothing is as it seemed before:

'I am married now, and settled down as Mrs Huntingdon of Grass-dale Manor. I have had eight weeks experience of matrimony. And do I regret the step I have taken? – No – though I must confess, in my secret heart, that Arthur is not what I thought him at first, and if I had known him in the beginning as thoroughly as I do now, I probably never should have loved him, and if I had loved him first, and then made the discovery, I fear I should have thought it my duty not to have married him. To be sure, I might have known him, for everyone was willing enough to tell me about him, and he himself was no accomplished hypocrite, but I was wilfully blind, and now, instead of regretting that I did not discern his full character before I was indissolubly bound to him, I am *glad*; for it has saved me a great deal of battling with my conscience, and a great deal of consequent trouble and pain; and, whatever I *ought* to have done, my duty, now, is plainly to love him and to cleave to him; and this just tallies with my inclination.

He is very fond of me — almost *too* fond. I could do with less caressing and more rationality: I should like to be less of a pet and more of a friend, if I might choose.'
Chapter 23

It is not hard to see Anne, the unmarried woman, exploring her ideas here. In the following description of the honeymoon, in which Arthur Huntingdon shows his selfishness, she skilfully suggests how much freedom an individual can lose in any relationship:

'The first instance he gave was on the occasion of our bridal tour. He wanted to hurry it over, for all the continental scenes were already familiar to him: many had lost their interest in his eyes, and others had never had anything to lose. The consequence was, that, after a flying transit through part of France and part of Italy, I came back nearly as ignorant as I went, having made no acquaintance with persons and manners, and very little with things, — my head swarming with a motley confusion of objects and scenes — some, it is true, leaving a deeper and more pleasing impression than others, but these embittered by the recollection that my emotions had not been shared by my companion, but that, on the contrary, when I had expressed a particular interest in anything that I saw or desired to see, it had been displeasing to him in as much as it proved that I could take delight in anything disconnected with himself.'
Chapter 23

The marriage falls rapidly into argument and misunderstanding in scenes bearing an uncomfortable ring of truth:

'— Arthur is getting tired — not of me, I trust, but of the idle, quiet life he leads — and no wonder, for he has so few sources of amusement; he never reads anything but newspapers and sporting magazines; and when he sees me occupied with a book, he won't let me rest till I close it. In fine weather he generally manages to get through the time pretty well; but on rainy days, of which we have had a good many of late, it is quite painful to witness his ennui. I do all I can to amuse him, but it is impossible to get him to feel interested in what I most like to talk about; while, on the other hand, he likes to talk about things that cannot interest me — or even that annoy me —

and these please him the most of all; for his favourite amusement is to sit or loll beside me on the sofa and tell me stories of his former amours, always turning upon the ruin of some confiding girl or the cozening of some unsuspecting husband; and when I express my horror and indignation, he lays it all to the charge of jealousy, and laughs till the tears run down his cheeks. I used to fly into passions or melt into tears at first, but seeing that his delight increased in proportion to my anger and agitation, I have since endeavoured to suppress my feelings and receive his revelations in the silence of calm contempt; but still, he reads the inward struggle in my face, and misconstrues my bitterness of soul for his unworthiness into the pangs of wounded jealousy; and when he has sufficiently diverted himself with that, or fears my displeasure will become too serious for his comfort, he tries to kiss and soothe me into smiles again –'
Chapter 24

As Huntingdon's behaviour, his adultery and drunken disregard for his wife, condemns the marriage to breakdown, Helen Huntingdon emerges as an ever stronger woman. She becomes a worthy opponent to her debauched husband. After she finds him with another woman, he is made to feel her strength:

'"Will you *never* learn?" he continued, more boldly, "that you have

Drinking scene.

nothing to fear from me? that I love you wholly and entirely? – or if," he added, with a lurking smile, "I ever give a thought to another, you may well spare it, for those fancies are here and gone like a flash of lightning, while my love for you burns on steadily, and for ever like the sun. You little exorbitant tyrant, will not *that* – "

"Be quiet a moment, will you, Arthur," said I, "and listen to me – and don't think I'm in a jealous fury: I am perfectly calm. Feel my hand." And I gravely extended it towards him – but closed it upon his with an energy that seemed to disprove the assertion, and made him smile. "You needn't smile, sir," said I, still tightening my grasp, and looking steadfastly on him till he almost quailed before me. "You may think it all very fine, Mr Huntingdon, to amuse yourself with rousing my jealousy; but take care you don't rouse my hate instead. And when you have once extinguished my love, you will find it no easy matter to kindle it again."'
Chapter 27

Helen Huntingdon's resolve to leave her husband and to take her young son with her was not only controversial in 1847 but also illegal. A married woman had no right to take a child from its father nor did she have any right to property or freedom. The fugitive wife and single parent that Helen becomes was as challenging a figure as Markham and his family suggested at the outset of the novel.

A case in Haworth is recorded where Anne's father advised the wife of a clergyman to leave her drunken husband and to take her children with her. Certainly the Brontës were never conformist nor do any of their heroes or heroines follow predictable paths. The Rev. Brontë seems, at any rate, to have taught his girls to follow their own consciences and to value integrity above all else. In their quiet way, each of the Brontë sisters lights a fuse of revolution in her novel. In *The Tenant of Wildfell Hall* Anne Brontë creates a woman who faces reality, makes up her own mind about possible courses of action and is prepared to act for her own and her child's good. However much she may be criticized or misunderstood, Helen Huntingdon cannot be accused of inertia or lack of resolve. In this she echoes the spirit that took Charlotte unchaperoned to Brussels and that made her such an unpatronizable authoress at London dinner parties.

Helen Huntingdon's plan to leave her husband, to 'escape', as Anne Brontë put it, derived from her husband's attempts to debauch the child:

'My greatest source of uneasiness, in this time of trial, was my son, whom his father and his father's friends delighted to encourage in all the embryo vices a little child can show, and to instruct in all the evil habits he could acquire – in a word, to "make a man of him" was one of their staple amusements; and I need say no more to justify my alarm on his account, and my determination to deliver him at any hazard from the hands of such instructors.'
Chapter 39

The boy's father taught him to swear and to drink:

The Tenant of Wildfell Hall

'. . . he was not going to have the little fellow moped to death between an old nurse and a cursed fool of a mother. So the little fellow came down every evening, in spite of his cross mamma, and learnt to tipple wine like papa, to swear like Mr Hattersley, and to have his own way like a man, and sent mamma to the devil when she tried to prevent him. To see such things done with the roguish naïveté of that pretty little child and hear such things spoken by that small infantile voice, was as peculiarly piquant and irresistibly droll to them as it was inexpressibly distressing and painful to me; and when he had set the table in a roar, he would look round delightedly upon them all, and add his shrill laugh to theirs. But if that beaming blue eye rested on me, its light would vanish for a moment, and he would say, in some concern, "Mamma, why don't *you* laugh? Make her laugh, papa – she never will."
Chapter 39

Drunks with children, one of the moral concerns of this novel.

If we see this in the context of Rev. Brontë's concern to provide proper schooling for the 'little creatures' of the poor of Haworth, and of Anne's experiences as a governess, it is clear that the family involvement with education is never far from their work. The proper treatment of the young is very much a Brontë theme. Helen is resolute:

'But this should not continue; my child must not be abandoned to this corruption: better far that he should live in poverty and obscurity with a fugitive mother, than in luxury and affluence with such a father.'
Chapter 31

The kind of company Arthur Huntingdon keeps is summed up in a scene of dissipation where we can almost hear the voice of a drunkard, perhaps Branwell's:

'Grimsby repulsed him with a solemn wave of the hand, and then, turning to me, continued, with the same drawling tones, and strange uncertainty of utterance, and heavy gravity of aspect as before, "But as I was saying, Mrs Huntingdon, – they have no head at all: they can't take half a bottle without being affected some way; whereas I – well, I've taken three times as much as they have tonight, and you see I'm perfectly steady. Now that may strike you as very singular, but I think I can explain it: – you see *their* brains – I mention no names, but you'll understand to whom I allude – *their* brains are light to begin with, and the fumes of the fermented liquor render them lighter still, and produce an entire light-headedness, or giddiness, resulting in intoxication; whereas my brains, being composed of more solid materials, will absorb a considerable quantity of this alcoholic vapour without the production of any sensible result – "

"I think you will find a sensible result produced on that tea," interrupted Mr Hargrave, "by the quantity of sugar you have put into it. Instead of your usual complement of one lump you have put in six."

"Have I so?" replied the philosopher, diving with his spoon into the cup and bringing up several half-dissolved pieces in confirmation of the assertion. "Um! I perceive. Thus, madam, you see the evil of absence of mind – of thinking too much while engaged in the common concerns of life. Now if I had had my wits about me, like ordinary men, instead of within me like a philosopher, I should not have spoiled this cup of tea, and been constrained to trouble you for another. – With your permission, I'll turn this into the slop-basin."

"That is the sugar-basin, Mr Grimsby."'
Chapter 31

Helen flees with her son and thus comes to be the tenant of Wildfell Hall, the property of her brother.

Her plan is to earn a living from her hobby of painting. In this she emulates her creator. All the Brontë children took painting and drawing lessons and at one stage or another considered exploiting their talent, Branwell as a portrait painter, the girls as teachers.

The Tenant of Wildfell Hall

The rest of the tale, after Gilbert Markham has discovered the truth about Mrs Graham's (Helen Huntingdon's) relationship with his supposed rival Mr Lawrence, is something of a suspense story that deserves not to be spoiled by telling.

Biography has favoured the image of Anne Brontë as 'the gentle Anne' following the young Charlotte's playful description of her as a mere nothing. Anne's ability to work away from Haworth belies this image and her novels certainly show her as a robust observer of life as it is and a fearless reporter. Indeed, we can argue that she is more explicit than Charlotte or Emily in scenes where her heroine witnesses infidelity and drunkenness. An early passage in the novel shows the control and the balance of her writing and also illustrates how she unflinchingly included violence in her work.

Opposite Portrait by Patrick Branwell Brontë.

Letter by Patrick Branwell Brontë with drawings showing scenes of drunken revelling.

The Tenant of Wildfell Hall

Markham, having mistaken Mrs Graham's brother as a rival for her hand, meets him on a journey:

'As I trotted along, however, chewing the cud of – *bitter* fancies, I heard another horse at no great distance behind me; but I never conjectured who the rider might be – or troubled my head about him, till on slackening my pace to ascend a gentle acclivity – or rather suffering my horse to slacken its pace into a lazy walk; for, lost in my own reflexions, I was letting it jog on as leisurely as it thought proper – I lost ground, and my fellow-traveller overtook me. He accosted me by name; for it was no stranger – it was Mr Lawrence! Instinctively the fingers of my whip-hand tingled, and grasped their charge with convulsive energy; but I restrained the impulse, and answering his salutation with a nod, attempted to push on; but he pushed on beside me and began to talk about the weather and the crops. I gave the briefest possible answers to his queries and observations, and fell back. He fell back too, and asked if my horse was lame. I replied with a *look* – at which he placidly smiled. . . .'

"Markham," said he, in his usual quiet tone, "why do you quarrel with your friends, because you have been disappointed in one quarter? You have found your hopes defeated; but how am *I* to blame for it? I warned you beforehand, you know, but you would not – "

He said no more; for, impelled by some fiend at my elbow, I had seized my whip by the small end, and – swift and sudden as a flash of lightning – brought the other down upon his head. It was not without a feeling of savage satisfaction that I beheld the instant, deadly pallor that overspread his face, and the few red drops that trickled down his forehead, while he reeled a moment in his saddle, and then fell backward to the ground. The pony, surprised to be so strangely relieved of its burden, started and capered, and kicked a little, and then made use of its freedom to go and crop the grass of the hedge bank; while its master lay as still and silent as a corpse. Had I killed him? – an icy hand seemed to grasp my heart and check its pulsation, as I bent over him, gazing with breathless intensity upon the ghastly, upturned face. But no; he moved his eyelids and uttered a slight groan. I breathed again – he was only stunned by the fall. It served him right – it would teach him better manners in future. Should I help him to his horse? No. For any other combination of offences I would; but his were too unpardonable. He might mount it himself, if he liked – in a while already he was beginning to stir and look about him – and there it was for him, quietly browsing on the roadside.'
Chapter 14

Anne Brontë's form of aversion therapy, the means whereby Helen Huntingdon cured her son of a liking for wine, has all the indications of a real method which may well derive from the Brontë family's desperation over Branwell's condition. It is chilling to think of Anne's book being published in the July of 1848 and her brother dying of alcohol and drug abuse in September of the same year:

'I had much trouble at first in breaking him of those evil habits his father had taught him to acquire, but already that difficulty is nearly vanquished now: bad language seldom defiles his mouth, and I have succeeded in giving him an absolute disgust for all intoxicating liquors, which I hope not even his father or his father's friends will be able to overcome. He was inordinately fond of them for so young a creature, and, remembering my unfortunate father as well as his, I dreaded the consequences of such a taste. But if I had stinted him in his usual quantity of wine or forbidden him to taste it altogether, that would only have increased his partiality for it, and made him regard it as a greater treat than ever. I therefore gave him quite as much as his father was accustomed to allow him – as much indeed, as he desired to have, but into every glass I surreptitiously introduced a small quantity of tartar-emetic – just enough to produce inevitable nausea and depression without positive sickness. Finding such disagreeable consequences invariably to result from this indulgence, he soon grew weary of it, but the more he shrank from the daily treat the more I pressed it upon him, till his reluctance was strengthened to perfect abhorrence. When he was thoroughly disgusted with every kind of wine, I allowed him, at his own request, to try brandy and water and then gin and water; for the little toper was familiar with them all, and I was determined that all should be equally hateful to him. This I have now effected; and since he declares that the taste, the smell, the sight of any one of them is sufficient to make him sick, I have given up teasing him about them, except now and then as objects of terror in cases of misbehaviour: "Arthur, if you're not a good boy I shall give you a glass of wine," or "Now Arthur, if you say that again you shall have some brandy and water," is as good as any other threat; and, once or twice, when he was sick, I have obliged the poor child to swallow a little wine and water without the tartar-emetic, by way of medicine; and this practice I intend to continue for some time to come; not that I think it of any real service in a physical sense, but because I am determined to enlist all the powers of association in my service: I wish this aversion to be so deeply grounded in his nature that nothing in afterlife may be able to overcome it.'
Chapter 41

Detail from a drawing by Patrick Branwell Brontë – 'A Parody'–. Branwell decorated many of his letters with such crude sketches.

VIII

THE PROFESSOR

'This little book was written before either Jane Eyre *or* Shirley *and yet no indulgence can be solicited for it on a plea of a first attempt. A first attempt it certainly was not, as the pen that wrote it had been previously worn a good deal in a practice of some years.'*

Charlotte Brontë wrote this in the Preface to the book which she had hoped would signal her literary debut as a novelist.

Of the three manuscripts that the Brontë sisters sent out for publication as novels, Charlotte's *The Professor* is something of a curiosity. Never published in her lifetime, it enjoyed some success after her death but has never been held by critics to be entirely satisfactory. In being persuaded to allow its publication, Arthur Bell Nicholls, Charlotte's widower, suggested that although Charlotte had made use of material from *The Professor* in *Villette* the two 'stories were in most respects unlike'. It is arguable that this is not the case. Indeed it can be shown that material from this book found its way into *Jane Eyre* as well as *Villette*.

Written and sent to publishers in 1846, Charlotte was still trying to have it published as late as 1851, after the publication of *Shirley* and before she had written *Villette*:

Writing to George Smith who had published her other work, Charlotte begins:

'*The Professor*' has now had the honour of being rejected nine times by the 'Tr-de' (three rejections go to your own share) . . . I must regard this martyrized MS. as repulsed . . . Few, I flatter myself, have earned an equal distinction, and, of course my feelings towards it can only be paralleled by those of a doting parent towards an idiot child. . . .'
Charlotte Brontë to George Smith. 5 February 1851

She continues by declining Smith's offer to take the manuscript into safe keeping, suggesting that he might light a cigar from the odd page. No, she would rather keep it in a cupboard in the dark on its own. This she did, after making use of much of its scenes, setting and theme.

Opposite Portrait thought to be of Aunt Elizabeth Branwell, who came to live at Haworth Parsonage at the death of her younger sister, and who financed Charlotte and Emily Brontës' stay in Brussels.

The Professor

Originally entitled *The Master*, the novel is uncompromisingly about education, about teaching, about classroom behaviour and about the differences between the education of boys and girls. It is also a romantic love story, but again, it is the love of one teacher for another and the story of how a shy orphan assistant teacher becomes the owner and headmistress of a successful school, a happy wife and mother.

Beginning in Yorkshire, the story moves to Brussels and then back to England again. Charlotte uses her own knowledge of Haworth and her Belgian experiences throughout the book.

Too much and too little has been made of Charlotte's time in Brussels. It was to have a lasting and profound influence on herself and on Emily, who was for a while her companion, and not only because of the relationship that developed between Charlotte and M. Heger, her teacher and the husband of her employer.

The idea of going to Brussels, at first of simply going abroad, seems to have arisen while Charlotte was a governess with the White family at Upperwood House, Rawdon, not far from Leeds. Here Charlotte confessed to her usual homesickness:

'... Home sickness afflicts me sorely, I like Mr White extremely. Respecting Mrs White I am for the present silent. I am trying hard to like her. The children are not such little devils incarnate as the Sidgwicks, but they are over-indulged, and at times hard to manage. ...'
Charlotte Brontë to Ellen Nussey. 21 March 1841

While Charlotte tried to like her employer and subdue the children, her former school friend Mary Taylor was writing of the delights of travel. Her letters fired Charlotte's imagination:

'... Mary's letter spoke of some of the pictures and cathedrals she had seen – pictures the most exquisite and cathedrals the most venerable – I hardly know what swelled to my throat as I read her letter – such a vehement impatience of restraint and steady work. Such a strong wish for wings – wings such as wealth can furnish – such an urgent thirst to see – to know – to learn. ...'
Charlotte Brontë. Letter to Ellen Nussey, 7 August 1841

By the following month Charlotte was sounding out her aunt and father about the possibility of herself and Emily tasting some of the delights that Mary Taylor reported. The 'impatience of restraint and steady work' would not abate.

Somehow Charlotte, herself so susceptible to letters, found the right way to introduce the idea to her aunt who alone in the family would have the means to finance such a venture. The aunt was already considering lending her nieces money to set up their own school. This became the starting point for Charlotte. The money would be better spent helping the girls gain more accomplishments and in turn become better teachers.

Opposite Typical schoolroom scene from a contemporary engraving.

The Professor

'I would go to Brussels, in Belgium.
The cost of the journey there, at the dearest rate of travelling, would be £5; living is there little more than half as dear as in England, and the facilities for education are equal or superior to any other place in Europe. . . . I know no other friend in the world to whom I could apply on this subject except yourself. . . .'

and then Charlotte added a master stroke:

'Papa will perhaps think it a wild and ambitious scheme; but whoever rose in the world without ambition? When he left Ireland to go to Cambridge University, he was as ambitious as I am now. I want us all to go on. I know we have talents, and I want them to be turned to account.'
Charlotte Brontë to Elizabeth Branwell. 29 September 1841

Charlotte had reminded her aunt of the extraordinary energy that had indeed brought her father from poverty to the parsonage at Haworth. In due course the money was found for both Charlotte and Emily to attend as pupil-teachers at a school in Brussels. The letter to her aunt was written in September; by the next February the girls, accompanied by their father, were on their way to Brussels.

The destination of the young women – Charlotte was 25 and Emily 23 years old – was the Pensionnat Heger, owned by a married lady, and a school of good reputation where the education of girls was given considerable importance. The young Englishwomen would have the anomalous role of pupils and assistant teachers, improving themselves while offering some lessons in English in return. Not an enviable role in any school.

Charlotte's journey to Belgium and her arrival in Brussels are all described in close detail in *The Professor* where its hero Crimsworth makes the same journey:

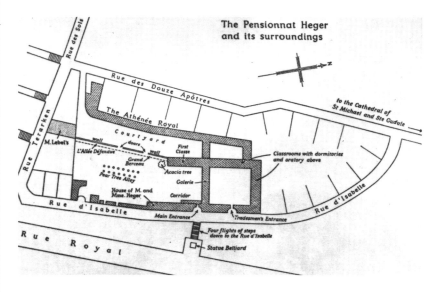

Plan of the immediate surroundings of the Pensionnat Heger as it was in 1842, showing the proximity of the Royal Park which Emily and Charlotte knew so well.

'This is Belgium, reader. Look! don't call the picture a flat or a dull one – it was neither flat nor dull to me when I first beheld it. When I left Ostend on a mild February morning, and found myself on the road to Brussels, nothing could look vapid to me. My sense of enjoyment possessed an edge whetted to the finest, untouched, keen, exquisite. I was young; I had good health; pleasure I had never met; no indulgence of hers had enervated or sated one faculty of my nature. Liberty I clasped in my arms for the first time, and the influence of her smile and embrace revived my life like the sun and the west wind. Yes, at that epoch I felt like a morning traveller who doubts not that from the hill he is ascending he shall behold a glorious sunrise . . .

I gazed often, and always with delight, from the window of the diligence (these, be it remembered, were not the days of trains and railroads). Well! and what did I see? I will tell you faithfully. Green, reedy swamps; fields fertile, but flat, cultivated in patches that made them look like magnified kitchen-gardens; belts of cut trees, formal as pollard willows, skirting the horizon; narrow canals, gliding slow by the roadside; painted Flemish farm-houses; some very dirty hovels; a grey, dead sky; wet road, wet fields, wet house-tops: not a beautiful, scarcely a picturesque object met my eye along the whole route; yet to me, all was beautiful, all was more than picturesque.'
Chapter 7

Crimsworth also introduces us to the school and its proximity to the Royal Palace and gardens in Brussels that Charlotte and Emily would come to know so well:

The Royal Park in Brussels.

The Professor

'I remarked the sparkling clearness of the air, the deep blue of the sky, the gay clean aspect of the white-washed or painted houses; I saw what a fine street was the Rue Royale, and, walking leisurely along its broad pavement, I continued to survey its stately hotels, till the palisades, the gates, the trees of the park appearing in sight, offered to my eye a new attraction. I remember, before entering the park, I stood a while to contemplate the statue of General Belliard, and then I advanced to the top of the great staircase just beyond, and I looked down into a narrow back street, which I afterwards learnt was called the Rue d'Isabelle. I well recollect that my eye rested on the green door of a rather large house opposite, where, on a brass plate, was inscribed, "Pensionnat de Demoiselles." Pensionnat! The word excited an uneasy sensation in my mind; it seemed to speak of restraint. Some of the demoiselles, externats no doubt, were at that moment issuing from the door – I looked for a pretty face amongst them, but their close, little French bonnets hid their features; in a moment they were gone.'
Chapter 7

Statue of General Belliard, a landmark in *The Professor* and one that remains in the exact spot, above the steps leading to Rue d'Isabelle, site of Mme Heger's school, today.

Charlotte made no attempt to disguise places or addresses in *The Professor*. The school belonging to Mme Heger was in the Rue d'Isabelle, precisely as Crimsworth described it. His excitement was clearly that of his creator.

As Brussels plays its part in the novel, so too does Yorkshire, for it is there there the novel begins. Edward Crimsworth, having just left Eton College, is seeking a means of earning a living. An orphan, he has the temerity to turn down his uncle's suggestion that he become a clergyman and chooses to endure his guardians' wrath and become a tradesman, applying to his brother for a post as clerk in his mill. Eton College may seem a strange choice of school for a Brontë character, but in the event it was not at all odd. Charlotte had a young cousin in Cornwall, Charles Henry Branwell, who entered Eton College as a King's Scholar in 1841, the very year that she was organizing her departure for Belgium.

The Brontë family's interest in education was far-reaching and curiously responsive to movements and developments throughout the land. The Eton College that Crimsworth, and Charlotte's cousin, attended was the unreformed school where beatings and a rule of undisciplined behaviour bordering upon anarchy were the order of the day. The references to the college in *The Professor* are not flattering. Crimsworth's brother questions Edward's abilities: 'What can you do? Do you know anything besides that useless trash of college learning – Greek and Latin and so forth?'

Charlotte could have asked the same question of her brother Branwell, who had learnt Greek and was able to translate an ode by Horace but painfully failed to find any permanent employment in the industrial world of the mid-19th century. Later in the novel another character challenges Crimsworth to take his intellect and refinement to the market and see what it is worth. It is as if in the rejection of a curacy Crimsworth is turning his back on his training, and seeking to find his way in the future developing world.

Charlotte briefly but effectively runs the Eton theme through the novel, ending with Crimsworth preparing to send his son to the college 'where,' his mother suggests, 'I suspect, his first year or two will be utter wretchedness.'

The only positive reference to the school is when Crimsworth saves a young boy from drowning and Charlotte suggests that swimming was the one useful thing that he had learnt at Eton.

Crimsworth's stay in Yorkshire is brief, for he quickly learns that he will never make a living in trade. Thus, like Charlotte, but for different reasons, he arrives in Brussels.

Unlike her sisters, Charlotte Brontë created and retained a male narrator for *The Professor*, thereby restricting herself and possibly condemning the novel to be a pale shadow of her true feelings. This certainly seems the case when we read her preface to the intended edition of the 1850s that did not appear until after her death.

'I said to myself that my hero should work his way through life as I had seen real living men work theirs – that he should never get a shilling he had not earned – that no sudden turns should lift him a moment to wealth and high station. . . .

. . . In the sequel, however, I find the publishers in general scarcely approved of this system, but would have liked something more imaginative and poetical – something more consonant with a highly wrought fancy, with a taste for pathos . . . Men in business are usually thought to prefer the real; on trial the idea will often be found fallacious: a passionate preference for the wild, wonderful and thrilling – the

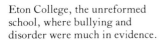

Eton College, the unreformed school, where bullying and disorder were much in evidence.

The Professor

strange, startling, and harrowing – agitates divers souls that show a calm sober surface.'
Author's Preface

Distancing herself from the events of the story by adopting Edward Crimsworth as her narrator and keeping the plot within the bounds of possibility may have tamed the novel too much for her publishers. It should perhaps warn us against too biographical an approach to this text. Charlotte's apparent carelessness with identities and location – she seemed not to care one jot that schools would be identified and teachers matched with her fictional characters – suggest that she was confident that her story was not of personalities but ideas.

The ideas of *The Professor* are those of the Brontë sisters themselves, Crimsworth's ambitions theirs. These ambitions, ideas or concerns can be listed. They begin with the anxiety of a would-be teacher and comprise thoughts about school systems, classroom behaviour and the description of good and bad pupils. Frances Henri, another orphan teacher in *The Professor*, is anatomized by Crimsworth in a perceptive analysis of what it takes to be a teacher:

'So much for her perseverance . . . her success as a teacher rested partly, perhaps chiefly, upon the will of others; it cost her a most painful effort to enter into conflict with this foreign will, to endeavour to bend it into subjection to her own; for in what regarded people in general the action of her will was impeded by many scruples; it was as unembarrassed as strong where her own affairs were concerned, and to it she could at any time subject her inclination, if that inclination went counter to her convictions of right; yet when called upon to wrestle with the propensities, the habits, the faults of others, of children especially, who are deaf to reason, and, for the most part, insensate to persuasion, her will sometimes almost refused to act; then came in the sense of duty, and forced the reluctant will into operation. A wasteful expense of energy and labour was frequently the consequence; Frances toiled for and with her pupils like a drudge, but it was long ere her conscientious exertions were rewarded by anything like docility on their part, because they saw that they had power over her, inasmuch as by resisting her painful attempts to convince, persuade, control – by forcing her to the employment of coercive measures – they could inflict upon her exquisite suffering. Human beings – human children especially – seldom deny themselves the pleasure of exercising a power which they are conscious of possessing, even though that power consist only in a capacity to make others wretched; a pupil whose sensations are duller than those of his instructor, while his nerves are tougher and his bodily strength perhaps greater, has an immense advantage over that instructor, and he will generally use it relentlessly, because the very young, very healthy, very thoughtless, know neither how to sympathize nor how to spare.'
Chapter 16

A letter Charlotte wrote to her publisher's reader, W. S. Williams,

Opposite View over Haworth today from the moors above.

when his daughters were thinking of becoming teachers, shows how interwoven were her fiction and beliefs:

'. . . the great qualification . . . necessary to the task: the faculty, not merely of *acquiring* but of imparting knowledge – the power of influencing young minds – that natural fondness for, that innate sympathy with, children. . . . He or she who possesses this faculty, this sympathy – though perhaps not otherwise highly accomplished – need never fear failure in the career of instruction. Children will be docile with them, will improve under them. . . .

. . . The young teacher's chief anxiety, when she sets out in life, always is to know enough. Brief experience will, in most instances, show her that this anxiety has been misdirected. She will rarely be found too ignorant for her pupils; the demand on her knowledge will not often be larger than she can answer. But on her patience – on her self-control, the requirement will be enormous; on her animal spirits (and woe be to her if these fail) the pressure will be immense.'
Letter to W.S. Williams, 12 May 1848

There is an understanding here which shows that governessing was more than a chore to Charlotte, and teaching a topic about which she had well-formed and considered opinions.

The character and personality of fellow teachers, the struggle to teach and learn in foreign languages, the shock of different cultures; these are the true themes of *The Professor*. Charlotte, as we might expect, coming from a parsonage home in the evangelical north, with a father who published anti-Catholic tracts, would be extremely critical of the Catholicism that she encountered in Brussels. This prejudice is borne out in her descriptions of her pupils, both in her fiction and in actual life:

'The least exceptionable pupil was the poor little Sylvie I have mentioned once before. Sylvie was gentle in manners, intelligent in mind; she was even sincere, as far as her religion would permit her to be so, but her physical organization was defective; weak health stunted her growth and chilled her spirits, and then, destined as she was for the cloister, her whole soul was warped to a conventual bias, and in the tame, trained subjection of her manner, one read that she had already prepared herself for her future course of life, by giving up her independence of thought and action into the hands of some despotic confessor. She permitted herself no original opinion, no preference of companion or employment; in everything she was guided by another. With a pale, passive, automaton air, she went about all day long doing what she was bid; never what she liked, or what, from innate conviction, she thought it right to do. The poor little future religieuse had been early taught to make the dictates of her own reason and conscience quite subordinate to the will of her spiritual director. She was the model pupil of Mdlle Reuter's establishment; pale, blighted image, where life lingered feebly, but whence the soul had been conjured by Romish wizard-craft!'
Chapter 12

In real life Charlotte wrote home again and again betraying her partial view:

'If the national character of the Belgians is to be measured by the character of most of the girls in this school, it is a character singularly cold, selfish, animal and inferior ... their principles are rotten to the core. We avoid them, which is not difficult to do, as we have the brand of Protestantism and Anglicism upon us. People talk of the danger which Protestants expose themselves to in going to reside in Catholic countries. ... My advice to all Protestants who are tempted to do anything so besotted as to turn Catholics is, to walk over the sea on to the Continent; to attend Mass sedulously for a time; to note well the mummeries thereof; also the idiotic, mercenary aspect of all the priests; and *then*, if they are still disposed to consider Papistry ... let them turn Papists at once – that's all. I consider Methodism, Quakerism and the extremes of High and Low Churchism foolish, but Roman Catholicism beats them all.'
Charlotte Brontë to Ellen Nussey, July 1842

We should not underestimate the effect of the Brussels visit on Charlotte and Emily, and in turn upon their writing. The sharp contrast between Haworth and Brussels must always be borne in mind. Brussels was an ancient city with its great Gothic cathedral, its medieval traditions, and its thriving expatriate population among whom were not

Left The pulpit in the Cathedral of Ste Gudule, the cathedral depicted in both *The Professor* and *Villette*.

Right The pulpit in St Michael's and All Angels in Haworth. Comparison of the two pulpits suggests the contrast between the two cultures of Yorkshire and Belgium. It is easy to underestimate the impact that life in Brussels made on Charlotte and Emily Brontë.

The Professor

a few revolutionaries. The art exhibitions, concerts, celebrations in the park only a stone's throw from the school where they lived; all contributed to enrich the young Englishwomen's experience. Their regular attendance at the Chapel Royal, given to the Protestants of Brussels by Napoleon, brought them close to a world that was as far as possible from Haworth and Yorkshire as could be imagined.

Charlotte may satirize the English abroad but she greatly enjoyed the style and variety of what she saw around her. Crimsworth, searching for Frances Henri, describes the scene after the service at the Chapel Royal:

'. . . I turned from the door of the chapel-royal which the door-keeper had just closed and locked, and followed in the wake of the last of the congregation, now dispersed and dispersing over the square. I had soon outwalked the couples of English gentlemen and ladies. (Gracious goodness! why don't they dress better? My eye is yet filled with visions of the high-flounced, slovenly, and tumbled dresses in costly silk and satin, of the large unbecoming collars in expensive lace: of the ill-cut coats and strangely fashioned pantaloons which every Sunday, at the English service, filled the choirs of the chapel-royal, and after it, issuing forth into the square, came into disadvantageous contrast with freshly and trimly attired foreign figures, hastening to attend salut at the church of Coburg.) I had passed these pairs of Britons, and the groups of pretty English children, and the British footmen and waiting-maids; I had crossed the Place Royale, and got into the Rue Royale, thence I had diverged into the Rue de Louvain – an old and quiet street. I remember that, feeling a little hungry, and not desiring to go back and take my share of the "goûter," now on the refectory-table at Pelet's – to wit, pistolets and water – I stepped into a baker's and refreshed myself on a *couc* (?) – it is a Flemish word, I don't know how to spell it – *à Corinthe – anglicé*, a currant bun – and a cup of coffee; and then I strolled on towards the Porte de Louvain.'
Chapter 19

Rue Royale as it was when Charlotte Brontë lived in Brussels, a sharper contrast with her home in Haworth is hard to imagine. Mme Heger's school was only a step away from this fashionable part of this city.

There is much in *The Professor* to support the view that Charlotte's

Porte de Louvain, one of the medieval gates in Brussels known to both Emily and Charlotte Brontë.

initial enjoyment of Brussels did not fall short of her expectations. Work in the school might be hard but Haworth could not offer the scenes and the passers by of the elegant quarters by the Royal Park. Towards the end of *The Professor* she wrote:

'Novelists should never allow themselves to weary of the study of real life.'
Chapter 19

Following her own advice, Charlotte would find much to write about during her stay in Belgium. Yet she was never overwhelmed by what she saw or experienced; her eye was clear and her feelings under control.

Using her own relationships in teaching, she explores the real nature of that profession:

'Know, O incredulous reader! that a master stands in a somewhat different relation towards a pretty, light-headed, probably ignorant girl, to that occupied by a partner at a ball, or a gallant on the promenade. A professor does not meet his pupil to see her dressed in satin and muslin, with hair perfumed and curled, neck scarcely shaded by aërial lace, round white arms circled with bracelets, feet dressed for the gliding dance. It is not his business to whirl her through the waltz, to feed her with compliments, to heighten her beauty by the flush of gratified vanity. Neither does he encounter her on the smooth-rolled, tree-shaded Boulevard, in the green and sunny park, whither she repairs clad in her becoming walking dress, her scarf thrown with grace over her shoulders, her little bonnet scarcely screening her curls, the red rose under its brim adding a new tint to the softer rose on her cheek: her face and eyes, too, illumined with smiles, perhaps as transient as the sunshine of the gala-day, but also quite as brilliant; it is not his office to walk by her side, to listen to her lively chat, to carry her parasol, scarcely larger than a broad-green leaf, to lead in a ribbon her Blenheim spaniel or Italian greyhound. No: he finds her in the schoolroom, plainly dressed, with books before her. Owing to her education or her nature books are to her a nuisance, and she opens them with aversion, yet her teacher must instil into her mind the contents of these books; that mind resists the admission of grave information, it recoils, it grows restive, sullen tempers are shown, disfiguring frowns spoil the symmetry of the face, sometimes coarse gestures banish grace from the deportment, while muttered expressions, redolent of native and ineradicable vulgarity, desecrate the sweetness of the voice. Where the temperament is serene though the intellect be sluggish, an unconquerable dullness opposes every effort to instruct.'
Chapter 14

With Frances Henri the two themes of Charlotte's writing merge. Education and the need for love and affection walk hand in hand. Charlotte's decision to write the story of Edward rather than that of Frances is rather like a version of *Jane Eyre* with that other Edward,

The Professor

Edward Fairfax Rochester, as narrator. Sustaining the male narrator may in the end have limited the scope of *The Professor*, may have ruled out just those qualities of romance, the imaginative and poetical, that her publishers felt the book lacked. Certainly when Charlotte reversed the narration, making Frances the central figure and Edward secondary, adding enough 'strange, startling and harrowing' occurrences to fill a Gothic novel, as she did when she wrote *Jane Eyre*, the result was a book that was an instant and continuing success.

There are two love stories in *The Professor*: that of Crimsworth and Mlle Reuter, his employer, is false, but the love of Crimsworth and Frances is real. The contrast between the two women is as clear as that between Jane Eyre and Blanche Ingram. Charlotte uses an overheard trumpet call from the royal gardens to announce, or herald the beginning of the true love story in *The Professor*. It is a master-pupil relationship where, subtly, the pupil takes over; as Crimsworth's pupil progresses, and Frances emerges as her true self, so she becomes a force to be reckoned with. Her greatest moment of integrity comes when Crimsworth suggests that once married she will, of course, give up her work as a teacher. Frances's reply that not only will she not relinquish her work, but that it will make more sense if Crimsworth follows her career, has all the force of Charlotte's strong sense of her own value and the strength of a woman's point of view. It was an advanced view for the 1800s and one that all the Brontë sisters shared.

The contrast between Mlle Zoraïde Reuter and Frances Henri is of wealth, sophistication and guile compared with modesty, poverty and integrity. It is also an opportunity for Charlotte Brontë to make a further comparison, that between bourgeois living and the life of the poor.

Edward Crimsworth's first visit to Frances's home suggests the simplicity of poverty familiar to the Brontë sisters, where everything was cared for and valued through necessity:

'Stepping over a little mat of green wool, I found myself in a small room with a painted floor and a square of green carpet in the middle; the articles of furniture were few, but all bright and exquisitely clean; order reigned through its narrow limits — such order as it soothed my punctilious soul to behold. And I had hesitated to enter the abode, because I apprehended after all that Mdlle Reuter's hint about its extreme poverty might be too well founded, and I feared to embarrass the lace-mender by entering her lodgings unawares! Poor the place might be; poor truly it was; but its neatness was better than elegance, and had but a bright little fire shone on that clean hearth, I should have deemed it more attractive than a palace. No fire was there, however, and no fuel laid ready to light; the lace-mender was unable to allow herself that indulgence, especially now when, deprived by death of her sole relative, she had only her own unaided exertions to rely on. Frances went into an inner room to take off her bonnet, and she came out a model of frugal neatness, with her well-fitting black stuff dress, so accurately defining her elegant bust and taper waist, with her spotless white collar turned back from a fair and shapely neck, with her plenteous brown hair arranged in smooth bands on her temples, and in a large Grecian plait behind: ornaments she had none – neither brooch, ring, nor ribbon; she did well enough without them – perfection of fit, proportion of form, grace of carriage, agreeably supplied their place. Her eye, as she re-entered the small sitting-room, instantly sought mine, which was just then lingering on the hearth; I knew she read at once the sort of inward ruth and pitying pain which the chill vacancy of that hearth stirred in my soul: quick to penetrate, quick to determine, and quicker to put in practice, she had in a moment tied a holland apron round her waist; then she disappeared, and reappeared with a basket; it had a cover; she opened it, and produced wood and coal; deftly and compactly she arranged them in the grate.

"It is her whole stock, and she will exhaust it out of hospitality," thought I.

"What are you going to do?" I asked: "not surely to light a fire this hot evening? I shall be smothered."

"Indeed, Monsieur, I feel it very chilly since the rain began; besides, I must boil the water for my tea, for I take tea on Sundays; you will be obliged to try and bear the heat."'

Chapter 19

Later in the story Frances encounters a harsh view of England when Crimsworth's Yorkshire acquaintance, Hunsden, visits her:

Interior of an English labourer's cottage showing the poverty and simplicity of a cottager's home in the mid-19th century.

The Professor

'"You understand English?" was the prefatory question.

"A little."

"Well, then, you shall have plenty of it; and first, I see you've not much more sense than some others of my acquaintance" (indicating me with his thumb), "or else you'd never turn rabid about that dirty little country called England; for rabid, I see you are; I read Anglophobia in your looks, and hear it in your words. Why, Mademoiselle, is it possible, that anybody with a grain of rationality should feel enthusiasm about a mere name, and that name England? I thought you were a lady-abbess five minutes ago, and respected you accordingly; and now I see you are a sort of Swiss sibyl, with high Tory and high Church principles!"

"England is your country?" asked Frances.

"Yes."

"And you don't like it?"

"I'd be sorry to like it! A little corrupt, venal, lord-and-king-cursed nation, full of mucky pride (as they say in ——shire), and helpless pauperism; rotten with abuses, worm-eaten with prejudices!"

"You might say so of almost every state; there are abuses and prejudices everywhere, and I thought fewer in England than in other countries."

"Come to England and see. Come to Birmingham and Manchester; come to St Giles' in London, and get a practical notion of how our system works. Examine the footprints of our august aristocracy; see how they walk in blood, crushing hearts as they go. Just put your head in at English cottage doors; get a glimpse of Famine crouched torpid on black hearthstones; of Disease lying bare on beds without coverlets, of Infamy wantoning viciously with Ignorance, though indeed Luxury is her favourite paramour, and princely halls are dearer to her than thatched hovels – "

"I was not thinking of the wretchedness and vice in England; I was thinking of the good side – of what is elevated in your character as a nation."

"There is no good side – none at least of which you can have any knowledge; for you cannot appreciate the efforts of science: narrowness of education, and obscurity of position quite incapacitate you from understanding these points; and as to historical and poetical associations, I will not insult you, Mademoiselle, by supposing that you alluded to such humbug."'

Chapter 24

Charlotte's experience of the cottagers of her father's parish together with her life as governess lend weight to Hunsden's outburst.

The Professor, however, is no social document; in its exploration of the testing of a man's education and character it takes personal relationships as its theme rather than wider social issues. A turning point in the plot is when Edward's time at Eton serves him well.

On a school trip, Jean Baptiste Vandenhuten, a pupil, ventures into a rowing boat:

'It chanced that Jean was the first lad to step into the boat; he stumbled, rolled to one side, the boat revolted at his weight and capsized. Vandenhuten sank like lead, rose, sank again. My coat and waistcoat were off in an instant; I had not been brought up at Eton and boated and bathed and swam there ten long years for nothing; it was a natural and easy act for me to leap to the rescue. The lads and the boatmen yelled; they thought there would be two deaths by drowning instead of one; but as Jean rose the third time, I clutched him by one leg and the collar, and in three minutes more both he and I were safe landed. To speak heaven's truth, my merit in the action was small indeed, for I had run no risk, and subsequently did not even catch cold from the wetting: but when M. and Madame Vandenhuten, of whom Jean Baptiste was the sole hope, came to hear of the exploit, they seemed to think I had evinced a bravery and devotion which no thanks could sufficiently repay. Madame, in particular, was "certain I must have dearly loved their sweet son, or I would not thus have hazarded my own life to save his." Monsieur, an honest-looking, though phlegmatic man, said very little, but he would not suffer me to leave the room, till I had promised that in case I ever stood in need of help I would, by applying to him, give him a chance of discharging the obligation under which he affirmed I had laid him.'
Chapter 21

St John's College, Cambridge, where Rev. Patrick Brontë was enrolled as a sizar in 1802.

The spontaneous act leads in time to just the kind of help from Jean Baptiste's parents that Crimsworth needs. There is more of interest in this passage, however, in the light of *Jane Eyre*. The boy's name finds an echo in the naming of St John Rivers, Jane's cousin who wishes to marry her and take her off to be a missionary – a name which is perhaps partly derived from Charlotte's father's attending St John's College, Cambridge.

There are other links with *Jane Eyre* which suggest that Charlotte consciously used material and ideas from it in her later and more successful work. Frances Henri writes verses which Edward reads. The verses incorporated in the novel were written while Charlotte was at school in Brussels, and some of them find their way into *Jane Eyre*. It is interesting that Frances calls herself Jane in the poems, and that when Crimsworth first reads them, he idly makes marks in their margin, implying that he corrects them. Such was Charlotte's insight into teachers.

The Professor deals with Charlotte's experience of Brussels, her commitment to education, teaching and learning, and her deep desire for love and friendship. The path of Edward and Frances's love is gentle and romantic to the extent that some find it insipid. This is a mistake, for it is a pattern of kindness and shared happiness that borders, in its closing scenes of the flower-embraced cottage in Daisy Lane, on the picturesque idyll. The chapter announcing the birth of their son Victor exemplifies the Brontë sisters' natural curiosity about childbirth and motherhood, a subject easy to overlook in their works. There are babies and a simple enjoyment of infancy throughout their writing:

'But whether she read to me, or talked with me ... always at nine o'clock I was left – abandoned. She would extricate herself from my arms, quit my side, take her lamp, and be gone. Her mission was upstairs; I have followed her sometimes and watched her. First she opened the door of the dortoir (the pupils' chamber), noiselessly she glided up the long room between the two rows of white beds, surveyed all the sleepers; if any were wakeful, especially if any were sad, spoke to them and soothed them; stood some minutes to ascertain that all was safe and tranquil; trimmed the watch-light which burned in the apartment all night, then withdrew, closing the door behind her without sound. Thence she glided to our own chamber; it had a little cabinet within; this she sought; there, too, appeared a bed, but one, and that a very small one; her face (the night I followed and observed her) changed as she approached this tiny couch; from grave it warmed to earnest; she shaded with one hand the lamp she held in the other; she bent above the pillow and hung over a child asleep; its slumber (that evening at least, and usually, I believe) was sound and calm; no tear wet its dark eyelashes; no fever heated its round cheek; no ill dream discomposed its budding features. Frances gazed, she did not smile and yet the deepest delight filled, flushed her face; feeling, pleasurable, powerful, worked in her whole frame, which still was motionless. I saw, indeed, her heart heave, her lips were a little apart, her breathing grew somewhat hurried; the child smiled; then at last the mother smiled too, and said in low soliloquy, "God bless my little son!" She stooped closer over him, breathed the softest of kisses on his brow, covered his minute hand with hers, and at last started up and came away. I regained the parlour before her. Entering it two minutes later she said quietly as she put down her extinguished lamp:

"Victor rests well: he smiled in his sleep; he has your smile, Monsieur."

The said Victor was of course her own boy, born in the third year of our marriage . . .'
Chapter 25

The Brontë sisters' ability, and indeed need, to explore the experience of motherhood recurs in their juvenile writing and adult works. Even as a governess, Charlotte, who is so often thought to have disliked children, could admit:

'by dint of nursing the fat baby it has got to know me and be fond of me – occasionally I suspect myself of growing rather fond of it – but this suspicion clears away the moment its mamma takes it and makes a fool of it – from a bonny, rosy little morsel it sinks in my estimation into a small, petted nuisance.'
Charlotte Brontë to Ellen Nussey, 4 May 1841

The desire to marry and the hope for children are often expressed in the Brontë sisters' writing. There is an added sense of loss when we recall that Charlotte was to die in the sixth month of pregnancy after less than a year of married life.

Only after that double tragedy was *The Professor* to be taken from the dark cupboard where Charlotte had placed it to appear in print alongside *Jane Eyre* and *Villette*, both of which owe much to this earlier work.

Towards the end of the novel, Charlotte had Mlle Reuter speak Robert Southey's warning to Charlotte that literature could never be the right pursuit for a woman:

'"I think, Monsieur – it appears to me that ambition, *literary* ambition especially, is not a feeling to be cherished in the mind of a woman: would not Mdlle Henri be much safer and happier if taught to believe that in the quiet discharge of social duties consists her real vocation, than if stimulated to aspire after applause and publicity? She may never marry; scanty as are her resources, obscure as are her connections, uncertain as is her health (for I think her consumptive, her mother died of that complaint), it is more than probable she never will; I do not see how she can rise to a position, whence such a step would be possible; but even in celibacy it would be better for her to retain the character and habits of a respectable decorous female."'
Chapter 18

Charlotte seemed determined to prove Southey wrong and seldom missed the opportunity of holding his advice up for her own and the world's scrutiny. Perhaps the challenge thrown to her by the Poet Laureate did more for the cause of literature than could have been achieved had Southey written urging Charlotte to forsake her puddings and sewing and take up the pen of a poet and novelist.

Photograph of the Pensionnat Heger in Brussels, where Charlotte and Emily were pupils and where Charlotte later taught.

IX

PRELUDE TO SHIRLEY

In 1845 Emily and Charlotte were both at home caring for their father. Anne joined them on relinquishing her post as governess with the Robinson family at Thorp Green, a month before Branwell was dismissed in disgrace from his position there as tutor. His return to Haworth reassembled the family for the first time in several years; but because of his behaviour, his increasing reliance on drink and laudanum, and his morbid self-pity, the former feeling of deep affection between brother and sisters was seldom present.

Anne Brontë spoke little of her experiences at Thorp Green, save that she had been exposed to deep humiliation and shame. Branwell, characteristically, had a highly implausible explanation for his departure, flattering to himself and detrimental to those who had injured him. He declared that he was in love with Lydia Robinson, that she loved him and that on the death of her invalid husband, they were to be wed. Mrs Robinson was many years Branwell's senior, and history, through the version given to the world by Elizabeth Gaskell, has made her the villain of the piece. It is hard to know the truth. In the event, after Mr Robinson's death Lydia Robinson forbade Branwell to visit her and subsequently remarried.

Branwell's dismissal from his post was merely the last in a sequence of such fiascos. Whenever he left Haworth — to apply for admission at the Royal Academy, to become tutor, to be a railway clerk or to take up portrait painting in Bradford — the outcome was always the same. The high hopes would founder and he would return home usually in debt and armed with fanciful but lame excuses.

So while the girls were industriously writing and sending manuscripts to publishers, they were also nursing and caring for their troublesome brother. Although Charlotte sometimes despaired, regarding him as a hopeless being, she and the others would usually rally to support and help him. Anne transposed such episodes into her powerful condemnation of drunkenness in *The Tenant of Wildfell Hall*, which skilfully anatomized the effects of intemperance in terms far from melodramatic. Emily, we are told, kept watch late at night, leaving bolts drawn and a lamp lighting the way to the parsonage from the Black Bull Inn.

Opposite George Richmond's portrait of Charlotte Brontë, a present given to her by her publisher George Smith, 1850.

Prelude to Shirley

Branwell's death at 31 seems to have surprised the family, none of them realizing how ill he had become:

'The event . . . came upon us with startling suddenness and was a severe shock to us all. My poor brother has long had a shaked constitution, and during the summer his appetite had been diminished, and he had seemed weaker, but neither we, not himself, nor any medical man who was consulted on his case, thought it one of immediate danger: he was out of doors two days before his death, and was only confined to bed one single day.'
Charlotte Brontë to Ann Nussey, 14 October 1848

Patrick Branwell Brontë.

Writing to Mr Williams in London, Charlotte adopts a harsher tone:

'We have buried our dead out of sight. A lull begins to succeed the gloomy tumult of last week. It is not permitted us to grieve for him who has gone as others grieve for those they lose. The removal of our only brother must necessarily be regarded by us rather in the light of a mercy than a chastisement. Branwell was his father's and his sisters' pride and hope in boyhood, but since manhood the case has been otherwise. It has been our lot to see him take a wrong bent; to hope, expect, wait his return to the right path; to know the sickness of hope deferred, the dismay of prayer baffled; to despair at last – and now to behold the sudden early obscure close of what might have been a noble career.'
Charlotte Brontë to W.S. Williams, 2 October 1848

Understandably, Charlotte found herself unable to continue with her writing:

'My book, alas! is laid aside for the present; both head and hand seem to have lost their cunning: imagination is pale, stagnant, mute.'
Charlotte Brontë to W.S. Williams, 18 October 1848

By the middle of November Emily too had fallen ill and was visibly weakening. It was soon clear to Charlotte that the situation was desperate. The entire family were stunned by what was happening:

'The details of her illness are deep-branded in my memory, but to dwell on them, either in thought or narrative, is not in my power. Never in all her life had she lingered over any task that lay before her, and she did not linger now. She sank rapidly. She made haste to leave us. Yet, while physically she perished, mentally, she grew stronger than we had yet known her. Day by day, when I saw with what a front she met suffering, I looked on her with an anguish of wonder and love. I have seen nothing like it; but, indeed, I have never seen her parallel in anything. Stronger than a man, simpler than a child, her nature stood alone. The awful point was, that, while full of ruth for others, on herself she had no pity; the spirit was inexorable to the flesh; from the trembling hand, the unnerved limbs, the faded eyes, the same service was exacted as they had rendered in health. To stand by and witness this, and not dare to remonstrate, was a pain no words can render.

   Two cruel months of hope and fear passed painfully by, and the day came at last when the terrors and pains of death were to be undergone by this treasure, which had grown dearer and dearer to our hearts as it wasted before our eyes. Towards the decline of that day, we had nothing left of Emily but her mortal remains as consumption left them. She died December 19, 1848.'
Charlotte Brontë. Biographical Notice to 1850 edition of Wuthering Heights.

   Emily had steadfastly refused to see any doctor until she was beyond help. Once again it was to Williams in London that Charlotte wrote of her sadness:

'Emily is nowhere here now — her wasted mortal remains are taken out of the house; we have laid her cherished head under the church-aisle beside my mother's, my two sisters', dead long ago, and my poor, hapless brother's. But a small remnant of the race is left — so my poor father thinks . . . some sad comfort I take, as I hear the wind blow and feel the cutting keenness of the frost, in knowing that the elements bring her no more suffering — their severity cannot reach her grave — her fever is quieted, her restlessness soothed, her deep, hollow cough is hushed for ever; we do not hear it in the night nor listen for it in the morning . . .'
Charlotte Brontë to W.S. Williams, 23 December 1848

   But even as Charlotte and her father made their way home from Emily's funeral, they realized that Anne, too, was now ill:

'She was not buried ere Anne fell ill. She had not been committed to the grave a fortnight, before we received distinct intimation that it was necessary to prepare our minds to see the younger sister go after the elder. Accordingly, she followed in the same path with slower steps, and with a patience that equalled the other's fortitude. I have said that she was religious, and it was by leaning on those Christian doctrines in which she firmly believed, that she found support through her most painful journey. I witnessed their efficacy in her latest hour and greatest trial, and must bear my testimony to the calm triumph with which they brought her through.'
Charlotte Brontë. Biographical Notice

   Charlotte began to think that Currer Bell would never write another word.
   Unlike Emily, Anne had sought all possible medical help once she realized how ill she was. This included seeking the advice of Thomas Teale of Leeds, a founder of the Leeds School of Medicine:

'Mr Teale said it was a case of tubercular consumption, with congestion of the lungs — yet he intimated that the malady had not yet reached so advanced a stage as to cut off all hope; he held out a prospect that a truce

Prelude to Shirley

and even an arrest of disease might yet be procured.'
Charlotte Brontë to George Smith, 22 January 1849

As her illness developed, Teale's optimism proving ill-founded, Anne craved more and more for Scarborough. She wanted to be near the sea and back where she had enjoyed summers and visits with the Robinson family. Her father was in a quandary. It was doubtful whether Anne would survive a journey. With a profound generosity of spirit, he let Anne have her wish. As soon as Mr Teale agreed to the experiment and the chill of winter gave way to the promise of spring, Charlotte enlisted Ellen Nussey's help and arranged lodgings in Scarborough.

Informing Williams of the plan, she also told him how impossible it was for her to work on her novel:

'I try to write now and then. The effort was a hard one at first. It renewed the terrible loss of last December strangely. Worse than useless did it seem to attempt to write what there no longer lived an "Ellis Bell" to read; the whole book, with every hope founded on it, faded to vanity and vexation of spirit.'
Charlotte Brontë to W.S. Williams, 16 April 1849

Charlotte even found it hard to find time to read. She had to point out that Mr Currer Bell now knew the real disadvantages of his sex. Charlotte lent a little dubious veracity to Southey's warning that literature could never be a suitable occupation for women:

'You will perhaps think I am a slow reader, but remember, Currer Bell is a country housewife, and has sundry little matters connected with the needle and kitchen to attend to which take up half his day, especially now, when alas! there is but one pair of hands where once there were three.'
Charlotte Brontë to W.S. Williams, 16 April 1849

There may be more truth in Charlotte's gentle humour than is at first apparent. Had Charlotte been an only child, she might well have had no time to read or write. By dividing up the household chores, the three sisters made room for more fulfilling creative activities. Between the lines of Charlotte's letter it is easy to read the loneliness and vulnerability of the sister who was more concerned to be a good nurse to Anne than a best-selling author.

The trip to Scarborough would involve some kind of horse-drawn vehicle from Haworth to Keighley (there was no coach), a train from Keighley to Leeds, another from Leeds to York and a third from York to Scarborough. Making final arrangements with Ellen Nussey, Charlotte warned her friend not to be shocked at the invalid's wasted appearance:

'It is with a heavy heart I prepare – and earnestly do I wish the fatigue of the journey were well over – it may be borne better than I expect – but

Pencil drawing of Anne Brontë by Charlotte Brontë, evidently a drawing exercise for her drawing-master.

when I see the daily increasing weakness – I know not what to think.

I fear you will be shocked when you see Anne – but be on your guard not to express your feelings – indeed I can trust both your self-possession and your kindness.'
Charlotte Brontë to Ellen Nussey, 16 May 1849

The sad trio made their farewells at Haworth, and it must have been obvious to Patrick Brontë and the servants Tabby and Martha that they were saying their last goodbye to Anne.

Charlotte's account book for the journey survives as an eloquent but sad chronicle of some details of the expedition.

The trip to Scarborough, the last that Anne Brontë ever made, was emblematic of her constant striving for individual dignity and strength. Scarborough was the setting for the close of her first novel, a story that ended hopefully in an atmosphere of serenity and peace. Like her heroine Agnes, Anne journeyed to Scarborough tranquil and undismayed, taking whatever comfort and pleasure she could from memories of her stronger days. A night stop was made at York, allowing her to visit York Minster, which always thrilled her. Arriving at Scarborough, she and her companions were lodged close to the apartments she had known with the Robinson girls, overlooking the sweeping bay where Agnes Grey had found her husband, her best earthly companion. Anne was content:

'Our lodgings are pleasant. As Anne sits at the window she can look down at the sea, which this morning is calm as glass. She says if she could breathe more freely she would be comfortable at this moment – but she cannot breathe freely.'
Charlotte Brontë to W.S. Williams, 27 May 1849

North-west view of York Minster, circa 1840.

Prelude to Shirley

Anne Brontë died peacefully on Monday 28 May, 29 years old, near the sea, the ruined castle and the old church which she loved so fondly. Charlotte arranged for her to be buried in the churchyard high on a cliff where, much visited, the grave overlooks the bay and the old town of Scarborough.

Patrick Brontë warned Charlotte not to return home until she felt strong enough to endure the bitterness of her new solitude. She took his advice. From nearby Filey she wrote once more to Williams:

'A year ago – had a prophet warned me how I should stand in June 1849 – how stripped and bereaved – had he foretold the autumn, the winter, the spring of suffering to be gone through – I should have thought – this can never be endured. It is over. Branwell – Emily – Anne – are gone like dreams – gone as Maria and Elizabeth went twenty years ago. One by one I have watched them fall asleep on my arm – and closed their glazed eyes – I have seen them buried one by one . . .'
Charlotte Brontë to W.S. Williams, 13 June 1849

23 June 1849

'Dear Ellen,
. . . I got home a little before eight o'clock. All was clean and bright waiting for me – Papa and the servants were well – and all received me with an affection which should have consoled. The dogs seemed in a strange ecstasy. I am certain they regarded me as the harbinger of others – the dumb creatures thought that as I was returned – those who had been so long absent were not far behind.

I left Papa soon and went into the dining room – I shut the door – I tried to be glad that I was come home – I have always been glad before – except once – even then I was cheered, but this time joy was not to be the sensation. I felt that the house was all silent – the rooms were all empty – I remembered where the three were laid – in what narrow dark dwellings . . .

. . . I do not know how life will pass . . .

. . . Solitude may be cheeered and made endurable beyond what I can believe. The great trial is when evening closes and night approaches – At that hour we used to assemble in the dining room – we used to talk – Now I sit by myself – necessarily I am silent – I cannot help thinking of their last days – remembering their sufferings and what they said and did and how they looked in mortal affliction – perhaps this will become less poignant in time.'
Charlotte Brontë to Ellen Nussey

Somehow in her solitude Charlotte found the courage to return to her manuscript even before she knew how she was going to manage without the companionship of her sisters. By the end of August the same year; the book was finished, for we find Charlotte discussing possible titles.

The suggestions for titles (there appear to have been at least three possibilities) indicate the disparate elements of the work. The first, 'Hollows Mill', clearly places the emphasis on the industrial unrest of the first decades of the century; the second, 'Fieldhead', would suggest that the book was about the families and occupants of various houses; the third, 'Shirley', lends weight to the argument that the central female character was a portrait of Emily, had she been strong and wealthy, making the story of Shirley Keeldar the central theme of the work. The choice was left to the publisher, Charlotte subsequently agreeing to 'Shirley', 'without any explanation or addition'.

On 29 August Charlotte bade the manuscript 'good riddance', claiming that whatever its value in the world, 'the occupation of writing it has been a boon to me. It took me out of dark and desolate reality into an unreal but happier region'. Now it would be dealt with by her publisher.

That Charlotte was able to complete the work at all is seen by many as remarkable. Not only had her personal circumstances altered completely, but for the first time in her life she was adrift in the loneliness of a world devoid of the sustaining talk and sharing of ideas that the Brontë children had always held so dear.

Between starting to write the novel in 1847 and completing it in 1849, Charlotte's life had undergone sudden and tragic changes. The story of her own sufferings during those years quite overshadows anything she ever wrote or imagined. In less than twelve months she and her father found themselves sole survivors of the original family of eight. A letter from a time much earlier in her life sums up the depth of her loss:

'My home is humble and unattractive to strangers, but to me it contains what I shall find nowhere else in the world – the profound, and intense affection which brothers and sisters feel for each other when their minds are cast in the same mould, their ideas drawn from the same source – when they have clung to each other from childhood, and when disputes have never sprung up to divide them.'
Charlotte Brontë to Henry Nussey, 9 May 1841

That special relationship had now vanished. The Currer Bell who completed *Shirley* now stood alone.

Copy by Patrick Branwell Brontë of a vignette by Thomas Bewick.

X

SHIRLEY

*'Out of obscurity I came, to obscurity I can easily return
Standing afar off, I now watch to see what will become of* Shirley.'
Charlotte Brontë to G.H. Lewes, 1 November 1849

Shirley was a deliberate attempt by Charlotte Brontë to broaden her canvas. Convinced that her sheltered existence severely limited the experiences she could draw upon for her writing, she designed the book to be quite different from *Jane Eyre*. It is her one attempt at an historical novel.

She did not have to look far for a subject. In 1812, the year of her mother and father's wedding, there had been considerable unrest in the manufacturing districts. Riots in Yorkshire culminated in an attack by Luddites on Rawfolds Mill near Dewsbury. Croppers fearing for their livelihoods had smashed frames that were being introduced into mills as part of a process of industrial change. During the rioting a man was murdered and the ringleaders subsequently caught, tried and hung in a trial that was notorious for its harsh sentence. At that time Patrick Brontë was in charge of the parish of St Peter's-cum-Clifton at Hartshead, not far from the mill, and it was rumoured that some of the rioters who died from wounds during the attack were secretly buried in his churchyard. Certainly Patrick Brontë knew much of what happened and with his own peasant background may well have had considerable sympathy with the weavers and mill-workers.

To augment her father's tale Charlotte sent to Leeds for copies of the newspapers of the time, the *Leeds Intelligencer* and the *Leeds Mercury*.

The troubles at Rawfolds Mill thus became one thread of the tale:

'The period of which I write was an overshadowed one in British history, and especially in the history of the northern provinces. War was then at its height. Europe was all involved therein. England, if not weary, was worn with long resistance: yes, and half her people were weary too, and cried out for peace on any terms. National honour was become a mere empty name, of no value in the eyes of many, because their sight was dim with famine; and for a morsel of meat they would have sold their birthright.

Opposite Factory children taken from George Walker's *The Costumes of Yorkshire*.

175

Shirley

The "Orders in Council", provoked by Napoleon's Milan and Berlin decrees, and forbidding neutral powers to trade with France, had, by offending America, cut off the principal market of the Yorkshire woollen trade, and brought it consequently to the verge of ruin. Minor foreign markets were glutted, and would receive no more: the Brazils, Portugal, Sicily, were all overstocked by nearly two years' consumption. At this crisis, certain inventions in machinery were introduced into the staple manufactures of the north, which, greatly reducing the number of hands necessary to be employed, threw thousands out of work, and left them without legitimate means of sustaining life. A bad harvest supervened. Distress reached its climax. Endurance, overgoaded, stretched the hand of fraternity to sedition. The throes of a sort of moral earthquake were felt heaving under the hills of the northern counties. But, as is usual in such cases, nobody took much notice. When a food-riot broke out in a manufacturing town, when a gig-mill was burnt to the ground, or a manufacturer's house was attacked, the furniture thrown into the streets, and the family forced to flee for their lives, some local measures were or were not taken by the local magistracy; a ringleader was detected, or more frequently suffered to elude detection; newspaper paragraphs were written on the subject, and there the thing stopped. As to the sufferers, whose sole inheritance was labour, and who had lost that inheritance – who could not get work, and consequently could not get wages, and consequently could not get bread – they were left to suffer on; perhaps inevitably left: it would not do to stop the progress of invention, to damage science by discouraging its improvements; the war could not be terminated, efficient relief could not be raised: there was no help then; so the unemployed underwent their destiny – ate the bread and drank the waters of affliction.'
Chapter 2

Drawing by Wimperis of Briarfield Church from an earlier edition of *Shirley*.

From the general historical background Charlotte swiftly brought the conflict to Yorkshire:

'Misery generates hate: these sufferers hated the machines which they believed took their bread from them; they hated the buildings which contained those machines; they hated the manufacturers who owned those buildings. In the parish of Briarfield, with which we have at present to do, Hollow's-Mill was the place held most abominable; Gérard Moore, in his double character of semi-foreigner and thorough-going progressist, the man most abominated. And it perhaps rather agreed with Moore's temperament than otherwise to be generally hated; especially when he believed the thing for which he was hated a right and an expedient thing; and it was with a sense of warlike excitement he, on this night, sat in his counting-house waiting the arrival of his frame-laden waggons.'
Chapter 2

Charlotte had been at school in the Calder Valley where the attack on the frames and mill had taken place and knew the landscape well. She also had school friends who belonged to mill-owning families.

Curates provide much of the comedy in *Shirley*, and were also, at the time of publication, the cause of much controversy. Charlotte was fearless in her portrayal of a particular kind of clergy who cared more for their own wellbeing, convivial living and flirting than they did for theology, and who cared little for the poor souls in their care. She insisted that they were 'real' and refused to expunge them from the tale when her publishers warned of the prejudice they would arouse. Curates provide the opening paragraphs of the book:

'Of late years, an abundant shower of curates has fallen upon the north of England: they lie very thick on the hills ... A certain favoured district in the West Riding of Yorkshire could boast three rods of Aaron blossoming within a circuit of twenty miles. You shall see them, reader. Step into this neat garden-house on the skirts of Whinbury, walk forward into the little parlour – there they are at dinner. Allow me to introduce them to you: Mr Donne, curate of Whinbury; Mr Malone, curate of Briarfield; Mr Sweeting, curate of Nunnely. These are Mr Donne's lodgings, being the habitation of one John Gale, a small clothier. Mr Donne has kindly invited his brethren to regale with him. You and I will join the party, see what is to be seen, and hear what is to be heard. At present, however, they are only eating; and while they eat we will talk aside.

The gentlemen are in the bloom of youth; they possess all the activity of that interesting age – an activity which their moping old vicars would fain turn into the channel of their pastoral duties, often expressing a wish to see it expended in a diligent superintendence of the schools, and in frequent visits to the sick of their respective parishes. But the youthful Levites feel this to be dull work; they prefer lavishing their energies on a course of proceeding, which, though to other eyes it appear more heavy with ennui, more cursed with monotony, than the toil of the

Rawfolds Mill, the original for Hollow's Mill in *Shirley*, from a drawing by Wimperis in an early illustrated edition of the novel.

Shirley

weaver at his loom, seems to yield them an unfailing supply of enjoyment and occupation.

I allude to a rushing backwards and forwards, amongst themselves, to and from their respective lodgings: not a round – but a triangle of visits, which they keep up all the year through, in winter, spring, summer, and autumn. Season and weather make no difference; with unintelligible zeal they dare snow and hail, wind and rain, mire and dust, to go and dine, or drink tea, or sup with each other.'
Chapter 1

Just as Hollows Mill had its counterpart in life, so too did each of the curates. Mr Donne was drawn from her father's curate, Joseph Brett Grant, who was to become the first vicar of Oxenhope Church when, in 1845, it was built in a corner of Haworth parish. He, like the character in the book, was a great raiser of funds for the church. Mr Malone was based on J.W. Smith, a curate at Haworth from 1842–4 who became a subject of censure for taking an interest in Charlotte's friend Ellen Nussey because of her prospects as an heiress. In the novel he carries pistols and a shillelagh, a detail which, along with his Irish accent, Charlotte took from her father. It was her father's custom to carry a small loaded pistol at the time of the rioting near Dewsbury. Mr Sweeting derives from J.C. Bradley who was curate at Oakworth, a neighbouring parish. A fourth curate, kindly if rather sombrely depicted in *Shirley*, was Mr McCarthey, a mild man only roused to anger over dissenters; he was a sketch of Arthur Bell Nicholls, whom Charlotte eventually married in June 1854, still confessing that she found him well-intentioned but a little solemn.

The discovery that the new machinery for Moore's mill has been smashed is the prelude to later rioting:

Canon Roberson upon whom it is thought Charlotte Brontë based her character Helstone, the anti-Luddite rector in *Shirley*.

St Peter's Hartshead, Rev. Patrick Brontë's first living as priest in charge, a parish that was the setting of much disturbance during the Luddite and Chartist unrest.

'The night was still, dark, and stagnant: the water yet rushed on full and fast: its flow almost seemed a flood in the utter silence. Moore's ear, however, caught another sound – very distant, but yet dissimilar – broken and rugged: in short, a sound of heavy wheels crunching a stony road. He returned to the counting-house and lit a lantern, with which he walked down the mill-yard, and proceeded to open the gates. The big waggons were coming on; the dray-horses' huge hoofs were heard splashing in the mud and water. Moore hailed them.

"Hey, Joe Scott! Is all right?"

Probably Joe Scott was yet at too great a distance to hear the inquiry; he did not answer it.

"Is all right, I say?" again asked Moore when the elephant-like leader's nose almost touched his.

Some one jumped out from the foremost waggon into the road; a voice cried aloud, "Ay, ay, divil, all's raight! We've smashed 'em."

And there was a run. The waggons stood still: they were now deserted.

"Joe Scott!" No Joe Scott answered. "Murgatroyd! Pighills! Sykes!" No reply. Mr Moore lifted his lantern, and looked into the vehicles; there was neither man nor machinery: they were empty and abandoned.

Now Mr Moore loved his machinery: he had risked the last of his capital on the purchase of these frames and shears which to-night had been expected; speculations most important to his interests depended on the results to be wrought by them: where were they?

The words "we've smashed 'em!" rung in his ears.'
Chapter 2

As the mill-owner and friends set out in the night to find Joe Scott, they meet others, including the rector, Mr Helstone. It is agreed that he will write a suitable article to appear in the local newspaper, *The Stilbro' Courier*:

'"We're eleven strong men, and there's both horses and chariots amang us. If we could only fall in wi' some of these starved ragamuffins of frame-breakers, we could win a grand victory; we could iv'ry one be a Wellington – that would please ye, Mr Helstone; and sich paragraphs as we could contrive for t' papers! Briarfield suld be famous: but we'se hev a column and a half i' th' *Stilbro' Courier* ower this job, as it is, I daresay: I'se expect no less."

"And I'll promise you no less, Mr Yorke, for I'll write the article myself," returned the Rector.

"To be sure! sartainly! And mind ye recommend weel that them 'at brake t' bits o' frames, and teed Joe Scott's legs wi' band, suld be hung without benefit o' clergy. It's a hanging matter, or suld be; no doubt o' that."

"If I judged them, I'd give them short shrift!" cried Moore; "but I mean to let them quite alone this bout, to give them rope enough, certain that in the end they will hang themselves."

Shirley

"Let them alone, will ye, Moore? Do you promise that?"

"Promise? No. All I mean to say is, I shall give myself no particular trouble to catch them; but if one falls in my way" –

"You'll snap him up, of course: only you would rather they would do something worse than merely stop a waggon before you reckon with them. Well, we'll say no more on the subject at present. Here we are at my door, gentlemen, and I hope you and the men will step in: you will none of you be the worse of a little refreshment."'
Chapter 3

Patrick Brontë was in the habit of writing for newspapers on remarkable happenings in his parish, and Charlotte read all her father's articles. Encouraged by him, she was an avid reader of newspapers, and the question of their suitability for women is discussed later in the novel. Caroline Helstone and Shirley Keeldar are outside the church when Joe Scott, one of Miss Keeldar's mill-hands, comes out:

'"Young ladies," continued Joe, assuming a lordly air, "ye'd better go into th' house."

"I wonder what for?" inquired Shirley, to whom the overlooker's somewhat pragmatical manners were familiar, and who was often at war with him; for Joe, holding supercilious theories about women in general, resented greatly, in his secret soul, the fact of his master and his master's mill being, in a manner, under petticoat government, and had felt as wormwood and gall certain business-visits of the heiress to the Hollow's counting-house.

"Because there is naught agate that fits women to be consarned in."

"Indeed! There is prayer and preaching agate in that church: are we not concerned in that?"

"Ye have been present neither at the prayer nor preaching, ma'am, if I have observed aright. What I alluded to was politics: William Farren, here, was touching on that subject, if I'm not mista'en."

"Well, what then? Politics are our habitual study, Joe. Do you know I see a newspaper every day, and two of a Sunday?"

"I should think you'll read the marriages, probably, Miss, and the murders, and the accidents, and sich like?"

"I read the leading articles, Joe, and the foreign intelligence, and I look over the market prices: in short, I read just what gentlemen read."

Joe looked as if he thought this talk was like the chattering of a pie. He replied to it by a disdainful silence.

"Joe," continued Miss Keeldar, "I never yet could ascertain properly whether you are a Whig or a Tory: pray which party has the honour of your alliance?"

"It is rayther difficult to explain where you are sure not to be understood," was Joe's haughty response; "but, as to being a Tory, I'd as soon be an old woman, or a young one, which is a more flimsier article still. It is the Tories that carries on the war and ruins trade; and, if I be of any party – though political parties is all nonsense – I'm of that which is most favourable to peace, and, by consequence, to the mercantile interests of this here land."

"So am I, Joe," replied Shirley, who had rather a pleasure in teasing the overlooker, by persisting in talking on subjects with which he opined she – as a woman – had no right to meddle: "partly, at least. I have rather a leaning to the agricultural interest, too; as good reason is, seeing that I don't desire England to be under the feet of France, and that if a share of my income comes from Hollow's Mill, a larger share comes from the landed estate around it. It would not do to take any measure injurious to the farmers, Joe, I think?"

"The dews at this hour is unwholesome for females," observed Joe.'
Chapter 18

Shirley Keeldar teases her overlooker for his masculine prejudice. If equality for rich and poor is a principal theme in *Shirley*, so is equality for women. Politics and economics are of interest to everyone, and Charlotte will not agree that women should only read the 'marriages, murders and such like.' She clearly did not believe that 'all the wisdom in the world is lodged in male skulls'.

Charlotte, in fact, goes one step further. The debate with Joe Scott about newspaper reading occurs in a novel written by a woman, and that novel was partly created from newspaper articles. A pleasant irony is at work. Men are being put in their place. Even John Milton does not escape, for a little earlier in the same episode his description of 'Eve before the Fall of Man' is pilloried:

'The grey church and greyer tombs look divine with this crimson gleam on them. Nature is now at her evening prayers: she is kneeling before those red hills. I see her prostrate on the great steps of her altar, praying for a fair night for mariners at sea, for travellers in deserts, for lambs on moors, and unfledged birds in woods. Caroline, I see her! and I will tell you what she is like: she is like what Eve was when she and Adam stood alone on earth."

"And that is not Milton's Eve, Shirley."

"Milton's Eve! Milton's Eve! I repeat. No, by the pure Mother of God, she is not! Cary, we are alone: we may speak what we think. Milton was great; but was he good? His brain was right; how was his heart? He saw heaven: he looked down on hell. He saw Satan, and Sin his daughter, and Death their horrible offspring. Angels serried before him their battalions: the long lines of adamantine shields flashed back on his blind eyeballs the unutterable splendour of heaven. Devils gathered their legions in his sight: their dim, discrowned, and tarnished armies passed rank and file before him. Milton tried to see the first woman; but, Cary, he saw her not."

"You are bold to say so, Shirley."

"Not more bold than faithful. It was his cook that he saw; or it was Mrs Gill, as I have seen her, making custards, in the heat of summer, in the cool dairy, with rose-trees and nasturtiums about the latticed window, preparing a cold collation for the rectors, – preserves, and 'dulcet creams' – puzzled 'what choice to choose for delicacy best; what

Shirley

order so contrived as not to mix tastes, not well-joined, inelegant; but
bring taste after taste, upheld with kindliest change. "'
Chapter 18

Charlotte suggests that Milton envisaged Eve as a housewife, denying
her a true partnership with Adam. Even in Eden he saw woman's role as
that of provider and cook. Charlotte is indignant at the poet's failure to
see women clearly. It was all too reminiscent of Southey.

G.H. Lewes, in congratulating Currer Bell for the success of *Jane
Eyre*, had warned 'him' to beware of too much melodrama in his next
book. Charlotte heeded his advice, reading Jane Austen as he recommended, and promising that though her store of materials was small she
would try to enlarge the scope of her writing. Clearly *Shirley* does
represent a widening of focus, a broadening of issues.

Yet Charlotte did not eliminate all private matters from this her most
public book. In the creation of her two young women, Caroline and
Shirley, she seems to have celebrated, or perhaps explored, her feelings
about her dead sisters. There is a curious wish-fulfilment in her
treatment of illness and the reunion of a daughter with a long-lost
mother. Caroline's illness in Chapter 25 is clearly an account of Anne's
last illness, with the tragic conclusion transformed into a happy ending.
Charlotte, who could scarcely remember her own mother, writes
movingly of an ideal reunion and the steady progress out of sickness into
health which, in real life, her sisters never experienced. In the novel,

John Martin's painting *The
Great Day of His Wrath*. Martin
was a great favourite with the
Brontës , his dramatic landscapes
matching their passionate and
dramatic tales.

Mrs Prior nurses Caroline, the daughter with whom she has been reunited:

'Caroline's youth could now be of some avail to her, and so could her mother's nurture: both – crowned by God's blessing, sent in the pure west wind blowing soft as fresh through the ever-open chamber lattice – rekindled her long-languishing energies. At last Mrs Pryor saw that it was permitted to hope – a genuine, material convalescence had commenced. It was not merely Caroline's smile which was brighter, or her spirits which were cheered, but a certain look had passed from her face and eye – a look dread and indescribable, but which will easily be recalled by those who have watched the couch of dangerous disease. Long before the emaciated outlines of her aspect began to fill, or its departed colour to return, a more subtle change took place: all grew softer and warmer. Instead of a marble mask and glassy eye, Mrs Pryor saw laid on the pillow a face pale and wasted enough, perhaps more haggard than the other appearance, but less awful; for it was a sick, living girl – not a mere white mould, or rigid piece of statuary.

Now, too, she was not always petitioning to drink. The words "I am *so* thirsty" ceased to be her plaint. Sometimes, when she had swallowed a morsel, she would say it had revived her: all descriptions of food were no longer equally distasteful; she could be induced, sometimes, to indicate a preference. With what trembling pleasure and anxious care did not her nurse prepare what was selected! How she watched her as she partook of it!

Nourishment brought strength. She could sit up. Then she longed to breathe the fresh air, to revisit her flowers, to see how the fruit had ripened. Her uncle, always liberal, had bought a garden-chair for her express use: he carried her down in his own arms, and placed her in it himself, and William Farren was there to wheel her round the walks, to show her what he had done amongst her plants, to take her directions for further work.
Chapter 25

The 'emaciated outlines', the 'marble mask and glassy eye' were the very changes that Charlotte noticed in Anne during her last fatal illness.

Perhaps to a greater extent than any of the other Brontë novels, *Shirley* embodies the landscape its author knew and is peopled by her family and friends. Almost every aspect or quality of life in Haworth Parsonage is present at one point or another in the narrative. Discussion of church matters ranges from high church theology to congregational hymn singing and the purposes of pastoral visiting. There is political debate and concern for the divisions of rich and poor. The conversations of the characters are informed both by love of nature and by book learning, robust Yorkshire accents vying with cultured educated tones. In seeking to broaden her view, Charlotte manages to display the richness of her interests and demonstrates the wealth of learning and understanding contained within the walls of the small old parsonage. Above all, the folk in the novel are from real life, inhabiting houses and walking paths that can still be visited and explored today. Take, for example, the two principal houses of the novel – Briarmains and Fieldhead:

'Spring evenings are often cold and raw, and though this had been a fine day, warm even in the morning and meridian sunshine, the air chilled at sunset, the ground crisped, and ere dusk a hoar frost was insidiously stealing over growing grass and unfolding bud. It whitened the pavement in front of Briarmains (Mr Yorke's residence), and made silent havoc among the tender plants in his garden, and on the mossy level of his lawn. As to that great tree, strong-trunked and broad-armed, which guarded the gable nearest the road, it seemed to defy a spring-night frost to harm its still bare boughs; and so did the leafless grove of walnut-trees rising tall behind the house.

In the dusk of the moonless if starry night, lights from windows shone vividly: this was no dark or lonely scene, nor even a silent one. Briarmains stood near the highway; it was rather an old place, and had been built ere that highway was cut, and when a lane winding up through fields was the only path conducting to it. Briarfield lay scarce a mile off; its hum was heard, its glare distinctly seen. Briar-chapel, a large, new, raw, Wesleyan place of worship, rose but a hundred yards distant; and, as there was even now a prayer-meeting being held within its walls, the illumination of its windows cast a bright reflection on the road, while a hymn of a most extraordinary description, such as a very Quaker might feel himself moved by the spirit to dance to, roused cheerily all the echoes of the vicinage. The words were distinctly audible by snatches: here is a quotation or two from different strains; for the singers passed jauntily from hymn to hymn and from tune to tune, with an ease and buoyancy all their own.

> "Oh! who can explain
>   This struggle for life,
> This travail and pain,
>   This trembling and strife?
> Plague, earthquake, and famine,
>   And tumult and war,
> The wonderful coming
>   Of Jesus declare!"

(Terrible, most distracting to the ear was the strained shout in which the last stanza was given).

> "Here we raise our voices higher,
>   Shout in the refiner's fire;
> Clap our hands amidst the flame,
>   Glory give to Jesus' name!"

The roof of the chapel did *not* fly off; which speaks volumes in praise of its solid slating.

But if Briar-chapel seemed alive, so also did Briarmains: though certainly the mansion appeared to enjoy a quieter phase of existence than the temple; some of its windows too were a-glow: the lower casements opened upon the lawn, curtains concealed the interior, and partly obscured the ray of the candles which lit it, but they did not entirely muffle the sound of voice and laughter. We are privileged to enter that front-door, and to penetrate to the domestic sanctum.

It is not the presence of company which makes Mr Yorke's habitation lively, for there is none within it save his own family, and they are assembled in that farthest room to the right, the back-parlour.

This is the usual sitting-room of an evening. Those windows would be seen by daylight to be of brilliantly-stained glass – purple and amber the predominant hues, glittering round a gravely tinted medallion in the centre of each, representing the suave head of William Shakespeare, and the serene one of John Milton. Some Canadian views hang on the walls – green forest and blue water-scenery – and in the midst of them blazes a night-eruption of Vesuvius; very ardently it glows, contrasted with the cool foam and azure of cataracts, and the dusky depths of woods.

The fire illuminating this room, reader, is such as, if you be a southern, you do not often see burning on the hearth of a private apartment; it is a clear, hot, coal fire, heaped high in the ample chimney. Mr Yorke *will* have such fires even in warm summer weather: he sits beside it with a book in his hand, a little round stand at his elbow supporting a candle – but he is not reading, he is watching his children.'
Chapter 9

Briarmains is the Red House at Gomersal, red because it was one of the few brick-built houses in an area of stone buildings. The Red House was well known to Charlotte as the home of Mary and Martha Taylor, friends since her schooldays in the Calder Valley. Hiram Yorke is their

Briarmains, the house based on The Red House at Gomersal, home of Charlotte Brontë's friends the Taylors, and now a museum. Illustration taken from a drawing by Wimperis.

Shirley

father, Joshua Taylor, who had built near his house a chapel for his own brand of Methodism. Joshua Taylor was a man Charlotte respected; she had found much to admire and enjoy in his household, with its French newspapers and lively discussions on the arts and politics. His wife in real life becomes the model for Hesther Yorke, his wife in the novel; and his daughters are also represented, Jessie Yorke being based on Martha, and Rose on Mary, who shared her father's radical views and was eventually to emigrate to New Zealand, where she ran a general store.

Fieldhead, in the novel, is the home of Shirley Keeldar:

'If Fieldhead had few other merits as a building, it might at least be termed picturesque: its irregular architecture, and the grey and mossy colouring communicated by time, gave it a just claim to this epithet. The old latticed windows, the stone porch, the walls, the roof, the chimney-stacks, were rich in crayon touches and sepia lights and shades. The trees behind were fine, bold, and spreading; the cedar on the lawn in front was grand, and the granite urns on the garden wall, the fretted arch of the gateway, were, for an artist, as the very desire of the eye.'
Chapter 11

Fieldhead is the 16th-century Oakwell Hall, belonging to relatives of Charlotte's friend Ellen Nussey. The dog-gates with which Malone saved his fellow curate Donne from Tartar, are still to be seen.

In sharp contrast to life in the comfortable houses of mill-owner and rector are Charlotte's descriptions of mills and poverty. One scene set early on a February morning is a reminder that the majority of children in Haworth were much less privileged than Charlotte and her sisters:

'The breath of this morning was chill as its aspect; a raw wind stirred the mass of night-cloud, and showed, as it slowly rose – leaving a colourless, silver-gleaming ring all round the horizon – not blue sky, but a stratum of paler vapour beyond. It had ceased to rain, but the earth was sodden, and the pools and rivulets were full.

Fieldhead Hall, the house based on Oakwell Hall which Charlotte visited through her friendship with Ellen Nussey.

The mill-windows were alight, the bell still rung loud, and now the little children came running in, in too great a hurry, let us hope, to feel very much nipped by the inclement air; and, indeed, by contrast, perhaps the morning appeared rather favourable to them than otherwise; for they had often come to their work that winter through snow-storms, through heavy rain, through hard frost.

Mr Moore stood at the entrance to watch them pass: he counted them as they went by; to those who came rather late he said a word of reprimand, which was a little more sharply repeated by Joe Scott when the lingerers reached the work-rooms. Neither master nor overlooker spoke savagely; they were not savage men either of them, though it appeared both were rigid, for they fined a delinquent who came considerably too late: Mr Moore made him pay his penny down ere he entered, and informed him that the next repetition of the fault would cost him twopence.

Rules, no doubt, are necessary in such cases, and coarse and cruel masters will make coarse and cruel rules, which, at the time we treat of at least, they used sometimes to enforce tyrannically; but, though I describe imperfect characters (every character in this book will be found to be more or less imperfect, my pen refusing to draw anything in the model line), I have not undertaken to handle degraded or utterly infamous ones. Child-torturers, slave masters and drivers, I consign to the hands of jailers; the novelist may be excused from sullying his page with the record of their deeds.

Rawfolds Mill where the Luddite riots in Yorkshire in 1812 culminated in an attack which left Horsfall, a local mill owner fatally wounded. The subsequent trial of the ringleaders was notorious for its harsh sentences.

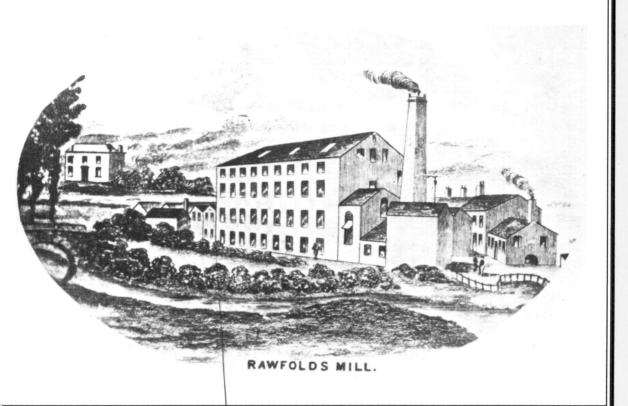

RAWFOLDS MILL.

Shirley

Instead, then, of harrowing up my reader's soul, and delighting his organ of Wonder, with effective descriptions of stripes and scourgings, I am happy to be able to inform him that neither Mr Moore nor his overlooker ever struck a child in their mill. Joe had, indeed, once very severely flogged a son of his own for telling a lie and persisting in it; but, like his employer, he was too phlegmatic, too calm, as well as too reasonable a man, to make corporeal chastisement other than the exception to his treatment of the young.'
Chapter 5

The battle at Hollows Mill is set at the centre of the novel. Throughout it is faithful to the newspaper accounts and to Patrick Brontë's experiences. Any Church of England parson could be a target for rioters, and it is said that during the 1812 troubles Patrick, on account of his outspoken Tory views, had a price on his head. He knew what it was to wait behind locked doors as a mob paused and then passed by. In the 1840s similar gatherings and riots took place around Haworth and Halifax, as poor harvests and economic depression drove working men to desperation:

Working conditions in the 19th century. Many children of Haworth worked in factories, many dying before their fourteenth birthday. Their death certificates merely said 'worn out'.

'The dog recommenced barking furiously; suddenly he stopped, and seemed to listen. The occupants of the dining-room listened too, and not merely now to the flow of the mill-stream: there was a nearer, though a muffled sound on the road below the churchyard; a measured, beating, approaching sound; a dull tramp of marching feet.

It drew near. Those who listened by degrees comprehended its extent. It was not the tread of two, nor of a dozen, nor of a score of men: it was the tread of hundreds. They could see nothing: the high shrubs of the garden formed a leafy screen between them and the road. To hear, however, was not enough; and this they felt as the troop trod forwards, and seemed actually passing the Rectory. They felt it more when a human voice – though that voice spoke but one word – broke the hush of the night.

"Halt."

A halt followed: the march was arrested. Then came a low conference, of which no word was distinguishable from the dining-room.

"We *must* hear this," said Shirley.

She turned, took her pistols from the table, silently passed out through the middle window of the dining-room, which was, in fact, a glass door, stole down the walk to the garden wall, and stood listening under the lilacs. Caroline would not have quitted the house had she been alone, but where Shirley went she would go. She glanced at the weapon on the side-board, but left it behind her, and presently stood at her friend's side. They dared not look over the wall, for fear of being seen: they were obliged to crouch behind it: they heard these words –

"It looks a rambling old building. Who lives in it besides the damned parson?"

"Only three women: his niece and two servants."

"Do you know where they sleep?"

"The lasses behind: the niece in a front room."

"And Helstone?"

"Yonder is his chamber. He uses burning a light: but I see none now."

"Where would you get in?"

"If I were ordered to do his job – and he desarves it – I'd try yond' long window: it opens to the dining-room: I could grope my way upstairs, and I know his chamber."

"How would you manage about the women-folk?"

"Let 'em alone except they shrieked, and then I'd soon quieten 'em. I could wish to find the old chap asleep: if he waked, he'd be dangerous."

"Has he arms?"

"Fire-arms, allus – and allus loadened."

"Then you're a fool to stop us here; a shot would give the alarm: Moore would be on us before we could turn round. We should miss our main object."

"You might go on, I tell you. I'd engage Helstone alone."

A pause. One of the party dropped some weapon, which rang on the stone causeway: at this sound the Rectory dog barked again furiously – fiercely.

"That spoils all!" said the voice; "he'll awake: a noise like that might rouse the dead. You did not say there was a dog. Damn you! Forward!"

Forward they went, – tramp, tramp, – with mustering manifold, slow-filing tread. They were gone.

Shirley stood erect; looked over the wall, along the road.

"Not a soul remains," she said.

She stood and mused. "Thank God!" was the next observation.'
Chapter 19

Nineteenth-century caricature of Luddites who believed that the introduction of machinery into the mills would deprive them of their livelihoods. Their desperation led to violent attacks on mills and their owners.

Shirley

The young women follow the rioters to the mill and are witness to the attack:

'"Shirley – Shirley, the gates are down! That crash was like the felling of great trees. Now they are pouring through. They will break down the mill doors as they have broken the gate: what can Robert do against so many? Would to God I were a little nearer him – could hear him speak – could speak to him! With my will – my longing to serve him – I could not be a useless burden in his way: I could be turned to some account."

"They come on!" cried Shirley. "How steadily they march in! There is discipline in their ranks – I will not say there is courage: hundreds against tens are no proof of that quality; but" (she dropped her voice) "there is suffering and desperation enough amongst them – these goads will urge them forwards."

"Forwards against Robert – and they hate him. Shirley, is there much danger they will win the day?"

"We shall see. Moore and Helstone are of 'earth's first blood' – no bunglers – no cravens" –

A crash – smash – shiver – stopped their whispers. A simultaneously-hurled volley of stones had saluted the broad front of the mill, with all its windows; and now every pane of every lattice lay in shattered and pounded fragments. A yell followed this demonstration – a rioters' yell – a North-of-England – a Yorkshire – a West-Riding – a West-Riding-clothing-district-of-Yorkshire rioters' yell. You never heard that sound, perhaps, reader? So much the better for your ears – perhaps for your heart; since, if it rends the air in hate to yourself, or to the men or principles you approve, the interests to which you wish well. Wrath wakens to the cry of Hate: the Lion shakes his mane, and rises to the howl of the Hyena: Caste stands up ireful against Caste; and the indignant, wronged spirit of the Middle Rank bears down in zeal and scorn on the famished and furious mass of the Operative class. It is difficult to be tolerant – difficult to be just – in such moments.

Caroline rose, Shirley put her arm round her: they stood together as still as the straight stems of two trees. That yell was a long one, and when it ceased, the night was yet full of the swaying and murmuring of a crowd.

"What next?" was the question of the listeners. Nothing came yet. The mill remained mute as a mausoleum.

"He *cannot* be alone!" whispered Caroline.

"I would stake all I have, that he is as little alone as he is alarmed," responded Shirley.

Shots were discharged by the rioters. Had the defenders waited for this signal? It seemed so. The hitherto inert and passive mill woke: fire flashed from its empty window-frames; a volley of musketry pealed sharp through the Hollow.

"Moore speaks at last!" said Shirley, "and he seems to have the gift of tongues; that was not a single voice."

"He has been forbearing; no one can accuse him of rashness," alleged Caroline: "their discharge preceded his; they broke his gates and his windows; they fired at his garrison before he repelled them."

What was going on now? It seemed difficult in the darkness, to distinguish, but something terrible, a still-renewing tumult, was obvious; fierce attacks, desperate repulses; the mill-yard, the mill itself, was full of battle-movement: there was scarcely any cessation now of the discharge of firearms; and there was struggling, rushing, trampling, and shouting between. The aim of the assailants seemed to be to enter the mill, that of the defendants to beat them off. They heard the rebel leader cry, "To the back, lads!" They heard a voice retort, "Come round, we will meet you!"

"To the counting-house!" was the order again.

"Welcome! – We shall have you there!" was the response. And accordingly, the fiercest blaze that had yet glowed, the loudest rattle that had yet been heard, burst from the counting-house front, when the mass of rioters rushed up to it.

The voice that had spoken was Moore's own voice. They could tell by its tones that his soul was now warm with the conflict: they could guess that the fighting animal was roused in every one of those men there struggling together, and was for the time quite paramount above the rational human being. Both the girls felt their faces glow and their pulses throb: both knew they would do no good by rushing down into the mêlée: they desired neither to deal nor to receive blows; but they could not have run away – Caroline no more than Shirley; they could not have fainted; they could not have taken their eyes from the dim, terrible scene – from the mass of cloud, of smoke – the musket-lightning – for the world.

"How and when would it end?" was the demand throbbing in their throbbing pulses. "Would a juncture arise in which they could be useful?" was what they waited to see; for, though Shirley put off their too-late arrival with a jest, and was ever ready to satirize her own or any other person's enthusiasm, she would have given a farm of her best land for a chance of rendering good service.

The Peterloo Massacre. The most infamous incident in the Chartist riots in 1819, where a large crowd, including women and children were dispersed by yeomanry galloping into their midst, sabres drawn.

Shirley

The chance was not vouchsafed her; the looked-for juncture never came: it was not likely. Moore had expected this attack for days, perhaps weeks: he was prepared for it at every point. He had fortified and garrisoned his mill, which in itself was a strong building: he was a cool, brave man: he stood to the defence with unflinching firmness; those who were with him caught his spirit, and copied his demeanour. The rioters had never been so met before. At other mills they had attacked, they had found no resistance; an organized, resolute defence was what they never dreamed of encountering. When their leaders saw the steady fire kept up from the mill, witnessed the composure and determination of its owner, heard themselves coolly defied and invited on to death, and beheld their men falling wounded round them, they felt that nothing was to be done here. In haste, they mustered their forces, drew them away from the building: a roll was called over, in which the men answered to figures instead of names: they dispersed wide over the fields, leaving silence and ruin behind them. The attack, from its commencement to its termination, had not occupied an hour.'
Chapter 19

Despite its many themes and varied discussions on spinsterhood, marriage, education, politics and poetry, *Shirley* is particularly notable and worth reading for its action and humour. At its best it is a successful historical novel, dealing with the implications of poverty and industrial change in human terms. It succeeds, too, as a satirical novel, ridiculing young clergymen for their insensitivity and pastoral incompetence. The comedy in *Shirley* shows Charlotte at her finest, suggesting the laughter that she and her sisters enjoyed at curates' expense:

'It was a fact to be noted that at whatever house in Briarfield, Whinbury, or Nunnely one curate dropped in to a meal – dinner or tea, as the case might be – another presently followed; often two more. Not that they gave each other the rendezvous, but they were usually all on the run at the same time; and when Donne, for instance, sought Malone at his lodgings and found him out, he inquired whither he had posted, and having learned of the landlady his destination, hastened with all speed after him: the same causes operated in the same way with Sweeting. Thus it chanced on that afternoon that Caroline's ears were three times tortured with the ringing of the bell, and the advent of undesired guests: for Donne followed Malone and Sweeting followed Donne . . .'

The curates, to Caroline's dismay, stay to tea:

'Yorkshire people, in those days, took their tea round the table; sitting well into it, with their knees duly introduced under the mahogany. It was essential to have a multitude of plates of bread and butter, varied in sorts and plentiful in quantity: it was thought proper, too, that on the centre-plate should stand a glass dish of marmalade; among the viands was expected to be found a small assortment of cheesecakes and tarts: if there was also a plate of thin slices of pink ham garnished with green

Opposite Rev. Arthur Bell Nicholls, Charlotte Brontë's husband, a photograph believed to have been taken at the time of their marriage in 1854.

parsley, so much the better.

Eliza, the Rector's cook, fortunately knew her business as provider: she had been put out of humour a little at first, when the invaders came so unexpectedly in such strength; but it appeared that she regained her cheerfulness with action, for in due time the tea was spread forth in handsome style; and neither ham, tarts, nor marmalade were wanting among its accompaniments.

The curates, summoned to this bounteous repast, entered joyous; but at once, on seeing the ladies, of whose presence they had not been forewarned, they came to a stand in the doorway. Malone headed the party; he stopped short and fell back, almost capsizing Donne, who was behind him. Donne, staggering three paces in retreat, sent little Sweeting into the arms of old Helstone, who brought up the rear. There was some expostulation, some tittering: Malone was desired to mind what he was about, and urged to push forward; which at last he did, though colouring to the top of his peaked forehead a bluish purple. Helstone, advancing, set the shy curates aside, welcomed all his fair guests, shook hands and passed a jest with each, and seated himself snugly between the lovely Harriet and the dashing Hannah; Miss Mary he requested to move to the seat opposite to him, that he might see her if he couldn't be near her. Perfectly easy and gallant, in his way, were his manners always to young ladies; and most popular was he amongst them: yet, at heart, he neither respected nor liked the sex, and such of them as circumstances had brought into intimate relation with him had ever feared rather than loved him.

The curates were left to shift for themselves.'
Chapter 7

Although it is a delightful exercise to trace back fictional characters to their real counterparts (as Patrick Brontë's parishioners did once they got hold of *Shirley*), we should not forget Charlotte's warning to her friend Ellen Nussey:

'You are not to suppose any of the characters in *"Shirley"* intended as

Rev. Patrick Brontë's study in the Parsonage. The room well illustrates the occupations of the house: paintings hang by Emily's piano, books lie on the table. Meetings in this room brought the whole world of the parish into the Brontë children's home.

literal portraits. It would not suit the rules of art, nor my own feelings, to write in that style. We only suffer reality to *suggest*, never to *dictate*.'
Charlotte Brontë to Ellen Nussey, 16 November 1849

Arthur Nicholls, Patrick Brontë's curate and eventually Charlotte's husband, delighted in *Shirley*. Charlotte wrote to Ellen Nussey:

'Mr Nicholls has finished reading *Shirley*, he is delighted with it. John Brown's wife seriously thought that he had gone wrong in the head as she heard him giving vent to roars of laughter as he sat alone, clapping his hands and stamping on the floor. He would read all the scenes about the curates aloud to papa, he triumphed in his own character.'
Charlotte Brontë to Ellen Nussey, 28 January 1850

This is how Currer Bell depicted 'his' future husband, in the final chapter of *Shirley*:

'Perhaps I ought to remark that, on the premature and sudden vanishing of Mr Malone from the stage of Briarfield parish . . . there came as his successor another Irish curate, Mr Macarthey. I am happy to be able to inform you, *with truth*, that this gentleman did as much credit to his country as Malone had done it discredit: he proved himself as decent, decorous, and conscientious, as Peter was rampant, boisterous, and – (this last epithet I choose to suppress, because it would let the cat out of the bag). He laboured faithfully in the parish: the schools, both Sunday and day-schools, flourished under his sway like green bay-trees. Being human, of course he had his faults; these, however, were proper, steady-going, clerical faults; what many would call virtues: the circumstance of finding himself invited to tea with a dissenter would unhinge him for a week; the spectacle of a Quaker wearing his hat in the church, the thought of an unbaptized fellow-creature being interred with Christian rites – these things could make strange havoc in Mr Macarthey's physical and mental economy; otherwise he was sane and rational, diligent and charitable.'

Interior of cottage, from George Walker's *Costumes of Yorkshire*, far removed from the Brontë children's own childhood in Haworth Parsonage, but a common enough way of life in the parish.

XI

VILLETTE

'Villette *touches on no matter of public interest. I cannot write books handling the topics of the day; it is no use trying. Nor can I write a book for its moral.'*
Charlotte Brontë to George Smith, 30 October 1852

As late as October 1850 Charlotte still found her suffering at the loss of Emily and Anne difficult to overcome:

'I feel to my deep sorrow, to my humiliation, that it is not in my power to bear the canker of constant solitude. I had calculated that when shut out from every enjoyment, from every stimulus but what could be derived from intellectual exertion, my mind would rouse itself perforce. It is not so. Even intellect, even imagination, will not dispense with the ray of domestic cheerfulness, with the gentle spur of a family discussion.'
Charlotte Brontë to W.S. Williams, 2 October 1850

Twelve months later she still found that inspiration flagged:

'It is not at all likely that my book (*Villette*) will be ready at the time you mention. If my health is spared I shall get on with it as fast as is consistent with its being done, if not well, yet as well as I can do it, *not one whit* faster. When the mood leaves me (it has left me now, without vouchsafing so much as a word of a message when it will return) I put by the MS and wait till it comes back again; and God knows I sometimes have to wait long – *very* long it seems to me.'
Charlotte Brontë to George Smith, 28 November 1851

It was to be another year before *Villette* would be finished, and it is not surprising that solitude should be its theme.

Villette is in many ways a predictable book. It is the story of Lucy Snowe who, like Jane Eyre, Agnes Grey and Frances Henri, is a teacher. Like Crimsworth, Lucy goes to Brussels where many of her experiences derive from Charlotte's memories of the Pensionnat Heger. School and

Opposite The Grand Place in Brussels, the scene of medieval splendour and pageantry with architecture that must have overwhelmed the Yorkshire Brontës.

Villette

schooling are familiar ground for the Brontë imagination, but the superficial theme of education does not provide the true power of the story. It is a mature exploration of loneliness, depression and suffering, its success attributable to its depth of insight and psychological truth.

Lucy Snowe, as her name suggests, is incapable of warmth; indeed, until just before publication Charlotte had called her Lucy Frost, making the alteration only at the last moment:

'As to the name of the heroine, I can hardly express what subtelty of thought made me decide upon giving her a cold name; but at first I called her "Lucy Snowe" (spelt with an "e"), which Snowe I afterwards changed to "Frost". Subsequently I rather regretted the change, and wished it Snowe again. If not too late I should like the alteration to be made now throughout the MS. A *cold* name she must have . . .'
Charlotte Brontë to W.S. Williams, 6 November 1852

Villette has one of the quietest openings of any novel, signalling nothing of the storm and emotion that lies in store:

'My godmother lived in a handsome house in the clean and ancient town of Bretton. Her husband's family had been residents there for generations, and bore, indeed, the name of their birthplace — Bretton of Bretton: whether by coincidence, or because some remote ancestor had been a personage of sufficient importance to leave his name to his neighbourhood, I know not.

When I was a girl I went to Bretton about twice a year, and well I liked the visit. The house and its inmates specially suited me. The large peaceful rooms, the well-arranged furniture, the clear wide windows, the balcony outside, looking down on a fine antique street, where Sundays and holidays seemed always to abide — so quiet was its

Gawthorpe Hall, home of Sir James Kay Shuttleworth, through whom Charlotte Brontë was to meet Mrs Gaskell and other society figures.

atmosphere, so clean its pavement – these things pleased me well.

One child in a household of grown people is usually made very much of, and in a quiet way I was a good deal taken notice of by Mrs Bretton, who had been left a widow, with one son, before I knew her; her husband, a physician, having died while she was yet a young and handsome woman.

She was not young, as I remember her, but she was still handsome, tall, well-made, and though dark for an Englishwoman, yet wearing always the clearness of health in her brunette cheek, and its vivacity in a pair of fine, cheerful black eyes. People esteemed it a grievous pity that she had not conferred her complexion on her son, whose eyes were blue – though, even in boyhood, very piercing – and the colour of his long hair such as friends did not venture to specify, except as the sun shone on it, when they called it golden.'
Chapter 1

Charlotte described her heroine as weak, claiming that anybody 'living her life would necessarily become morbid'. *Villette* is the story of that life.

The peaceful days at the Bretton's come to an end and Lucy Snowe seeks and finds employment with a maiden lady. Thus the theme of the loneliness of women is developed:

'I know not that I was of a self-reliant or active nature; but self-reliance and exertion were forced upon me by circumstances, as they are upon thousands besides; and when Miss Marchmont, a maiden lady of our neighbourhood, sent for me, I obeyed her behest, in the hope that she might assign me some task I could undertake.

Miss Marchmont was a woman of fortune, and lived in a handsome residence; but she was a rheumatic cripple, impotent, foot and hand, and had been so for twenty years. She always sat upstairs: her drawing-room adjoined her bed-room. I had often heard of Miss Marchmont, and of her peculiarities (she had the character of being very eccentric), but till now had never seen her. I found her a furrowed, grey-haired woman, grave with solitude, stern with long affliction, irritable also, and perhaps exacting. It seemed that a maid, or rather companion, who had waited on her for some years, was about to be married; and she, hearing of my bereaved lot, had sent for me, with the idea that I might supply this person's place. She made the proposal to me after tea, as she and I sat alone by her fireside.

"It will not be an easy life," said she candidly, "for I require a good deal of attention, and you will be much confined; yet perhaps, contrasted with the existence you have lately led, it may appear tolerable."

I reflected. Of course it ought to appear tolerable, I argued inwardly; but somehow, by some strange fatality, it would not.'
Chapter 4

Miss Marchmont's story is heralded by a storm – a storm, moreover, that recalls *Wuthering Heights*:

Villette

'One February night – I remember it well – there came a voice near Miss Marchmont's house, heard by every inmate, but translated, perhaps, only by one. After a calm winter, storms were ushering in the spring. I had put Miss Marchmont to bed; I sat at the fireside sewing. The wind was wailing at the windows: it had wailed all day; but, as night deepened, it took a new tone – an accent keen, piercing, almost articulate to the ear; a plaint, piteous and disconsolate to the nerves, trilled in every gust.

"Oh, hush! hush!" I said in my disturbed mind, dropping my work, and making a vain effort to stop my ears against that subtle, searching cry. I had heard that very voice ere this, and compulsory observation had forced on me a theory as to what it boded. Three times in the course of my life, events had taught me that these strange accents in the storm – this restless, hopeless cry – denote a coming state of the atmosphere unpropitious to life. Epidemic diseases, I believed, were often heralded by a gasping, sobbing, tormented, long-lamenting east wind. Hence, I inferred, arose the legend of the Banshee. I fancied, too, I had noticed – but was not philosopher enough to know whether there was any connection between the circumstances – that we often at the same time hear of disturbed volcanic action in distant parts of the world; of rivers suddenly rushing above their banks; and of strange high tides flowing furiously in on low sea-coasts. "Our globe," I had said to myself, "seems at such periods torn and disordered; the feeble amongst us wither in her distempered breath, rushing hot from steaming volcanoes."

I listened and trembled; Miss Marchmont slept.

About midnight, the storm in one half-hour fell to a dead calm. The fire, which had been burning dead, glowed up vividly. I felt the air change, and become keen. Raising blind and curtain, I looked out, and saw in the stars the keen sparkle of a sharp frost.'
Chapter 4

The two women, one an elderly cripple, the other young, consider the plight of a grieving woman. Miss Marchmont tells Lucy of her lover:

'"For what crime was I condemned, after twelve months of bliss, to undergo thirty years of sorrow?"

"I do not know," she continued, after a pause: "I cannot – *cannot* see the reason; yet at this hour I can say with sincerity, what I never tried to say before – Inscrutable God, They will be done! And at this moment I can believe that death will restore me to Frank. I never believed it till now."

"He is dead, then?" I inquired in a low voice.

"My dear girl," she said, "one happy Christmas Eve I dressed and decorated myself, expecting my lover, very soon to be my husband, would come that night to visit me. I sat down to wait. Once more I see that moment – I see the snow-twilight stealing through the window over which the curtain was not dropped, for I designed to watch him ride up the white walk; I see and feel the soft firelight warming me, playing on my silk dress, and fitfully showing me my own young figure in a glass. I see the moon of a calm winter night float full, clear, and cold, over the inky mass of shrubbery, and the silvered turf of my grounds. I wait, with some impatience in my pulse, but no doubt in my breast. The flames had died in the fire, but it was a bright mass yet; the moon was mounting high, but she was still visible from the lattice; the clock neared ten; he rarely tarried later than this, but once or twice he had been delayed so long.

"Would he for once fail me? No – not even for once; and now he was coming – and coming fast – to atone for lost time. 'Frank! you furious rider,' I said inwardly, listening gladly, yet anxiously to his approaching gallop, 'you shall be rebuked for this: I will tell you it is *my* neck you are putting in peril; for whatever is yours is, in a dearer and tenderer sense, mine.' There he was: I saw him; but I think tears were in my eyes, my sight was so confused. I saw the horse; I heard it stamp – I saw at least a mass; I heard a clamour. *Was* it a horse? or what heavy, dragging thing was it, crossing, strangely dark, the lawn? How could I name that thing in the moonlight before me? or how could I utter the feeling which rose in my soul?

"I could only run out. A great animal – truly Frank's black horse – stood trembling, panting, snorting before the door; a man held it: Frank, as I thought.

"'What is the matter?' I demanded. Thomas, my own servant, answered by saying sharply, 'Go into the house, madam.' And then calling to another servant, who came hurrying from the kitchen as if summoned by some instinct, 'Ruth, take missis into the house directly.' But I was kneeling down in the snow beside something that lay there – something that I had seen dragged along the ground – something that sighed, that groaned on my breast, as I lifted and drew it to me. He was not dead; he was not quite unconscious. I had him carried in; I refused to be ordered about and thrust from him. I was quite collected enough, not only to be my own mistress, but the mistress of others. They had begun by trying to treat me like a child, as they always do with people struck by God's hand; but I gave place to none except the surgeon; and when he had done what he could, I took my dying Frank to myself. He had strength to fold me in his arms; he had power to speak my name; he heard me as I prayed over him very softly; he felt me as I tenderly and fondly comforted him.

"'Maria,' he said, 'I am dying in Paradise.' He spent his last breath in faithful words for me. When the dawn of Christmas morning broke, my Frank was with God.

"And that," she went on, "happened thirty years ago. I have suffered since. I doubt if I have made the best use of all my calamities. Soft, amiable natures they would have refined to saintliness; of strong, evil spirits they would have made demons; as for me, I have only been a woe-struck and selfish woman.'"
Chapter 4

Later that night Miss Marchmont dies and Lucy Snowe is forced again to think of her future. The solution to her problem is startling and

Villette

sudden, both in the story and in the structure of the novel. She simply goes to London and thence abroad, to Belgium.

Lucy Snowe's journey to Belgium follows closely Charlotte's own solitary journey in 1843 when she returned to the Pensionnat Heger. In London she stays at the Chapter Coffee House near St Paul's:

'The street on which my little sitting-room window looked was narrow, perfectly quiet, and not dirty: the few passengers were just such as one sees in provincial towns: here was nothing formidable; I felt sure I might venture out alone.

Having breakfasted, out I went. Elation and pleasure were in my heart: to walk alone in London seemed of itself an adventure. Presently I found myself in Paternoster Row – classic ground this. I entered a bookseller's shop, kept by one Jones: I bought a little book – a piece of extravagance I could ill afford; but I thought I would one day give or send it to Mrs Barrett. Mr Jones, a dried-in man of business, stood behind his desk; he seemed one of the greatest, and I one of the happiest of beings.

Prodigious was the amount of life I lived that morning. Finding myself before St Paul's, I went in; I mounted to the dome: I saw thence London, with its river, and its bridges, and its churches; I saw antique Westminster, and the green Temple Gardens, with sun upon them, and a glad, blue sky, of early spring above; and, between them and it, not too dense a cloud of haze.

Descending, I went wandering whither chance might lead, in a still ecstasy of freedom and enjoyment; and I got – I know not how – I got into the heart of city life. I saw and felt London at last: I got into the Strand; I went up Cornhill; I mixed with the life passing along; I dared the perils of crossings. To do this, and to do it utterly alone, gave me, perhaps an irrational, but a real pleasure. Since those days, I have seen the West End, the parks, the fine squares; but I love the city far better. The city seems so much more in earnest: its business, its rush, its roar, are such serious things, sights, and sounds. The city is getting its living – the West End but enjoying its pleasure. At the West End you may be amused, but in the city you are deeply excited.'
Chapter 6

St Paul's dominated the Brontë children's imaginations as they grew up in Haworth. Charlotte clearly was invoking a family memory when she placed it in *Villette*.

Boarding the vessel likewise derives from personal experience. All that Lucy did was founded upon Charlotte's own obstinacy and vulnerability:

'I had nothing to lose. Unutterable loathing of a desolate existence past forbade return. If I failed in what I now designed to undertake, who, save myself, would suffer? If I died far away from – home, I was going to say, but I had no home – from England, then, who would weep?

I might suffer; I was inured to suffering: death itself had not, I

Opposite St Paul's looking up Ludgate Hill. It was close by that the Brontë sisters stayed on their way to Brussels. The great dome of St Paul's fascinated all the children.

thought, those terrors for me which it has for the softly reared. I had, ere this, looked on the thought of death with a quiet eye. Prepared, then, for any consequences, I formed a project.

That same evening I obtained from my friend, the waiter, information respecting the sailing of vessels for a certain continental port, Boue-Marine. No time, I found, was to be lost: that very night I must take my berth. I might, indeed, have waited till the morning before going on board, but would not run the risk of being too late.

"Better take your berth at once ma'am," counselled the waiter. I agreed with him, and having discharged my bill, and acknowledged my friend's services at a rate which I now know was princely, and which in his eyes must have seemed absurd – and indeed, while pocketing the cash, he smiled a faint smile which intimated his opinion of the donor's *savoir-faire* – he proceeded to call a coach. To the driver he also recommended me, giving at the same time an injunction about taking me, I think, to the wharf, and not leaving me to the watermen; which that functionary promised to observe, but failed in keeping his promise. On the contrary, he offered me up as oblation, served me as a dripping roast, making me alight in the midst of a throng of watermen.

Chapter 6

Lucy Snowe has cast herself adrift. A chance meeting on the ferry offers a single sentence of advice: 'I wish you would come to Madame Beck's; she has some marmots whom you might look after.' Lucy accepts the casual invitation. She reaches the town of Villette, having lost the trunk with all her belongings, and quite by accident finds herself at Madame Beck's school; after passing a phrenological test, she is employed:

'M. Paul was summoned. He entered: a small, dark, and spare man, in spectacles.

"Mon cousin," began Madame, "I want your opinion. We know your skill in physiognomy; use it now. Read that countenance."

The little man fixed on me his spectacles. A resolute compression of the lips and gathering of the brow seemed to say that he meant to see through me, and that a veil would be no veil for him.

"I read it," he pronounced.

"Et qu'en dites vous?"

"Mais – bien des choses," was the oracular answer.

"Bad or good?"

"Of each kind, without doubt," pursued the diviner.

"May one trust her word?"

"Are you negotiating a matter of importance?"

"She wishes me to engage her as bonne or gouvernante; tells a tale full of integrity, but gives no reference."

"She is a stranger?"

"An Englishwoman, as one may see."

"She speaks French?"

"Not a word."

"She understands it?"

"No."

"One may then speak plainly in her presence?"

"Doubtless."

He gazed steadily. "Do you need her services?"

"I could do with them. You know I am disgusted with Madame Svini."

Still he scrutinized. The judgment, when it at last came, was as indefinite as what had gone before it.

"Engage her. If good predominates in that nature, the action will bring its own reward; if evil – eh bien! ma cousine, ce sera toujours une bonne œuvre." And with a bow and a "bon soir," this vague arbiter of my destiny vanished.

And Madame did engage me that very night – by God's blessing I was spared the necessity of passing forth again into the lonesome, dreary, hostile street.'

Chapter 7

To Lucy Snowe Belgium was a lonesome, dreary place, and the journey from the coast to Villette is faithful to Charlotte's own experience.

The lonely woman sees all in her terms, terms that were dictated by Charlotte Brontë's own loneliness:

'The evils that now and then wring a groan from my heart – lie in position – not that I am a *single* woman – but because I am a *lonely* woman and likely to be lonely. But it cannot be helped and therefore *imperatively must be borne.'*

Charlotte Brontë to Ellen Nussey, 25 August 1852

Accompanying the love story that develops between M. Paul Emanuel and Lucy Snowe there is a ghost story, as remarkable and full of

Mme Heger's school in Brussels upon which the school in *Villette* is modelled, taken from the Wimperis illustration of the actual school for an earlier edition.

Villette

atmosphere as the tale of Bertha Rochester in *Jane Eyre*:

'There went a tradition that Madame Beck's house had in old days been a convent. That in years gone by – how long gone by I cannot tell, but I think some centuries – before the city had overspread this quarter, and when it was tilled ground and avenue, and such deep and leafy seclusion as ought to embosom a religious house – that something had happened on this site which, rousing fear and inflicting horror, had left to the place the inheritance of a ghost story. A vague tale went of a black and white nun, sometimes, on some night or nights of the year, seen in some part of this vicinage. The ghost must have been built some ages ago, for there were houses all round now; but certain convent-relics, in the shape of old and huge fruit-trees, yet consecrated the spot; and, at the foot of one – a Methuselah of a pear-tree, dead, all but a few boughs which still faithfully renewed their perfumed snow in spring, and their honey-sweet pendants in autumn – you saw, in scraping away the mossy earth between the half-bared roots, a glimpse of slab, smooth, hard, and black. The legend went, unconfirmed and unaccredited, but still propagated, that this was the portal of a vault, imprisoning deep beneath that ground, on whose surface grass grew and flowers bloomed, the bones of a girl whom a monkish conclave of the drear middle ages had here buried alive for some sin against her vow. Her shadow it was that tremblers had feared, through long generations after her poor frame was dust; her black robe and white veil that, for timid eyes, moonlight and shade had mocked, as they fluctuated in the night-wind through the garden-thicket.'
Chapter 12

Madame Beck's school and its 'haunted' garden is an imaginative reconstruction of the school owned by Madame Heger. Tradition claims that there is much of Madame Heger in Madame Beck, and that M. Paul bears a striking resemblance to M. Heger, with whom Charlotte had been in love. Winifred Gerin argues forcefully for this point of view, offering a comparison between Heger, remembered by a pupil, and Paul, described in *Villette*:

'M. Heger is a very serious-minded man; on first impressions one would think him very hard, cold and uncommunicative, wrote a former intimate of the household, the Baronne de Willmar in 1846; that would be a mistake; M. Heger, like all learned men has a preoccupied air; nevertheless, he is more than ready to do kindnesses. ... He has very great qualities under that rather cold exterior; he has a will of iron and a really creative genius; he writes admirably and has as much talent as he has modesty.'
Willmar. Souvenirs

'A little dark man he certainly was, pungent and austere. Even to me he seemed a harsh apparition, with his close-shorn, black head, his broad, sallow brow, his thin cheek, his wide and quivering nostril, his

thorough glance and hurried bearing. Irritable he was; one heard that, as he apostrophized with vehemence the awkward squad under his orders.'
Chapter 14

Charlotte rejected such simple comparisons; her characters were 'natives of Dreamland'. She made no attempt to disguise Madame Beck's school; it was obviously the Pensionnat that she and Emily had attended, for the spot where it stood can be found from the directions in the novel. We are wrong, however, to look for Charlotte in Lucy Snowe, and just as wrong to seek Heger in Paul.

Lucy Snowe's love for M. Paul follows the usual pattern of hesitation and misunderstandings common to Charlotte Brontë's heroines. She is all unworthy, the men she admires adoring elsewhere. Lucy is more and more driven into herself until, a Protestant, she finds herself making her confession in the Catholic cathedral of St Gudule (disguised as St Jean Baptiste). Charlotte draws once more upon her own experience, as recounted to Emily, to furnish the details of Lucy's confession:

The Cathedral of Ste Gudule, close to Mme Heger's school where Charlotte went to make her confession and which she describes in the novel.

Villette

'I found myself opposite to Ste Gudule, and the bell, whose voice you know, began to toll for evening *salut*. I went in, quite alone (which procedure you will say is not much like me), wandered about the aisles where a few old women were saying their prayers, till vespers begun . . . An odd whim came into my head. In a solitary part of the Cathedral six or seven people still remained kneeling by the confessionals. In two confessionals I saw a priest. I felt I did not care what I did, provided it was not absolutely wrong, and that it served to vary my life and yield a moment's interest. I took a fancy to change myself into a Catholic and go and make a real confession to see what it was like . . . I made a real confession . . .'

Interior of St Michel, a striking contrast to the plain Protestant interior of the church at Haworth, and a reminder of the rich traditions of European culture that Charlotte and Emily experienced in Brussels.

Here is the version in *Villette*:

'The bells of a church arrested me in passing; they seemed to call me in to the *salut*, and I went in. Any solemn rite, any spectacle of sincere worship, any opening for appeal to God was as welcome to me then as bread to one in extremity of want. I knelt down with others on the stone pavement. It was an old solemn church, its pervading gloom not gilded but purpled by light shed through stained glass.

Few worshippers were assembled, and, the *salut* over, half of them departed. I discovered soon that those left, remained to confess. I did not stir. Carefully every door of the church was shut; a holy quiet sank upon, and a solemn shade gathered about us. After a space, breathless and spent in prayer, a penitent approached the confessional. I watched. She whispered her avowal: her shrift was whispered back; she returned consoled. Another went, and another. A pale lady, kneeling near me, said in a low, kind voice: –

"Go you, now; I am not quite prepared."

Mechanically obedient, I rose and went. I knew what I was about; my mind had run over the intent with lightning-speed. To take this step could not make me more wretched than I was; it might soothe me.

The priest within the confessional never turned his eyes to regard me; he only quietly inclined his ear to my lips. He might be a good man, but this duty had become to him a sort of form: he went through it with the phlegm of custom. I hesitated; of the formula of confession, I was ignorant: instead of commencing, then, with the prelude usual, I said: –

"Mon père, je suis Protestante."

He directly turned. He was not a native priest; of that class, the cast of physiognomy is, almost invariably, grovelling: I saw by his profile and brow he was a Frenchman; though grey and advanced in years, he did not, I think, lack either feeling or intelligence. He inquired, not unkindly, why, being a Protestant, I came to him?

I said, I was perishing for a word of advice or an accent of comfort. I had been living for some weeks quite alone; I had been ill; I had a pressure of affliction on my mind of which it would hardly any longer endure the weight.

"Was it a sin, a crime?" he inquired, somewhat startled.

I reassured him on this point, and, as well as I could, I showed him the mere outline of my experience.

He looked thoughtful, surprised, puzzled. "You take me unawares," said he. "I have not had such a case as yours before: ordinarily we know our routine, and are prepared; but this makes a great break in the common course of confession. I am hardly furnished with counsel fitting the circumstances."

Of course, I had not expected he would be; but the mere relief of communication in an ear which was human and sentient, yet consecrated – the mere pouring out of some portion of long accumulating, long pent-up pain into a vessel whence it could not be again diffused – had done me good. I was already solaced.
Chapter 15

The confession marks a crisis in Lucy's loneliness. On leaving the cathedral she becomes lost, a storm blows up and she falls in a swoon in the porch of another church, to regain consciousness among friends of earlier days.

The whole of Charlotte's experience in Brussels fed her creation of Villette. Visits to art galleries, theatre, and musical concerts – all have their counterpart, with details of programmes and even individual pictures taken directly from life. A fine example of this is the painting *Cleopatra*. An important chapter of the book bears its name:

'One day, at a quiet early hour, I found myself nearly alone in a certain gallery, wherein one particular picture of pretentious size, set up in the best light, having a cordon of protection stretched before it, and a cushioned bench duly set in front for the accommodation of worshipping connoisseurs, who, having gazed themselves off their feet, might be fain to complete the business sitting: this picture, I say, seemed to consider

Cleopatra, an engraving of a painting that Charlotte ridiculed in *Villette*.

itself the queen of the collection.

It represented a woman, considerably larger, I thought, than the life. I calculated that this lady, put into a scale of magnitude suitable for the reception of a commodity of bulk, would infallibly turn from fourteen to sixteen stone. She was, indeed, extremely well fed: very much butcher's meat – to say nothing of bread, vegetables, and liquids – must she have consumed to attain that breadth and height, that wealth of muscle, that affluence of flesh. She lay half-reclined on a couch: why, it would be difficult to say; broad daylight blazed round her; she appeared in hearty health, strong enough to do the work of two plain cooks; she could not plead a weak spine; she ought to have been standing, or at least sitting bolt upright. She had no business to lounge away the noon on a sofa. She ought likewise to have worn decent garments; a gown covering her properly, which was not the case: out of abundance of material – seven-and-twenty yards, I should say, of drapery – she managed to make inefficient raiment. Then, for the wretched untidiness surrounding her, there could be no excuse. Pots and pans – perhaps I ought to say vases and goblets – were rolled here and there on the foreground; a perfect rubbish of flowers was mixed amongst them, and an absurd and disorderly mass of curtain upholstery smothered the couch and cumbered the floor. On referring to the catalogue, I found that this notable production bore name "Cleopatra."

Well, I was sitting wondering at it (as the bench was there, I thought I might as well take advantage of its accommodation), and thinking that while some of the details – as roses, gold cups, jewels, etc., were very prettily painted, it was on the whole an enormous piece of claptrap; the room, almost vacant when I entered, began to fill. Scarcely noticing this circumstance (as, indeed, it did not matter to me) I retained my seat, rather to rest myself than with a view to studying this huge, dark-complexioned gipsy-queen; of whom, indeed, I soon tired, and betook myself for refreshment to the contemplation of some exquisite little pictures of still life: wild-flowers, wild fruit, mossy wood-nests, casketing eggs that looked like pearls seen through clear green sea-water; all hung modestly beneath that coarse and preposterous canvas.

Suddenly a light tap visited my shoulder. Starting, turning, I met a face bent to encounter mine; a frowning, almost a shocked face it was.

"Que faites vous ici?" said a voice.

"Mais, monsieur, je m'amuse."

"Vous vous amusez! et à quoi, s'il vous plait? Mais d'abord, faites-moi le plaisir de vous lever; prenez mon bras, et allons de l'autre côté."

I did precisely as I was bid. M. Paul Emanuel (it was he), returned from Rome, and now a travelled man, was not likely to be less tolerant of insubordination now, than before this added distinction laurelled his temples.

"Permit me to conduct you to your party," said he, as he crossed the room.

"I have no party."

"You are not alone?"

"Yes, monsieur."

"Did you come here unaccompanied?"

"No, monsieur. Dr Bretton brought me here."

"Dr Bretton and Madame his mother, of course?"

"No; only Dr Bretton."

"And he told you to look at *that* picture?"

"By no means; I found it out for myself."

M. Paul's hair was shorn close as raven down, or I think it would have bristled on his head. Beginning now to perceive his drift, I had a certain pleasure in keeping cool, and working him up.

"Astounding insular audacity," cried the professor. "Singulières femmes que ces Anglaises!"

"What is the matter, monsieur?"

"Matter! How dare you, a young person, sit coolly down, with the self-possession of a *garçon*, and look at *that* picture?"

"It is a very ugly picture, but I cannot at all see why I should not look at it."'

Chapter 19

Charlotte gently pursues her theme: the absurdity of a man's patronizing attitude. M. Paul directs Lucy to 'suitable' paintings: a set of four, catalogued 'La vie d'une femme':

'They were painted rather in a remarkable style – flat, dead, pale and formal. The first represented a "Jeune Fille", coming out of a church-door, a missal in her hand, her dress very prim, her eyes cast down, her

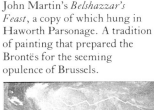

John Martin's *Belshazzar's Feast*, a copy of which hung in Haworth Parsonage. A tradition of painting that prepared the Brontës for the seeming opulence of Brussels.

mouth pursed up – the image of a most villainous little precocious she-hypocrite. The second, a "Mariée" with a long white veil, kneeling at a prie-dieu in her chamber, holding her hands plastered together, finger to finger, and showing the whites of her eyes in a most exasperating manner. The third, a "Jeune Mère", hanging disconsolate over a clayey and puffy baby with a face like an unwholesome full moon. The fourth, a "Veuve", being a black woman, holding by the hand a black little girl, and the twain studiously surveying an elegant French monument, set up in a corner of some Père la Chaise. All these four "Anges" were grim and grey as burglars, and cold and vapid as ghosts. What women to live with! insincere, ill-humoured, bloodless, brainless nonentities! As bad in their way as the indolent gipsy-giantess, the Cleopatra, in hers.

It was impossible to keep one's attention long confined to these masterpieces, and so, by degrees, I veered round, and surveyed the gallery.

A perfect crowd of spectators was by this time gathered round the Lioness, from whose vicinage I had been banished; nearly half this crowd were ladies, but M. Paul afterwards told me, these were "des dames", and it was quite proper for them to contemplate what no "demoiselle" ought to glance at. I assured him plainly I could not agree in this doctrine, and did not see the sense of it; whereupon, with his usual absolutism, he merely requested my silence, and also, in the same breath, denounced my mingled rashness and ignorance.'
Chapter 19

Villette is not limited by Charlotte's experiences in Brussels. As the loneliness and frustration in the novel was tempered by her anguish in the years after her sisters' deaths, so her other experiences are employed in the fiction.

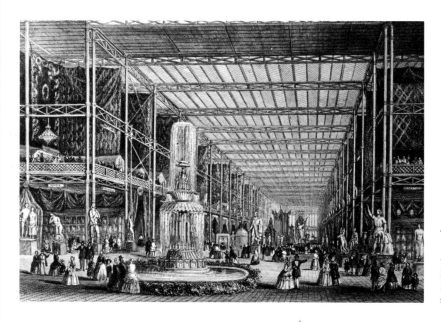

The Crystal Palace Exhibition, 1851. Charlotte made several visits to the exhibition during her various journeys away from Haworth after the death of her sisters.

In 1851, as well as visiting the Crystal Palace Exhibition, Charlotte had seen the celebrated actress Rachel:

'On Saturday I went to hear and see Rachel – a wonderful sight – "terrible as if the earth had cracked deep at your feet and revealed a glimpse of hell" – I shall never forget it – she made me shudder to the marrow of my bones: in her some fiend has certainly taken up an incarnate home. She is not a woman – she is a snake.'
Charlotte Brontë to Ellen Nussey, 24 June 1851

Rachel appears in *Villette* as 'Vashti':

'The theatre was full – crammed to its roof: royal and noble were there; palace and hotel had emptied their inmates into those tiers so thronged and so hushed. Deeply did I feel myself privileged in having a place before that stage; I longed to see a being of whose powers I had heard reports which made me conceive peculiar anticipations. I wondered if she would justify her renown: with strange curiosity, with feelings severe and austere, yet of riveted interest, I waited. She was a study of such nature as had not encountered my eyes yet: a great and new planet she was: but in what shape? I waited her rising.

She rose at nine that December night: above the horizon I saw her come. She could shine yet with pale grandeur and steady might; but that star verged already on its judgment-day. Seen near, it was a chaos – hollow, half-consumed: an orb perished or perishing – half lava, half glow.

I had heard this woman termed "plain," and I expected bony harshness and grimness – something large, angular, sallow. What I saw was the shadow of a royal Vashti: a queen, fair as the day once, turned pale now like twilight, and wasted like wax in flame.'
Chapter 23

In *Villette* Charlotte triumphantly assembles all the elements of her childhood, all the various interests and passions that she and her brother pursued together. The hours spent poring over drawings and paintings, the scrutinizing of reviews of books and plays, the love of the flamboyant in architecture and the heady delight in romantic poetry: all find their way into her latest novel. In some sense *Villette* struggles to assert the dignity and value of the life that the Brontë family believed was attainable. For Charlotte the struggle was a passionate struggle against loneliness. Lucy Snowe finds no easy release from her suffering; neither did Charlotte.

During the years when she was writing *Villette*, Charlotte was trying to come to terms with her solitude. Her letters embody her wish for happiness as a single woman, but her heart cried out for companionship. When she finally married she wrote eloquently on the subject, wishing that her single friends could find the same joy as she then experienced. Clearly, no matter how much she protested, she was never reconciled to a single life.

Lucy Snowe finds some release in art, in theatre, in musical concerts, but only momentarily. The public world of social events does not absorb her. She, like Charlotte, sits on the outside, a spectator seeking involvement but incapable of it.

Nowhere is this isolation more evident than in the climax of the novel. Disillusioned, sedated by an opiate, Lucy cannot settle in the loneliness of her dormitory. The moon lures her out into a night where she hovers on the fringe of a glittering, inviting world:

Wintry scene in the Worth valley near Haworth.

'The drug wrought. I know not whether Madame had over-charged or under-charged the dose; its result was not that she intended. Instead of stupor, came excitement. I became alive to new thought – to reverie peculiar in colouring. A gathering call ran among the faculties, their bugles sang, their trumpets rang an untimely summons. Imagination was roused from her rest, and she came forth impetuous and venturous. With scorn she looked on Matter, her mate –

"Rise!" she said; "Sluggard! this night I will have *my* will; nor shalt thou prevail."

"Look forth and view the night!" was her cry; and when I lifted the heavy blind from the casement close at hand – with her own royal gesture, she showed me a moon supreme, in an element deep and splendid.

To my gasping senses she made the glimmering gloom, the narrow limits, the oppressive heat of the dormitory, intolerable. She lured me to leave this den and follow her forth into dew, coolness, and glory.

She brought upon me a strange vision of Villette at midnight. Especially she showed the park, the summer-park, with its long alleys all silent, lone, and safe; among these lay a huge stone basin – that basin I knew, and beside which I had often stood – deep-set in the tree-shadows, brimming with cool water, clear, with a green, leafy, rushy bed. What of all this? The park-gates were shut up, locked, sentinelled: the place could not be entered.

Could it not? A point worth considering; and while revolving it, I mechanically dressed. Utterly incapable of sleeping or lying still – excited from head to foot – what could I do better than dress?

The gates were locked, soldiers set before them: was there, then, no admission to the park?

The other day, in walking past, I had seen, without then attending to the circumstance, a gap in the paling – one stake broken down: I now saw this gap again in recollection – saw it very plainly – the narrow, irregular aperture visible between the stems of the lindens, planted orderly as a colonnade. A man could not have made his way through that aperture, nor could a stout woman, perhaps not Madame Beck; but I thought I might: I fancied I should like to try, and once within, at this hour the whole park would be mine – the moonlit, midnight park!'
Chapter 38

Illustration by Wimperis from an early edition of *Villette* of the Park in Brussels.

With the park locked and guarded, Lucy finds the whole town alive. Her desire to be alone will go unheeded.

The scene that unfolds draws together the whole of Charlotte's writing life. It could as well appear in the heady and extravagant writing of her juvenilia as here in her last work, for it incorporates all that we know of her imaginative powers and passionate enjoyment of invented spectacle. Lucy's entire past parades before her that night: it is a night of revelations. The truth finally emerges of the ghostly nun whom Lucy has seen several times, and in that revelation is contained another: the truth of Lucy's character. For in all her suffering the girl of frost and snow appears to the world as hard:

'Did you shriek when you saw her? *I* should have gone mad; but then you have such nerves — real iron and bend leather! I believe you feel nothing. You haven't the same sensitiveness that a person of my consitution has. You seem to me insensible both to pain and fear and grief.'
Chapter 40

Lucy is locked in her own misery. Nobody seems to perceive her sadness or sorrow, her coldness separates her from others, from their warmth and comfort.

Always the outsider, Lucy attempts to reconcile herself to M. Paul's absence. She is convinced that he has no love for her and that she must endure the sorrow of loving unloved. But reality bears in on Lucy. At the town festivities the drug she had taken heightened her perception; now, returning to the dormitory, her judgment and emotions are shocked:

'Gaining the Rue Fossette, reaching the Pensionnat, all there was still; no fiacre had yet arrived with Madame and Désirée. I had left the great door ajar; should I find it thus? Perhaps the wind or some other accident may have thrown it to with sufficient force to start the spring-bolt? In that case, hopeless became admission; my adventure must issue in catastrophe. I lightly pushed the heavy leaf: would it yield?

Yes. As soundless, as unresisting, as if some propitious genius had waited on a sesame-charm, in the vestibule within. Entering with bated breath, quietly making all fast, shoelessly mounting the staircase, I sought the dormitory, and reached my couch.

* * *

Aye! I reached it, and once more drew a free inspiration. The next moment, I almost shrieked – almost, but not quite, thank Heaven!

* * *

Throughout the dormitory, throughout the house, there reigned at this hour the stillness of death. All slept, and in such hush, it seemed that none dreamed. Stretched on the nineteen beds lay nineteen forms, at full-length and motionless. On mine – the twentieth couch – nothing *ought* to have lain: I had left it void, and void should have found it. What, then, do I see between the half-drawn curtains? What dark, usurping shape, supine, long, and strange? Is it a robber who has made his way through the open street-door, and lies there in wait? It looks very black, I think it looks – not human. Can it be a wandering dog that has come in from the street and crept and nestled hither? Will it spring, will it leap out if I approach? Approach I must. Courage! One step! –

My head reeled, for by the faint night-lamp, I saw stretched on my bed the old phantom – the NUN.

A cry at this moment might have ruined me. Be the spectacle what it might, I could afford neither consternation, scream, nor swoon. Besides, I was not overcome. Tempered by late incidents, my nerves disdained hysteria. Warm from illuminations, and music, and thronging thousands, thoroughly lashed up by a new scourge, I defied spectra. In a moment, without exclamation, I had rushed on the haunted couch; nothing leaped out, or sprang, or stirred; all the movement was mine, so was all the life, the reality, the substance, the force; as my instinct felt. I tore her up – the incubus! I held her on high – the goblin! I shook her loose – the mystery! And down she fell – down all round me – down in shreds and fragments – and I trode upon her.

Here again – behold the branchless tree, the unstabled Rosinante; the film of cloud, the flicker of moonshine. The long nun proved a long bolster dressed in a long black stole, and artfully invested with a white veil. The garments in very truth – strange as it may seem – were genuine nun's garments, and by some hand they had been disposed with a view to illusion. Whence came these vestments? Who contrived this artifice? These questions still remained. To the head-bandage was pinned a slip of paper: it bore in pencil these mocking words: –

"The nun of the attic bequeaths to Lucy Snowe her wardrobe. She will be seen in the Rue Fossette no more."'
Chapter 39

The Pensionnat Heger from Rue d'Isabelle as it appeared at the time of Charlotte and Emily Brontë's sojourn in Brussels.

It is Lucy's response to events and people that is put to the test. She swears that she has seen a ghostly nun, and she believes that her love for M. Paul is unreturned. She now ponders the truth of her feelings about M. Paul who is about to leave the country:

'Shall I yet see him before he goes? Will he bear me in mind? Does he purpose to come? Will this day – will the next hour bring him? or must I again assay that corroding pain of long attent – that rude agony of rupture at the close, that mute, mortal wrench, which, in at once uprooting hope and doubt, shakes life; while the hand that does the violence cannot be caressed to pity because absence interposes her barrier?

It was the Feast of the Assumption; no school was held. The boarders and teachers, after attending mass in the morning, were gone a long walk into the country to take their goûter, or afternoon meal, at some farm-house. I did not go with them, for now but two days remained ere the *Paul et Virginie* must sail, and I was clinging to my last chance, as the living waif of a wreck clings to his last raft or cable.'
Chapter 41

The image of 'the living waif of a wreck' clinging to 'his last raft or cable', could be from Chapter 1 of *Jane Eyre*, from the Bewick illustrations that little Jane Eyre was pondering. There is a remarkable singularity of image throughout Charlotte's writing.

M. Paul takes Lucy for a walk, and they call at a house Lucy does not know:

'We were now returning from the long walk. We had reached the middle of a clean Faubourg, where the houses were small, but looked pleasant. It was before the white door-step of a very neat abode that M. Paul had halted.

"I call here," said he.

Wood engraving by Thomas Bewick of a shipwrecked mariner – an emblem that Charlotte was to use for her heroine both in *Jane Eyre* and *Villette*.

Villette

He did not knock, but taking from his pocket a key, he opened and entered at once. Ushering me in, he shut the door behind us. No servant appeared. The vestibule was small, like the house, but freshly and tastefully painted; its vista closed in a French window with vines trained about the panes, tendrils, and green leaves kissing the glass. Silence reigned in this dwelling.

Opening an inner door, M. Paul disclosed a parlour, or salon – very tiny, but I thought, very pretty. Its delicate walls were tinged like a blush; its floor was waxed; a square of brilliant carpet covered its centre; its small round table shone like the mirror over its hearth; there was a little couch, a little chiffonière; the half-open, crimson-silk door of which, showed porcelain on the shelves; there was a French clock, a lamp; there were ornaments in biscuit china; the recess of the single ample window was filled with a green stand, bearing three green flower-pots, each filled with a fine plant glowing in bloom; in one corner appeared a guéridon with a marble top, and upon it a work-box and a glass filled with violets in water. The lattice of this room was open; the outer air breathing through gave freshness, the sweet violets lent fragrance.

"Pretty, pretty place!" said I. M. Paul smiled to see me so pleased.

"Must we sit down here and wait?" I asked in a whisper, half awed by the deep pervading hush.

"We will first peep into one or two other nooks of this nutshell," he replied.

"Dare you take the freedom of going all over the house?" I inquired.

"Yes, I dare," said he, quietly.

He led the way. I was shown a little kitchen with a little stove and oven, with few but bright brasses, two chairs and a table. A small cupboard held a diminutive but commodious set of earthenware.

"There is a coffee service of china in the salon," said M. Paul, as I looked at the six green and white dinner-plates; the four dishes, the cups and jugs to match.

Conducted up the narrow but clean staircase, I was permitted a glimpse of two pretty cabinets of sleeping rooms; finally, I was once more led below, and we halted with a certain ceremony before a larger door than had yet been opened.

Producing a second key, M. Emanuel adjusted it to the lock of this door. He opened, put me in before him.

"Voici!" he cried.

I found myself in a good-sized apartment, scrupulously clean, though bare, compared with those I had hitherto seen. The well-scoured boards were carpetless; it contained two rows of green benches and desks, with an alley down the centre, terminating in an estrade, a teacher's chair and table; behind them a tableau. On the walls hung two maps; in the windows flowered a few hardy plants; in short, here was a miniature classe – complete, neat, pleasant.

"It is a school then?" said I, "Who keeps it? I never heard of an establishment in this faubourg."

"Will you have the goodness to accept of a few prospectuses for

Opposite Portrait of the Heger family by Ange François, painted shortly after the Brontë sisters were in Brussels.

Villette

distribution in behalf of a friend of mine?" asked he, taking from his surtout-pocket some quires of these documents, and putting them into my hand. I looked, I read – printed in fair characters: –

"Externat de demoiselles. Numéro 7, Faubourg Clotilde. Directrice, Mademoiselle Lucy Snowe."

* * *

And what did I say to M. Paul Emanuel?'
Chapter 41

What could Lucy Snowe say? Charlotte always believed that the good things in life would pass her by. She and her sisters shared two dreams: to become writers and to have their own school. Charlotte realized the first, and in her writing gave Lucy Snowe the second. Lucy speaks with Charlotte's surprise when she replies to M. Paul's generosity and loving contrivance:

'"Did you do this, M. Paul? Is this your house? Did you furnish it? Did you get these papers printed? Do you mean me? Am I the directress? Is there another Lucy Snowe? Tell me: say something."

But he would not speak.'
Chapter 41

The Brontë family's preoccupation with schools and schooling is as much in evidence at the end of Charlotte's writing career as it was at its beginning.

M. Paul, however, is still going away and Lucy is denied marriage. Charlotte withholds a happy ending. Whether or not in this she was bowing to her father's wish is conjecture, but the ambiguity of the end of the novel when, after three years of separation, Lucy awaits M. Paul's return, is true to the vision of the work:

'And now the three years are past: M. Emanuel's return is fixed. It is Autumn; he is to be with me ere the mists of November come. My school flourishes, my house is ready: I have made him a little library, filled its shelves with the books he left in my care: I have cultivated out of love for him (I was naturally no florist) the plants he preferred, and some of them are yet in bloom. I thought I loved him when we went away; I love him now in another degree; he is more my own.

The sun passes the equinox; the days shorten, the leaves grow sere; but – he is coming.

Frosts appear at night; November has sent his fogs in advance; the wind takes its autumn moan; but – he is coming.

The skies hang full and dark – a rack sails from the west; the clouds cast themselves into strange forms – arches and broad radiations; there rise resplendent mornings – glorious, royal, purple as monarch in his state; the heavens are one flame; so wild are they, they rival battle at its thickest – so bloody, they shame Victory in her pride. I know some signs of the sky; I have noted them ever since childhood. God, watch that sail! Oh! guard it!

The wind shifts to the west. Peace, peace, Banshee – "keening" at every window! It will rise – it will swell – it shrieks out long: wander as

I may through the house this night, I cannot lull the blast. The advancing hours make it strong: by midnight, all sleepless watchers hear and fear a wild south-west storm.

That storm roared frenzied for seven days. It did not cease till the Atlantic was strewn with wrecks: it did not lull till the deeps had gorged their full of sustenance. Not till the destroying angel of tempest had achieved his perfect work would he fold the wings whose waft was thunder – the tremor of whose plumes was storm.

Peace, be still! Oh! a thousand weepers, praying in agony on waiting shores, listened for that voice, but it was not uttered – not uttered till, when the hush came, some could not feel it: till, when the sun returned, his light was night to some!

Here pause: pause at once. There is enough said. Trouble no quiet, kind heart; leave sunny imaginations hope. Let it be theirs to conceive the delight of joy born again fresh out of great terror, the rapture of rescue from peril, the wondrous reprieve from dread, the fruition of return. Let them picture union and a happy succeeding life.'
Chapter 42

Charlotte, living on the moors, could indeed read the signs of the sky. Mrs Gaskell writes that Charlotte took as much pleasure from watching clouds as many get from watching the sea. Thus her home landscape finds its way into her fiction.

Haworth and its moors may have been one influence; the fruits of learning were another.

The end of *Villette* recalls the end of Shakespeare's *The Tempest*; Prospero's last speech is Charlotte's model. The reader's imagination must complete the story. What we have read and understood of Lucy Snowe and what we know of life must help us to decide whether Paul Emanuel is shipwrecked or safely borne home to his Lucy.

Two years after *Villette* was published, Charlotte married her Paul Emanuel, Arthur Bell Nicholls. Finally, it seemed her solitude was ended. Within less than a year, however, she was dead. The woman writer who knitted baby-socks for her publisher's family as a memento of Mr Currer Bell, her male pen-name, died six months pregnant. Her few months of marriage had been among the happiest of her life.

The wide expanse of sky on the high moorland above Haworth made clouds the companions of solitary walkers. Mrs Gaskell was impressed by Charlotte Brontë's ability to read the sky as others would read the surface of the sea.

INDEX

Numbers in italics refer to illustration captions

Index

ACKNOWLEDGEMENTS

Illustrations

Frontispiece: Detail from portrait of the Brontë sisters *c.* 1825 by Branwell Brontë. National Portrait Gallery, London.

BBC Hulton Picture Library: 28, 102, 188
Bridgeman Art Gallery: 18 (below) (Gavin Graham Gallery), 43 (Victoria & Albert Museum), 98 (Victoria & Albert Museum), 106 (Victoria & Albert Museum), 110 (Wolverhampton Art Gallery), 114 (British Museum), 127, 171 (below) (York City Art Gallery), 203 (Guildhall, London)
Brontë Parsonage Museum, Haworth: 12, 18 (above), 19 (all), 20 (both), 21 (below), 22, 25, 26 (above), 27, 31 (both), 32, 37 (both), 41 (both), 42, 44, 45, 46, 50, 52, 53, 54, 55, 57, 62, 63, 74, 87, 88, 101, 103, 115, 117, 118, 121, 123, 124, 129, 131, 146, 157 (right), 165, 168, 171 (above), 176, 177, 178 (both), 185, 186, 193, 194, 205, 206, 207, 209, 214 (below), 216, 217
Brotherton Collection, Leyland papers, University of Leeds: 26 (below), 72, 142, 143, 145, 173
Calderdale Museums, Halifax: 75
Laing Art Gallery, Newcastle-upon-Tyne: 211

Leeds City Libraries: 72
Mansell Collection: 161, 187, 189
Mary Evans Picture Library: 33, 78, 86, 96, 105, 109, 128, 135, 138, 140, 153, 158, 196, 212
National Trust: 122
National Portrait Gallery, London: 17, 40, 48, 65, 71, 166
René Pechère: 219
L.A. Schouten: 150
Simon Warner: 6, 7, 10, 14, 30, 34, 38, 68, 70, 79, 81, 82, 91, 94, 95, 155, 214 (above), 221
Tate Gallery: 182
Brian Wilks: 16, 21 (right), 66, 67, 73, 152, 198

Author

I should like to take this opportunity to thank the staff at the Brontë Parsonage Museum for their unending friendship and help over many years. I should also like to thank the scholars who have attended the International Brontë Conference at Leeds for the generosity with which they have shared ideas. In particular I wish to record my gratitude to Chris Sumner, Member of the Brontë Society Council for her encouragement, and Ian Dewhirst of Keighley for his enthusiasm and infectious delight in Brontë studies.